A CENTURY OF MOUNTAINEERING

A CENTENARY TRIBUTE TO THE ALPINE CLUB

SWISS FOUNDATION FOR ALPINE RESEARCH

Some other works by Arnold Lunn:

The Mountains of Youth
Mountain Jubilee
Mountains of Memory
The Alps
Switzerland and the English
A History of Ski-ing
The Story of Ski-ing
Alpine Ski-ing at all Heights and Seasons
Oxford Mountaineering Essays. A Symposium
The Englishman in the Alps. An Anthology
Switzerland in English Prose and Poetry
Memory to Memory

WETTERHORN
Ferdinand Hodler (1887)
(Federal Deposit, Solothurn Museum)

A CENTURY OF MOUNTAINEERING

1857—1957

BY ARNOLD LUNN

GEORGE ALLEN & UNWIN LTD, LONDON

PRINTED IN SWITZERLAND

CONTENTS

ILLUSTRATIONS

The time-honoured cover decoration is reproduced by special permission of the
Alpine Club Committee

Preface

In our attempt to achieve a real understanding of mountaineering epochs and trends we should be guided by two prominent beacons: mountain and man. A student of the history of mountaineering will discover that the learned historian mostly proceeded by classifying mountains by groups and men by schools, whereas the gifted essayist excelled in distinguishing feature and personality.

As this book was intended by the Swiss Foundation for Alpine Research as a centenary tribute to the Alpine Club, its scope became obvious during the search for an author. Had our first consideration in selecting an author been to choose a learned historian we might have run the risk of finding ourselves at the mercy of a bore. If, on the other hand, we gave preference to an essayist, he might open too many windows onto his favourite foregrounds and the resultant draught might sweep away too many essential facts. It was therefore with relief that our search ended when we decided on a writer who could combine the factual approach of the historian with the personal interpretation of an essayist, Arnold Lunn. Born a Victorian, old enough to have met Whymper and Freshfield, elastic enough to respect the achievements of the representatives of the modern school of climbers, he is not only deeply concerned with the actual records of what was climbed but also with the personalities and mountain philosophy of the great mountaineers of the past. Being a member of the Alpine Club, and a honorary member not only of the Climbers' Club and the Oxford Mountaineering Club but also of the Akademischer Alpen Club Bern, the Groupe de Haute Montagne and the Appalachian Mountaineering Club, he may be described as an internationalist holding an honorary citizenship of Chamonix and an honorary doctorship of Zurich University. An Irish strain may have helped this English patriot to see things from a not too insular point of view. As a fervent friend of Switzerland and her unerring defender in troubled times he earned a thoroughly deserved honour when his Sovereign knighted him for services to Anglo-Swiss relations.

It is with deep gratitude to Providence that this book is dedicated to the Alpine Club as a token of long proved friendship between British and Swiss mountaineers. In commemorating a century of mountaineering no epoch is closed. The centenary of the Alpine Club cannot be regarded either as a definite break. But by marking the event all true mountaineers from far and near will be joined together in their congratulations to the doyen of the mountain brotherhood.

Easter, 1957.
Swiss Foundation for Alpine Research
Zurich, Mythenquai 10.   *Othmar Gurtner*

Introduction

In planning this book it has been more difficult to decide what to omit than what to include. A volume far larger than this would barely suffice if I tried to do justice to all the important first ascents in the mountain ranges of the world. Such a digest of mountaineering history would be an invaluable reference book for specialists, but it would have little appeal to the general reader and contribute even less to the conversion into mountaineers of those who have never climbed. The fact that such and such a rock excrescence on the surface of our planet was first trodden by human foot on such and such a date is in itself of little significance, and the attempt to give importance to mountaineering by associating it with scientific research was soon killed by the ridicule of the mountaineers themselves.

The story of mountain conquest is significant because it is part of the story of man's self-conquest. And because the changing patterns of human behaviour find expression not only in art and literature but also in sport, the development of mountaineering in the nineteenth and twentieth centuries belongs to the cultural history of our age. Sport, like art, is influenced by the contemporary climate of opinion. The Alpine Club, for instance, was a perfect period piece, the Victorian ethos of which survived well into the present century. I am not, of course, using the adjective "Victorian" in that pejorative sense which was fashionable when I was an undergraduate. The modern attitude to the Victorians is far nearer that of the young girl of this age whom Mr. Charles Morgan quotes as exclaiming to her father: "The Victorians had walls. Your generation broke them down. It's draughty without them."

The Alpine Club had walls. The *pietas* of the Club in the nineteenth century may perhaps seem faintly ridiculous to some of the younger climbers of today, and it must be admitted that the reverence for the founding Fathers of our sport, and for the tradition which they created, sometimes acted as a brake on new and necessary developments, but Burke's profound saying, "A people will not look forward to posterity that never looked back to their ancestors", applies not only to the citizens of a State but also to the members of any clearly defined community, such as the community of mountaineers.

There are few things in nature which gain more from association than mountains, and it was not until I visited mountain ranges in other continents that I fully realised all that the Alps owe to that patina of human associations which has been enriched by every generation of mountaineers from the Victorian pioneers, who on the summit of the conquered Lyskamm sang the national anthem "with happy thoughts of home and fatherland and of the bright eyes that will sparkle at our success", to the more sophisticated masters of the technique of piton and etrier who match their superb courage and fantastic skill against the smooth gaunt precipices of the western face of the Dru.

Of the younger and more enterprising representatives of the modern school of climbers there are some who are only interested in contemporary exploits, but there are others who assure me that they have read with keen enjoyment the classics of our literature and still have an immense respect for the achievements of their predecessors.

Though this book is intended as a centenary tribute to the Alpine Club, its central theme is that which is indicated in the title: "A Century of Mountaineering."

Many of the biographical sketches in this book of famous mountaineers are based on personal knowledge and many others on conversations with surviving friends and relatives.

Within the necessary limitations of space I have thought it best to restrict the number of biographical sketches in order to write at greater length of mountaineers who might be considered to represent a particular epoch, and not to feel myself restricted to their mountaineering achievements. In the case, for instance, of Leslie Stephen, the most distinguished of the Victorian pioneers, it seemed relevant to define his status as a philosopher and literary critic, more particularly as some aspects both of his philosophy and of his literary criticism were influenced by his love of mountains.

A minor point should be clarified. It is the normal practice of *The Alpine Journal* to drop prefixes in mountain narratives. In this I have dropped the prefix "Mr" and "Herr" and used other prefixes only on the first occasion when a climber is mentioned. For the benefit of those writers who use this book for reference the correct prefixes, other than "Mr", are given in the index.

And now all that remains is to record my very sincere thanks to all who have helped to produce this book, first and foremost to the sponsors, Karl Weber and Ernst Feuz, for inviting me to write the book and for all the encouragement they have given me. I submitted the typescript of the whole book to Sir John Hunt, the President of the Alpine Club, to T. S. Blakeney, the Assistant Secretary of the Alpine Club and the later chapters to Geoffrey Young. I am very grateful to them for valuable suggestions, but this must not be taken to imply that they agree with everything that I have written. I alone am responsible for the views expressed in this book. I owe a very special debt to my old friend Othmar Gurtner, the Editor of *The Mountain World*. Our collaboration began nearly forty years ago when we produced the first ski map to the Bernese Oberland. I am grateful to him not only for his editorial skill but also for the immense trouble he has taken to produce a representative collection of oil paintings. For this purpose he made a special journey to London and bought for the Swiss Foundation a painting by E. T. Compton, who accompanied Martin Conway on his first journey to the Karakoram.

The proofs have been read and re-read by four great specialists in mountaineering history, Othmar Gurtner, Marcel Kurz, T. S. Blakeney and D. F. O. Dangar. I am deeply indebted to them and also to Miss Phyllis Holt-Needham who, thought not a specialist in Alpine history, is a specialist in Lunn typescripts for she has been reading my typescripts and proofs for a quarter of a century. I must also record my appreciation of the skill with which Miss Philippa Hussey deciphered my typewritings with many bewildering abbreviations, and to Frau Ruth Stummer for the admirable index.

April 15th, 1957.
Swiss Foundation for Alpine Research
Zurich, Mythenquai 10.

Arnold Lunn

8

CHAPTER I

THE DISCOVERY OF MOUNTAIN BEAUTY

Τὸν δ' ἄνθρωπον θεατὴν εἰσήγαγεν αὐτοῦ τε καὶ των ἔργων των αὐτοῦ, καὶ οὐ μόνον θεατήν, ἀλλὰ καὶ ἐξηγητὴν αὐτων.

"God has put man into the world to be a spectator of himself and of his works, and not merely a spectator but also an interpreter."—*Epictetus*.

Many of those who have fallen under the spell of mountain beauty have never felt the least desire to climb, but it is no accident that the beginnings of mountaineering as a sport coincided with the recognition that mountains were beautiful, for if the view that "There is nothing in nature more ill-figured than a mountain" had been as widely accepted in the nineteenth as it was in the eighteenth century, the Alpine Club would never have been founded. A brief attempt, therefore, to trace the evolution of man's attitude to the mountains from the Greeks to modern times, is not irrelevant to the central theme of this book.

The Greek attitude to Mountains

No historian denies that art and architecture are influenced by the dominant philosophy of the age, but it is less generally realised that man's attitude to Nature often reflects his attitude to the Architect of Nature, and nowhere is this relationship clearer than in the case of the Greeks. The dominant philosophy of classical Greece was a development of the humanism expressed in the famous maxim of Protagoras, *Man is the measure of all things*. Man was even the measure of the gods, for the Olympic gods were little more than magnified men with the characteristic vices of the mortals who sought their patronage and invoked their assistance in the accomplishment of crime no less than in the pursuit of virtue. If you were a thief you prayed to Hermes, if a Lothario to Venus, if a drunkard to Bacchus.

To the Greek this life alone mattered. He feared death more than those for whom death was the end, for to the Greek death was not the end but the beginning of a dreary spectral life drained alike of vital joy and sorrow. The "man himself", as Homer says in a moment of unconscious self-revelation, remains in the battlefield. His soul joins the wraiths who wander witlessly through Hades. "I would

9

rather", says Achilles to Odysseus during their meeting in Hades, "live on earth as the hind of a landless man, who had himself only a scanty sustenance, than reign a king among the dead."

A stream of invincible melancholy runs through Greek literature. "Not to have been born is better for mortals" (Baccylides). "Of all things not to be born in the world is best, nor to see the sun, but being born as swiftly as may be to pass the gates of Hades" (Theognis). "Weeping I came to life, weeping I go" (Palladas). "The world is a sty and we are nourished for death" (Palladas). Even the golden hours of sunlit youth were shadowed by this morbid terror of death and decay. Mimmermus begs for death to cut short his life when "golden love" is beyond his reach.

Spengler explained the contrast between the classical and Christian culture in art and literature by the theory that the Greeks had a different sense of time. They lived in and for "the bodily present moment". It was not, however, because the Greeks *could not* but because they *would not* allow their minds to dwell on a future which included age and death and Hades, that they tried to live in the bodily present moment.

The Greek had an almost mystical horror of the *apeiron*, that which has no limits. He could not tolerate the conception of infinity either in time or space. He would have been oppressed by the wide horizons visible from a mountain summit. There are no horizon lines in his landscape reliefs. The Gothic spire soars into the high heavens; the Greek temple is firmly married to earth. The lines of the Parthenon columns are subtly curved so as to direct the eye inwards; the entablature of the Greek temple binds the building to earth, and prevents the eye escaping upwards along the line of the columns.

The Greek dread of anything which suggested the passing of time, and consequently the approach of age and death, had a great influence on Greek art. Personality takes time to mature, and a statue which suggests personality also suggests duration, and for this reason there is nothing so impersonal as many of the most famous of the Greek statues. A statue by Donatello is a biography in stone, but the Hermes of Praxiteles is the translation into stone of the bodily surface of a young man of great beauty. The soul is missing. Similarly Greek drama is situation drama rather than a drama of personalities. "Man", as Lowes Dickinson remarks, "is the hero of Greek tragedy, Tom, Dick or Harry of the modern novel." Significant is the contrast between the suppression of personality, imposed on the Greek actor by the mask which he wore, and the cult of personality in modern drama.

It is therefore not in the least surprising that there is no trace of what Ruskin called the "pathetic fallacy" in the Greek attitude to Nature, no attempt—that is—to discover something analogous to human personality in peak or hill or sea.

Homer, like Praxiteles, concentrates on the physical surface of landscapes or seascapes which he describes. The epithets which he applies to waves and the sea are factual and descriptive of their physical appearance, "dark-clear", "violet coloured" and so on. But then Homer, like most Greeks, feared and disliked the open sea. He will describe the dawn as "rosy-fingered" or "golden throned", because he loved the dawn which restored warmth and colour to the world.

Homer is, what Plato is not, a true interpreter of the Greek attitude to Nature. The Greek had no sympathy for mountain, hill or sea. "What sympathy and fellowship he had", writes Ruskin, "were always for the spirit *in* the stream, not for the stream; always for the dryad *in* the wood, not for the wood." The Greek, as Chesterton somewhere says, could not see the wood for the dryads. "If one imagines", writes Mr. Ridley, "a being dwelling in a fountain, it is just because one does not think of a fountain as a being in itself."

Greek descriptions of Nature are bleak and unsatisfying because the Greek was only interested in Nature as a means to an end, as a minister to the well-being and comfort of man. Man was the centre of his humanistic philosophy. He was never tempted to interpret his feelings for Nature by means of human analogies, though he sometimes uses analogies from Nature to reinforce a description of human activities. Whymper compares the Matterhorn to a stubborn foe. He begins with the rock and compares it to man. Homer, on the other hand, begins with man and compares him to a rock, the stubborn Danaans resisting the Trojans to a sea cliff defying the waves. And Sappho, to quote another example, compares a young bride to a sweet apple. She wastes no time trying to suggest the colour of the apple. It is good to eat, and that is what the apple is for. It is not the apple but the human beings which interest her, the men who are irritated because the apple is on the topmost twig, and they just can't reach it ... οὐκ ἐδύναντ᾽ ἐπίκεσθαι.

Nature was interesting to the Greek in so far and only in so far as Nature was helpful to or hostile to man. Fertile soil, meadows, shady groves, fountains, these are the things which the Greek liked. Homer's Ithaca is not "rich in meadows" but at least there is "always rain", a tribute the full force of which will only be appreciated by those who have seen the arid dustiness of Greece in August. The sea is ἀτρύγετος (barren) in contrast to the ζείδωρος (grain-giving) earth. Long after the Phœnician sailors had braved the open sea the Greeks still hugged the coasts. "Who would *willingly*", exclaims Homer's Hermes, "hasten over the immensities of the sea?" Homer never uses καλός (beautiful) or περικαλλής (very beautiful) for the open sea, though the latter epithet is at least once linked with λίμνη, a generic word for land-locked water, or pool of standing water left by the sea. The Greeks hated the open sea, and had no appreciation of mountain scenery. They judged mountains by the criterion of the humanist. What was their value to man? And Homer answers in effect that mountains are only useful to bad men. "Mountains are covered with mists which are bad for shepherds but better than night for thieves." There were mountain shrines in Greece, because a pilgrimage to a shrine is intended as a test of devotion, and shrines were therefore placed where they were *inconvenient* of access. Since no sane man would climb a mountain for fun, a visit to a mountain shrine was clear evidence of great devotion to the god or goddess in whose honour the shrine had been raised. Olympus was the home of the gods, and because the gods were magnified men with the tastes and vices of men it was necessary, as Norman Young pointed out in his scholarly contribution to *Oxford Mountaineering Essays*, that they should be near enough to the earth to keep in close touch with human affairs, and equally necessary for the maintenance of their dignity that they should be able to look down on men. The only royal residence which satisfied both conditions was a mountain summit, but because *real* mountains are repulsive, Olympus had to be suitably reconditioned for the use of its divine tenants. "It is not shaken by winds nor wet with rain. The snow does not come near to it, but mist-clear air is spread above it cloudless, and the white light floats over it. There the blessed gods are happy for all their days."

So far as mountains are concerned it is surely significant that the Greeks instinctively thought of mountains when they wanted a standard of comparison for ugly people, the Cyclops, for instance, or the loathsome queen of the Laestry-gones. The only line in Homer which evokes a beautiful picture of mountains, the Phoenician mountains "which showed like a shield in the misty sea", $εἴσατο$ $δ'ὡς ὅτε ῥινὸν ἐν ἠεροειδέϊ πόντῳ$, is indirect evidence in support of my thesis. The only occasion on which a Greek would welcome the sight of a mountain would be when a mountain crest raised itself above Homer's "dread gulfs of the barren sea", and conveyed to the sailors the glad news that land was in sight.

The romantic Hellenist who tries to read the modern feeling for Nature into Greek prose and poetry can of course muster a dozen passages or so in support of his thesis, Aeschylus' "innumerable laughter of the sea" among others. Sir Gavin de Beer, for instance, quoting A. Souter, gives two instances of the uses of $καλός$ (beautiful) as applied to mountains in Greek literature, one of them from Plato who, in this as in all else, is an aberrant from the Greek norm. But if I were to maintain that the Greeks thought young men ugly, my critics would not have to go through Greek prose and poetry with a comb to find quotations to refute me, only to be rewarded by a dozen references to male beauty scraped together from the literature of many centuries.

Translations from the Greek are often misleading, for few translators can resist the temptation to soften the bleak realism which is one of the notes of Hellenism. Nothing could be more realistic than the Greek attitude to Nature, for to the man who can only wring a bare livelihood from the soil there is nothing romantic about undomesticated nature, and nothing in the least attractive about mountains or the sea. But this is just what most translators cannot tolerate. The Homeric wave "roars" (ἴαχε), in other words makes a noise which is the noise of a wave, no more and no less, but the wave which "roars" in Homer is only allowed to "sing" in the Loeb translation.

To the Homeric shepherd, mist, as we have seen, was "better than night for thieves", and the combination of mist and night was the worst imaginable. Therefore the Homeric shepherd rejoices when the mists vanish and "the stars about the heaven look very clear", but Tennyson in his famous translation of the Trojan campfires passages has to substitute "beautiful" for ἀριπρεπέα (very clear).

The contrast between the humanist and the mystical attitude to Nature may be illustrated by comparing an Idyll of Theocritus and a passage from Hilaire Belloc's *The Path to Rome*:

> We lay down with delight in beds of sweet tamarisk and fresh cuttings from the vines strewn on the ground. Many poplars and elm trees were waving over our heads, and not far off the running of the sacred water from the cave of the nymphs warbled to us in the shimmering branches; the sun-burnt grasshoppers were busy with their talk, and from afar little owls cried softly, out of the tangled thorns of the blackberry; the larks were singing and the hedgebirds and the turtledove moaned; the bees flew round and round fountains, murmuring softly; the scent of late summer and the fall of the year was everywhere as the pears fell from trees at our feet, and apples in number rolled down at our sides, and the young plum trees were bent to the earth with the weight of their fruit. *(Walter Pater's translation.)*

A perfect expression of the love of Nature domesticated by man, the cupboard love of Nature generous in her provision of pears and young plums. We move into the Platonic realm of timeless beauty when we turn to Hilaire Belloc:

> In very early youth the soul can still remember its immortal habitation and clouds and the edges of hills are of another kind from ourselves, and every scent and colour has a savour of Paradise. What that quality may be no language can tell, nor has man made any words, no, nor any music, to recall it—only in a transient way and elusive the recollection of what youth was, and purity, flashes on us in phrases of the poets, and is gone before we can fix it in our minds—oh! my friends, if we could but recall it! Whatever those sounds may be that are beyond our sounds, and whatever are those keen lives which remain alive there under memory—whatever is Youth—Youth came up that valley at evening, borne upon a southern air. If we deserve or attain beatitude, such things shall at last be our settled state; and their now sudden influence upon the soul in short ecstasies is the proof that they stand outside time, and are not subject to decay.

For all its loveliness the passage which I have quoted from Theocritus is three dimensional, whereas Hilaire Belloc's vision of Nature is four dimensional, for he is of the company of Wordsworth and Traherne, and all those for whom the three dimensions of the physical world are a medium through which we discern in rare and fleeting moments the metaphysical dimension of timeless beauty.

"Something infinite", writes Traherne, "behind everything appeared which talked with my expectation and moved my desire." For Traherne, as for Wordsworth, the visible beauty of the world was an expectation of the invisible beauty which time could not corrupt, a promise rather than a possession. To the Greek, beauty, whether of Nature or of man, was a fleeting possession stricken by the doom of mortality. Contrast the four-dimensional quality of Traherne's

> "The corn was orient and immortal wheat which never should be reaped nor was ever sown. I thought it had stood from everlasting to everlasting. The dust and stones of the street were as precious as gold, the gates were at first the end of the world."

with the three-dimensional Homeric hymn to Earth the Universal Mother:

> "from thee
> Fair babes are born and fruit on every tree
> Hang ripe and large, revered Divinity"

or, again, contrast the mortal beauty which inspired Virgil's *splendet tremulo sub lumine pontus* with the beauty incorruptible which Wordsworth saw in "the light that never was on sea or land".

It is only just to add that however much the Greeks may have disliked mountains it was to a Greek that we owe that mystical doctrine of beauty which provides a philosophical justification for our mystical worship of mountain beauty. Plato taught that there are moments when the soul can ascend to that plain of Reality where we behold the universals Truth and Beauty αὐτὸ τὸ καλὸν (Beauty in itself) rather than τὰ πολλὰ καλὰ (Beauty in her many manifestations). The soul who remembers most clearly the universal Beauty will be stirred into religious adoration by the sight of earthly Beauty because it recalls and reflects eternal Beauty. Mysticism is a cure for pessimism, for the mystic's vision is not confined to the physical world subject to change and decay, but is fortified by faith in eternal Beauty which time cannot corrupt.

If we had no other standard of comparison but the Greeks we could still classify modern interpreters of Nature in prose or poetry as Greek humanists or neo-Platonists. Francis Thompson, for instance, is of the household of Plato when he writes: "Nature from Alp to Alpine flowers rises lovely with betrayal of divine thought. Earthly beauty is but heavenly beauty taking to herself flesh."

14

"Whereas God is a conclusion to the Greek", writes Sir Richard Livingstone, "for the Hebrew he is the first premise." The Greek, as we have seen, accepts usefulness to man as the supreme criterion of scenery. Mountains he disliked because judged by this criterion they were, as Homer pointed out, only useful to bad men. To the Hebrew, on the other hand, the majesty of the mountains revealed the glory of God. "God shall come down from Lebanon and the holy one from the shady and thickly covered mountain. His majesty has covered the heavens, and the earth is full of his presence."

Greek similes, as we have seen, began with man. Homer compares Hector's child to a star, but the Hebrew began with the stars and proceeded thence to God. "The heavens declare the glory of God and the firmament sheweth his handiwork." Homer compared the ugly Cyclops to a mountain; but it is to the mountains that the Hebrew turns for a simile to suggest the supreme reality of the universe. "Thy righteousness is like the great mountains." And when Moses called the people of Israel together to bless them before he died, he gave thanks "for the chief things of the ancient mountains and for the precious things of the lasting hills". And it is to the summit of a mountain that the lover in the *Song of Solomon* invites his beloved: "Come with me from Lebanon, my spouse, with me from Lebanon; look from the top of Amana, from the top of Shenir and Hermon, from the lions' dens, from the mountains of the leopards."

The note of tenderness, so unusual in classical allusions to nature, is ever present in the Bible. "The mountains and the fields shall break forth before you into singing, and all the trees of the field shall clap their hands. . . ." "The little hills rejoice on every side ... the valleys also are covered with corn, they shout for joy and they also sing." The Hebrew never felt oppressed by the majesty of nature. A note not only of tenderness and affection but also of confidence and trust characterises many of his allusions to hills and mountains. "The mountains shall bring peace to the people and the little hills righteousness. ..." "I will lift up mine eyes unto the hills from whence cometh my help."

Gothic Man and the Mountains

The dryads and oreads who haunted Greek woods and hills seem romantic to us but not to the Greeks, for Greek religion was not a religion of love but a science of placating a whole hierarchy of unpredictable and potentially dangerous gods and godlets from Zeus on Olympus to the dryad in the next wood. The good news of Christianity was not only of a Heaven infinitely preferable to Hades, but also that the hierarchy of spirits was subjected to a Creator who loved mankind.

Christianity, by freeing man from the limitations of an earth-bound humanism, rendered tolerable the idea of duration in time and in space. The Greek with his tendency to concentrate on the present, and to avoid thinking of duration in time, left Troy buried for the product of a less time-fearing culture to excavate. No normal Greek, with his instinctive fear of the *apeiron*, that which has no limits, would have been anything but repelled by the far horizons seen from a mountain top.

The Gothic spire soaring upwards into the *apeiron* is the symbol of a new world outlook. It is significant that this new feeling for far horizons, both in time and in space, should have manifested itself in the poetry of Petrarch, first of the sentimental mountaineers. "Petrarch", writes Spengler, "the fine collector of antiquities, coins and manuscripts, the very type of historically sensitive man, viewing the distant past and scanning the distant prospect, was he not the first to attempt an Alpine peak?"

Petrarch climbed Mont Ventoux in Provence on April 26th, 1335, and he described the ascent in an enthusiastic letter to his father. He enjoyed all the little incidents of a laborious climb, and revelled in the glorious panorama from the summit.

My conviction that there was a perceptible growth of appreciation of mountain scenery in the Gothic age is based not on literature, but on art. Apart from Petrarch there is virtually no literary evidence to confirm the evidence of art. Dante (1265–1321) often mentions mountains, but his mountain epithets, like Homer's sea epithets, express either dislike *maligno* (malignant) or indifference, i. e. *erto* (steep), *duro* (hard), *rotto* (broken). Again, the formal and conventional rocks in the works of Ghirlandajo, Pesellino or Mantegna suggests the same attitude to mountains as Dante's formal and conventional epithets, but artists who look at mountains long enough to differentiate between one mountain and another, and to reproduce with fidelity not only the essential facts of mountain form, but also the subtler effects, the shadows, for instance, of clouds on snow, may be credited with a genuine appreciation of mountain beauty. The charming mountain background in Hubert Van Eyck's *Crucifixion* (Metropolitan Museum, New York), the mountains of storm in Titian's *Madonna with St. Catherine*, the snowy hills seen through the open windows in Lotto's *Portrait of the Protonotary Giulano* in our National Gallery, and some of Giovanni Bellini's backgrounds all bear witness to a genuine feeling for mountain beauty.

My belief that mountain painting began to decline with the Renaissance was confirmed when I reread *The Alps* by Sir Martin Conway, later Lord Conway of Allington. Conway was not only a famous mountaineer but also a distinguished art critic. After paying tribute to the excellence of the snowy peaks in many works by Hubert Van Eyck, "the Father of modern landscape", and to Albrecht

MONT BLANC
Alexandre Calame (1850)
(By Courtesy Bürgenstock Hotels)

Dürer's studies of mountain scenes, he continues, "Well-drawn mountains are of frequent occurrence in sixteenth century wood-cuts and drawings by the prolific masters of sixteenth century south German and Venetian schools. The fact is one of many proofs of the vitality of that first outburst of mountain enthusiasm which gradually faded as the sixteenth century advanced.

"It is the commonplace of seventeenth and eighteenth century writers, who chance to refer to mountain scenery, to describe it as of monstrous, horrible or even hideous character. Contemporary artists gave it corresponding expression. We are wrong to assume that their pictures and prints manifest any incapacity to draw because we do not recognise in them the peaks and landscapes which we know."

On the other hand it is easy to recognise Mont Blanc, its attendant peaks, and the Salève in a painting by Konrad Witz painted in 1444. The subject is the miraculous draught of fishes, but it is by the waters, not of Galilee but of Geneva, that St. Peter lays at the feet of our Lord "the net full of great fishes".

It is easy to understand the terror which mountains inspired in those who crossed the Alpine passes, but only the most superficial of critics will assume that the fear of alpine travel explains the extreme rarity of any sign of appreciation, at least in literature, of the distant views of the Alps seen from the security of the plains, the exquisite loveliness, for instance, of Mont Blanc mirrored and reversed in the blue waters of Lake Léman.

Though, as Martin Conway said, the first outburst of mountain enthusiasm faded as the sixteenth century advanced, and though articulate tributes to mountain beauty are extremely rare in the literature of the period, such tributes are not unknown in the sixteenth century. Conrad Gesner, for instance, who was born in 1516, and was a professor of philosophy at Zürich University for twenty-four years, made it a rule to climb one mountain a year, and has left us a charming account of an ascent of Pilatus. Everything delighted him, the discipline of hardship, the joys of remembered toil and danger, the summit panorama and the silence of the heights in which "one catches echoes of the harmony of the celestial spheres".

Gesner's intimate friend, Professor Marti of Berne, was also a lover of mountains. "I am never happier", he wrote, "than on the mountain crests, and there are no wanderings dearer to one than those on the mountains." Marti tells us that on the summit of the Stockhorn he discovered a Greek inscription, cut into a stone, which may be rendered: "The love of mountains is best."

The first English tribute to the beauty of mountains and the joys of mountain travel is the magnificent panegyric of Hermann Kirchner of Marburg (1580) quoted in *Coryat's Crudities*, which was published in 1611.

"What I pray you is more pleasant, more delectable, and more acceptable unto a man than to behold the height of hilles as it were the very Atlantes themselves of heaven? to admire *Hercules* his pillers, to see the mountaines Taurus and Caucasus? to view the hill Olympus, the seat of *Jupiter?* to passe over the Alpes that were broken by *Annibals* Vineger? to climbe up the Apennine promontory of Italy? from the hill Ida to behold the rising of the Sunne before the Sunne appeares? to visite Pernassus and Helicon, the most celebrated seates of the Muses? Neither indeed is there any hill or hillocke, which doth not containe in it the most sweete memory of worthy matters."

Renaissance Man and the Mountains

The slow growth of a genuine appreciation of mountain beauty was checked by the Renaissance, as was inevitable, for the Renaissance involved a partial return to the standards of Greek humanity and therefore to a revival of the Greek attitude to Nature. There is, as Ruskin said, "a mountain brotherhood between the cathedral and the alp", between a Gothic spire and a Chamonix aiguille. Mountains indeed might be classified as Gothic landscape, and at a time when the very word "Gothic" was invented as a term of contempt for an architectural style which the eighteenth century associated with Gothic barbarians, it is not surprising that Gothic landscape should be regarded as repulsive.

Mountains, like Gothic cathedrals, refused to conform to defined standards of taste. Gothic was an architecture of undisciplined genius. The eighteenth century connoisseur admired restraint and conformity to classic standards, the heroic couplets of Pope, the classical landscape as expressed in formal gardens, and in architecture, the accepted "recipes for beauty and sublimity" as formulated by writers who invoked Vitruvius to determine the exact proportions of the "five orders". Mountains were beyond the pale, for as Thomas Burnet had pointed out in 1681, "they have neither Form nor Beauty nor Shape, nor Order ... they do not consist of any Proportion of Parts that is referable to any Design, or that hath the least footsteps of Art or Counsel. There is nothing in Nature more shapeless and ill-figured than an old Rock or Mountain, and all that Variety that is among them, is but the various Modes of Irregularity."

The Influence of Gothic Revival on Mountain Appreciation

It is strange that the British, whose influence on mountain appreciation was so great in the nineteenth century, should only have discovered the beauty of their own lakeland mountains two centuries after the Swiss, Gesner and Marti, had published lyrical descriptions of the beauty of the Alps. In 1739 the poet Thomas Gray wrote an enthusiastic description of the mountain scenery near the Grande Chartreuse, and exactly thirty years later, in 1769, his effective and charming word-pictures of our own lakeland mountains helped to create a fashion.

> "Saddleback, whose furrowed sides were gilt by the noonday sun, whilst its brow appeared of a sad purple from the shadow of the clouds as they sailed slowly by it ... the shining purity of the lake reflecting rocks, woods, fields, and inverted tops of hills, just ruffled by the breeze, enough to show it is alive, with the white buildings of Keswick, Crosthwaite Church, and Skiddaw for a background at a distance.... In the evening I walked down to the lake by the side of Crow-park after sunset, and saw the solemn colouring of night draw on, the last gleam of sunshine fading away on the hill-tops, the deep serene of the waters, and the long shadows of the mountains thrown across them, till they nearly touched the hithermost shore. At a distance were heard the murmurs of many water falls, not audible in the day-time; I wished for the moon, but she was dark to me and silent."

The Gothic revival, which began in the eighteenth century, led to a new feeling for Gothic landscape, but where the taste for Gothic was a pose the admiration for mountains was equally insincere. The absurdities, for instance, of Horace Walpole's pseudo-Gothic mansion on Strawberry Hill have enriched our language with a term of contempt "Strawberry Hill Gothic". His own attitude to Gothic may be deduced from one of his letters to Horace Mann in Florence. "I perceive you have no idea what Gothic is. You have lived too long amid true taste to understand venerable barbarism." Walpole, who amused the modish world by his defence of "venerable barbarism", was, I suspect, as self-consciously eccentric in his defence of the Gothic landscape of the Grande Chartreuse:

> "... all shagged with hanging woods, obscured with pines and lost in clouds! ... Sheets of cascade forcing their silver speed, and hasting into the roughened river at the bottom! ... This sounds too bombast and romantic for one that has not seen it, too cold for one that has. If I could send you my letter post between two lovely tempests that echoed each other's wrath, you might have some idea of this noble roaring scene."

Something more than Walpole's dilletante patronage, the moral fevour of Ruskin, was needed to convert England to a love of Gothic architecture and Gothic landscape.

The Mountains of Ideology

Whereas Walpole's taste for mountain scenery was a pose, Rousseau's mountain worship was an ideological deduction from his political philosophy, and his philosophy was in turn greatly influenced by Albrecht von Haller's poem on the Alps. Haller was a distinguished Swiss physiologist, and his poem, published in 1732, was a panygeric of the virtues of the Alpine peasant uncorrupted by ambition and avarice.

The idealisation of man in a state of nature led by a natural transition to the idealisation of the Alpine peasant, and thence to the idealisation of the peasant's Alpine environment. Rousseau's encounters with Alpine peasants were as infrequent as those of Housman with Shropshire lads, and he took no risks of exposing his sympathy with the mountains to any coarse contacts with reality. His real sentiments about mountains emerge in the contrast which his hero St. Preux implies between the charming and luxuriant Vaudois shores of Lake Léman and the barren heights which rise from the Savoy shore.

Rousseau was only interested in the mountains of ideology. He was born in Geneva, but never once in all his writings does he mention the Salève or the distant view of Mont Blanc from the southern shores of Lake Geneva. He spent a great deal of time at Vevey, but never refers to the Dent du Midi. He knew Maggiore but never alludes to Monte Rosa which is visible from the southern reaches of the lake. Rousseau, as Dr. Engel[1] remarks, "neither knew nor loved the Alps".

Whereas the publication of Rousseau's *Nouvelle Heloïse* in 1760 sent many enthusiasts to the Alps in search of an idealised peasantry, it is to an English traveller, Archdeacon Coxe, that we are indebted for some discerning studies of the real Swiss and also for some very charming descriptions of Swiss scenery. Rousseau, as Dr. Engel acutely remarks, both formed and falsified the literary aspect of the mountains, but England by 1789 had "created without manifestos or sociology an authentic literature of the mountains, richer in original thought than the sudden and superficial enthusiasms inspired by Rousseau's novel".

Rousseau was not only in rebellion against the accepted canons of taste which condemned mountains as ugly because they did not conform to classical models, but also against the political orthodoxy of his day.

This association between the mountain heresy and revolutionary sentiments is, indeed, part of the indictment which Chateaubriand brings against the disciples of the mountain cult. Chateaubriand, that eloquent apologist for religious and political orthodoxy, proves to his complete satisfaction that mountains have neither form nor beauty, and adds as a rider that the sentimental ravings about mountain scenery are exactly what we might expect from such an unbalanced prophet of subversive ideas as Rousseau.

Mountains and the Romantic movement

Mountains became fashionable in the early nineteenth century largely due to the influence of Byron and Wordsworth. Wordsworth's main source of mountain inspiration were the lakeland mountains but he wrote one superb sonnet on the

[1] *La Littérature Alpestre en France et en Angleterre aux XVIII⁰ et XIX⁰ siècles.* An erudite and well documented work.

20

Simplon Pass, and his sister Dorothy Wordsworth's Journal of their Swiss tour contains many descriptions of mountain scenery which have rarely been surpassed.

Byron's visit to the Oberland in 1816, which provided the setting for his dramatic poem *Manfred*, was perhaps the greatest single influence in popularising the Oberland in general and the Kleine Scheidegg in particular.

Of all those who chose the Alps as the theme for literature or art none had a more decisive influence on the English speaking world than John Ruskin. He was not only unrivalled as a word painter of mountain scenery, but he was also one of the first English artists to reproduce mountains with fidelity. It is no accident that Ruskin should have helped to revolutionise English architectural taste, for there is, as I have already remarked, a natural relationship between mountain pinnacles and that Gothic architecture which Ruskin did so much to revive.

CHAPTER II

THE MOUNTAIN MOTIVE

Easque ipsas voluptates humanae vitae etiam non inopinatis et praeter voluntatem inruentibus, sed institutis et voluntariis molestiis homines adquirunt ... ubique majus gaudium molestia majore praeceditur.

The price which we pay for those very pleasures of life are the difficulties which we must overcome, difficulties which are neither unsought nor unwelcome, but intended and desired ... the greater joys are always ushered in by greater suffering.　　　　　　　　　　　　St. Augustine, *Confessions*, viii. 3.

The essence of sport is the invention of an artificial problem for the fun of solving it. Nobody plays golf because some obscure need is satisfied or complex resolved by putting little white balls into round holes, for if this were so people who were afflicted by this complex would just go round a golf course at dawn dropping balls into the holes. Golf is an artificial problem invented for the amusement of man, the problem of propelling a ball in the minimum number of strokes round an eighteen hole golf course.

Many travellers have crossed mountain passes not because they liked mountaineering, but because they wanted to get to the other side. Nobody however has climbed a difficult peak for purely practical reasons. The ascent of a virgin peak is an artificial problem which offers to the solver no other reward than the fun of finding the correct solution.

The essence of mountaineering as a sport is the contest between the spirit of man and inanimate matter, and the key to all developments of mountaineering is the attempt to preserve the reality of this contest by weighting the odds against man. A virgin peak is a problem, but once the peak has been climbed new complications must be introduced in order that a contest, which would lose interest if the outcome were certain, may be renewed with redoubled zest. The conquest of new routes on peaks no longer virgin, guideless climbing, winter mountaineering and ski mountaineering are all expressions of the same search for new problems. Artificial difficulties are invented in order that the game may continue, for a game in which victory is inevitable soon loses its attraction.

Infinite is the interest which man throughout the ages has derived from exploiting the ingenious mechanism of his body and developing its hidden resources so as to establish some new record in one or other of the many branches of athletic endeavour. The motive which makes one man try to lower the world record for running a mile is much the same as that which compels a rock climber to attempt a virgin ridge.

There can be few sports which bring into play so many varieties of athletic talent as mountaineering, particularly if we include, as we should, ski-mountaineering. The balance of the rock climber is wholly different from the balance of a good skier. Many first class rock climbers have been indifferent skiers. Rock climbing again calls for qualities very different from those which are necessary for quick and accurate step-cutting in steep ice.

The characteristic common to all sports is the invention of problems for the fun of solving them. The characteristic common to all hard sports is asceticism, and mountaineering is an ascetic sport. The word itself is derived from the Greek word which means exercise, a noun which was used to describe the severe training of the athlete. St. Paul in a famous passage compares the asceticism of the athlete training for a perishable, and the asceticism of the saint training for an imperishable crown. The comparison was valid in so far as the one thing common to all forms of asceticism is the conviction that the conquest of the flesh is the key to the higher forms of happiness.

"Hell", said Mahomed, "is veiled with delights and heaven in hardships and misery". There is no sport which illustrates more perfectly than mountaineering the ascetic principle that "hardships and misery" are the price which must be paid for the rewards which are, perhaps, a foretaste of what awaits us if we deserve and attain beatitude.

No man has summed up with greater insight this ascetic key to mountaineering than John Ruskin. In a letter to his father from Chamonix (1863) he writes:

> "That question of the moral effect of danger is a very curious one; but this I know and find, practically, that if you come to a dangerous place, and turn back from it, though it may have been perfectly right and wise to do so, still your *character* has suffered some slight deterioration; you are to that extent weaker, more lifeless, more effeminate, more liable to passion and error in future; whereas if you go through with the danger though it may have been apparently wrong and foolish to encounter it, you come out of the encounter a stronger and better man, fitter for every sort of work and trial, and *nothing but danger* produces this effect."

Mr. R. H. Wilenski, in his admirable biography, writes: "Ruskin was a man who, it seems to me, had only one fault in his character—self-indulgence", and it was, perhaps because he was self-indulgent that Ruskin never crossed the frontier which separates the mountain rambler from the mountaineer. It was, I am convinced, the envy that the ascetic so often evokes in the non-ascetic which explains his intemperate attack on the Alpine Club in *Sesame and Lilies*:

23

"The French revolutionists made stables of the cathedrals of France; you have made race-courses of the cathedrals of the earth ... the Alps themselves, which your own poets used to love so reverently, you look upon as soaped poles in a bear-garden, which you set yourselves to climb and slide down again, with 'shrieks of delight'. When you are past shrieking, having no human articulate voice to say you are glad with, you fill the quietude of their valleys with gunpowder blasts, and rush home, red with cutaneous eruption of conceit, and voluble with convulsive hiccough of self-satisfaction."

No attempt to describe the attitude and the behaviour of the Alpine pioneers could be more grotesquely remote from the truth, as indeed Ruskin must have realised, for he subsequently—in 1869—joined the Alpine Club. He was elected on a literary qualification—author of the Fourth Volume of "Modern Painters". His second and saner thoughts on mountaineering were expressed in the Preface to the second edition of *Sesame and Lilies* which was published shortly after the Matterhorn accident of 1865, and in which Ruskin writes:

"No blame ought to attach to the Alpine tourist for incurring danger ... some experience of distinct peril, and the acquirements of habits of quick and calm action in its presence, are necessary elements at some period of life, in the formation of manly character."

Ruskin may well have envied the mountaineer who had enjoyed the noble panoramas visible from the great peaks, and he rationalised his envy by an attempt to prove that "the real beauty of the Alps is to be seen, and seen only, where all may see it, the child, the cripple, and the man with grey hairs". As this chapter is intended primarily for those who have never climbed but who may be tempted to climb, some discussion of the sentence which I have quoted from Ruskin is desirable if only as a clarification of the mountaineer's attitude to Alpine scenery.

Mountain conquest (and self conquest) rather than the desire to enjoy panoramas are the primary motives of the mountaineer, but it is no accident that mountaineering as an organised sport began in the century which witnessed the widespread recognition of mountain beauty. Few men would have climbed had they not loved mountains for their beauty, and many of those who have loved them best would agree with Ruskin that the most beautiful of Alpine views are not those from the actual summits of great peaks. On the other hand your real lover of the Alps does not confine his appreciation to the best views. The Jungfrau is lovelier than Snowdon but our Welsh and Lakeland mountains have their own charm which is no less appealing because it is less potent than the Alpine spell.

Ruskin did not regard as wasted the time which he spent exploring many a little town in Italy far more troublesome to visit than Venice and far less lovely.

It is not only the most beautiful views which merit our appreciation. The true mountain lover is never satisfied until he has studied the mountains in all their moods and in all their aspects. I happen to prefer the view of the Oberland giants from Mürren to the summit panoramas from any of the peaks which face Mürren across the Lauterbrunnen valley, but something of the remembered beauty of quiet hours on mountain crests enriches the views from the lower heights. I never, for instance, see the Eiger without an odd sense of bilocation, as if I were not only lifting up my eyes to that noble peak but once again gazing down from the crest and revelling in the enchanting loveliness of the Grindelwald valley in May, the radiant green of the young grass, the sheets of buttercups transformed by distance into a woof of gold, the cherry blossoms into a thread of silver.

This hour on the Eiger crest was exceptional, for summit panoramas seldom etch themselves deeply into the copper plate of memory. The majesty, might and dominion of the great peaks is often far more impressive from the approaches than from the actual mountain crests—and more beautiful. The view which burst on me as we scrambled on to the Lauteraarsattel on a May morning nearly forty years ago was even lovelier than the panorama from the Eiger.

No mountain experience is more impressive than the oncoming of storm in the High Alps. I remember, as if it were yesterday, the opening movements of such a storm on one of the great ridges of the Grand Combin, the watery sun bleering through a smudge of dampness, the violent and angry red of the dawn snows, precarious splendour on the brink of impending calamity,

> Es wechselt Paradieseshelle
> Mit tiefer schauervoller Nacht.

I remember the rising mist which sucked projecting pinnacles into a grey smother, the little puffs of snow volleying off the crest of the pass, the full fury of the storm which broke as we reached the Col de Meiten, and the bellying surges of black cloud breaking on the ice-fretted bastions of the Combin and disintegrating into long feathery streamers of icy particles. . . .

Would even Ruskin have maintained that the terrible beauty of the storm-tormented ridges would be equally impressive if seen from the valley, seen that is "where all may see it, the child, the cripple, and the man of grey hairs"? The point that Ruskin failed to appreciate is that the summit panorama is only one of an ever changing succession of noble views, and that every phase of a great climb, whether in storm or in sunshine, has its own aesthetic appeal. "The real beauty of the Alps", Ruskin's phrase, is a beauty with many facets, most of which can only be appreciated and understood by the mountaineer.

A man who knew no Greek might appreciate a beautifully bound and beautifully printed edition of Homer, but the Iliad in Greek would mean infinitely less

25

to him than to a classical scholar, and similarly the famous views from Mürren or the Gornergrat or the Brévent would mean incomparably less to the non-climber than to the mountaineer who has mastered the alphabet of the hills and who can translate the detail of rock and ice into the memory of difficulties conquered and problems solved. Does anybody really suppose that "the child, the cripple, and the man of grey hairs" even see the same mountain as the man who has climbed it?

It is difficult to analyse that queer irrational sense of a real bond between oneself and the mountain that one has climbed, the mountain that seems to hold part of one's past life on its crests. The chief reward of the mountaineer is the enrichment of a mountain view which is the direct consequence of the personal memories with which it is associated, so that for many mountaineers the primary object of climbing a great peak is not to enjoy the summit view from the peak but to enjoy the view of the peak from the valley.

CHAPTER III

THE PRECURSORS

The mountaineer, in the true sense of the term, may be defined as a man who climbs, and who continues to climb because he enjoys trying to solve the technical problems of different ascents. The man who climbs one mountain, however difficult, as a stunt, is no mountaineer. The mountain-traveller who crosses a pass merely to get to the other side, the mountain-rambler who enjoys mountain scenery, but who has no appetite for mountain problems, the mountain-scientist for whom the main motive of mountain exploration is scientific research are not mountaineers in the proper sense of the term.

Thus Philip of Macedon who climbed Haemus to discover whether the Adriatic and the Aegean could both be seen from the summit; and Hadrian who climbed Aetna to see the sun rise, were mountain-ramblers. Rotario of Asti who climbed the Roche Melon (11,605 ft.) near Susa in 1358 was a mountain-pilgrim rather than a mountaineer, for his motive was devotional. He deposited a bronze triptych on the summit, where he hoped to found a chapel.

The first undisputed ascent of a peak still considered to be a difficult rock climb was achieved in 1492, the year during which Columbus discovered America. Charles VIII of France ordered his Chamberlain, De Beaupré, to climb Mont Aiguille, near Grenoble, a rocky peak which though only 6880 ft. above the sea is still considered difficult enough to merit the dubious compliment of fixed ropes attached at the trickier passages. Beaupré would seem to have been the prototype of our modern piton experts, for he scaled the peak by "subtle means and engines". He arranged for Mass to be said, and for three crosses to be erected on the summit. This remarkable ascent was not repeated until 1834.

In 1521 Cortez, who like Charles VIII, preferred to climb by proxy, ordered a detachment of soldiers to climb the Mexican volcano, Popocatepetl (17,850 ft.). These daring climbers brought back from the summit large quantities of sulphur for the manufacture of gunpowder.

In 1574 Josias Simler, a professor at Zürich, published the first book to give practical advice on mountaineering above the snow-line, but he was writing for travellers who were *forced* to cross the Alps, and had no more affection for mountains than a sea-sick traveller has for the Straits of Dover. His book, however, was a most useful manual for mountain-travellers. He understood the use of rope, crampons, dark spectacles, and paper as protection against cold, and much that he has to say about avalanches and concealed crevasses is very sound.

The Titlis (10,627 ft.) was climbed by four peasants from Engelberg in 1744. Twenty-six years later the brothers de Luc climbed the Buet (10,201 ft.) for the purposes of scientific research.

Many of the more enterprising pioneers of the eighteenth century were priests. Whereas the Titlis, climbed as we have seen in 1744, is one of the lesser peaks, the Velan (12,251 ft.) was the first of the greater peaks of the Alps to be climbed, its conqueror being Murith, one of the canons of the St. Bernard Hospice. It was, as we shall see, a parish priest of Gressoney who made the first ascent of the Signalkuppe (Monte Rosa).

The Dent du Midi (10,696 ft.) was climbed in 1784 by Clément, curé of the Val d'Illiez, and the Gross Glockner (12,461 ft.) in 1800 by the Bishop of Gurk. But by far the most distinguished of these ecclesiastical mountaineers was the Benedictine monk, Father Placidus à Spescha, whose career as a mountaineer was described by Coolidge as equal to that of de Saussure himself. Towards the end of the century he carried out a series of brilliant ascents in Eastern Switzerland. In his interesting introduction to the *Lonsdale Library* volume on Mountaineering, Professor T. Graham Brown, F.R.S., describes him as "perhaps the first of the true mountaineers".

I agree with this tribute, for I regard Father Placidus, a monk of the Benedictine monastery of Disentis in the Grisons, as the father of mountaineering. He climbed mountains because he loved mountaineering and was never happier than when attempting to solve the problem of a virgin peak. He did not belong to the "one man—one mountain" school. Between 1788 and 1824 he had nine climbing seasons to his credit in the course of which he made the first ascents of the Stockgron (11,214 ft.), the Piz Urlaun (11,063 ft.), the Rheinwaldhorn (11,149 ft.), the highest summit overlooking the sources of the Hinter Rhine, the Güferhorn (11,132 ft.), the second highest summit in that region; the Oberalpstock (10,932 ft.), the highest point near Disentis; the Piz Aul, Piz Scharboden and Piz Terri, and he organised and took part in the first ascent of the Tödi (11,887 ft.), the monarch of the Glarus Alps. From a gap, a thousand feet below the summit, he watched his companions reach the top. Disentis is in the Grisons which was then allied to, and which is now a canton of Switzerland.

In 1760 Horace Bénédict de Saussure, a distinguished Genevese scientist, visited Chamonix and was struck by the possibility of climbing Mont Blanc (15,782 ft.). He offered a reward to the pioneer who should make the first ascent, a reward which was claimed in 1786 by Jacques Balmat who was accompanied to the summit by the local doctor, Michel Paccard. The respective roles of

Paccard and Balmat on that famous climb have been the subject of controversy, but it is now established beyond all possible doubt that Paccard's share in the expedition was at least equal to that of Balmat, who was engaged and paid as a guide.[1]

In 1787, a year after the first ascent of Mont Blanc, Colonel Beaufoy reached the summit, and was thus the first Englishman to climb a first-class peak.

In the closing year of the century the Gross Glockner (12,461 ft.) was climbed, as we have seen, by a genial ecclesiastic whose name and style was Franz Altgraf von Salm-Reifferscheid Krantheim, Bishop of Gurk. The Bishop was adventurous enough to attack a great peak, but too little of an ascetic to enjoy needless discomfort, so he postponed the climb until a comfortable hut had been built to accommodate himself, ten other amateurs and nineteen guides and porters. A chef from the episcopal Palace accompanied them. On August 25th, 1799, they reached the summit only to discover with dismay that the highest point, at the other end of the ridge, was about 100 ft. above them. Next year the mistake was rectified but though the bishop was one of the party, he did not himself reach the highest point until 1802.

In 1804, Joseph Pichler, an Austrian chamois hunter of the Passeiertal, climbed the Ortler (12,802 ft.), the highest peak in Tirol and in 1841 a party of Austrians climbed the Gross Venediger (12,008 ft.).

In the early years of the nineteenth century the Meyers of Aarau made a notable contribution to the development of mountaineering. Johann Rudolph Meyer, the Swiss founder of this mountaineering dynasty, was a rich merchant of Aarau, who climbed the Titlis and who was sufficiently interested in mountaineering to finance Müller's excellent map of a part of the Oberland glaciers.

In 1811 his two sons, Johann Rudolph the second and Hieronymus, made the first crossing of the Beichpass and Lötschenlücke, and the first ascent of the Jungfrau (13,670 ft.). To refute the sceptics, another expedition was undertaken in the following year, led by the third generation of the Meyers, Rudolph and Gottlieb Meyer, sons of J. R. Meyer the second. The two Meyers separated after crossing the Oberaarjoch. Gottlieb made the second ascent of the Jungfrau and his brother Rudolph attempted the Finsteraarhorn. Rudolph Meyer remained some distance below the summit, while his guides, led by Arnold Abbühl, continued. Abbühl, at the time, claimed to have completed the ascent but later withdrew this claim, and the first complete ascent of the Finsteraarhorn (14,026 ft.), the monarch of the Oberland, was made in 1829 by two guides, Jakob Leuthold and Joh. Währen. Their employer was a well known Swiss scientist, F. J. Hugi, who stopped about 200 ft. below the summit. The Hugisattel still commemorates

[1] The Oxford University Press will publish in 1957 a book on the first ascent of Mont Blanc by Sir Gavin de Beer and Graham Brown. This book will contain every document relating to the first ascent and will undoubtedly be the authoritative work on the subject. This will be an official publication of the Alpine Club to mark the centenary year.

a great pioneer not only of summer mountaineering, but also, as we shall see, of winter mountaineering.

A deserved tribute was paid to the Meyers by that great mountaineer, Captain J. P. Farrar:

> "It has often seemed to me (wrote Captain Farrar) that the craft of mountaineering and even more the art of mountaineering description, distinctly retrograded for over fifty years after these great expeditions of the Meyers. It is not until the early sixties that rocks of equal difficulty are again attacked. It is again not until the sixties that Meyer's calm yet vivid descriptions of actualities are surpassed."

To this same period belong the glacial researches of a famous Swiss, Agassiz, whose name is perpetuated in the Agassizjoch. Agassiz spent more than one summer on the Unteraar Glacier investigating glacial movement in search for evidence to support the theory first suggested by a simple chamois hunter, Perraudin, that glaciers had at one time covered the plains of Switzerland. Agassiz' headquarters on the medial moraine of the Unteraar Glacier, ironically known as the "Hôtel des Neuchâtelois", consisted at first of an overhanging boulder, the entrance to which was screened by a blanket. Later Agassiz moved into a rough cabin covered with canvas.

"Agassiz and his companions" is a phrase which recurs in the story of his glacier researches. Of these companions two became famous, Edouard Desor, a German, and Dollfus-Ausset, an Alsatian who was the author of two books, both of which were widely read, *Materials for the Study of Glaciers*, and *Materials for the Dyeing of Stuffs*. His name was perpetuated in the Dollfus Hut on the Lauteraar Glacier. Desor was the first German to conquer a first-class peak. His ascent of the Lauteraarhorn (13,264 ft.) was a very fine performance for the period. Desor also made with Dollfus-Ausset the first ascent of the Galenstock (11,805 ft.) above the Rhone Glacier in 1845 and the southernmost peak of the Wetterhörner, the Rosenhorn (12,110 ft.).

In the closing years of the eighteenth and early years of the nineteenth century the Monte Rosa range was the scene of some remarkable mountaineering exploits. In times of old the peasants who lived in the Italian valleys of Monte Rosa firmly believed that somewhere, hidden away between the glaciers of the range, there was a happy valley where flowers bloomed even in winter. In 1778 Jean Joseph Beck of Gressoney, a domestic servant with the courage and enterprise of a great pioneer, determined to find this valley. He collected a large party, including "a man of learning" by name Finzens (Vincent), and set out with great secrecy on a Sunday morning in August 1778. Beck's party succeeded in reaching the Lysjoch (13,625 ft.) where to this day the rock below which they rested bears the appropriate name which they gave it, "The Rock of Discovery". The height which they reached was an Alpine record till Mont Blanc was climbed. Twenty-three years later Dr. Pietro Giordani of Alagna made a solitary ascent of one of the summits of Monte Rosa which still bears his name, the Punta Giordani (13,304 ft.).

Monte Rosa is a cluster of ten summits of which the Dufour Spitze (15,217 ft.) is the highest. The Punta Giordani was climbed in 1801, the Vincent Pyramid (13,829 ft.) in 1819 by a son of the "man of learning" who accompanied Beck on the ascent to the Lysjoch. He had previously attempted this peak with a German, Dr. Parrot, in 1813. Dr. Parrot was the first man to reach the summit of Ararat, for it is probable that the highest point reached by Noah was the gap between the greater and lesser Ararat, and Noah himself must be considered as the proto-Patriarch of those who do their climbing in funiculars rather than as a pioneer of mountaineering.

The Signalkuppe, or Punta Gnifetti (14,961 ft.), was first climbed by Giovanni Gnifetti, parish priest of Alagna, on August 9th 1842.

Of all the early explorers of Monte Rosa the most enterprising was J. Zumstein, the descendant of one of the many Valaisian families which had migrated to Italy or Italian Switzerland. Macugnaga and Gressoney were originally Valaisian colonies. You can still find in these colonies the descendants of Visptal families with such well known names as Imboden or Andermatten. Many of these ancient Valaisian families were encouraged to italianize their names. Zumstein was naturalised as Della Pietra, Knubel as Squinobale.[1]

Zumstein made five attempts to reach the highest summit of Monte Rosa, and in the course of his many explorations spent a night alone in a crevasse at a height of 14,000 ft. In 1820 he succeeded in climbing the Zumstein Spitze (15,004 ft.).

Three more climbs must be mentioned before completing this brief digest of first ascents up to the middle of the nineteenth century, a date which divides the era of isolated ascents from the beginning of mountaineering as an organised sport. In 1845 a Scotsman, S. T. Speer, climbed the highest point of the Wetter-hörner, the Mittelhorn (12,166 ft.). In 1848 Victor Puiseux, a Frenchman, climbed the Pelvoux (12,973 ft.), one of the more important peaks of the Dauphiny, and in 1850 Coaz of Switzerland made the first ascent of the Piz Bernina (13,295 ft.), the monarch of the Engadine.

I am afraid this chapter has necessarily been rather dull, consisting as it has done, in the main, of a catalogue of peaks climbed. It was, however, important to summarise first ascents in far greater detail up to 1850 than after 1850, and this for two reasons. First because ascents of important peaks prior to 1850 have a certain rarity interest, and secondly because there has been a tendency among the ill-informed to assume that because the Alpine Club is the world's senior

---

[1] I have written at greater length about these Valaisian colonies in *Zermatt and the Valais*, pp. 101-103.

mountaineering club, mountaineering was invented by Englishmen. Even well-informed members of the Alpine Club, who should have known better, have tried to date the beginnings of "sporting" mountaineering from Alfred Wills' ascent of the Wetterhorn in 1854.

It is, of course, not in the least surprising that the natives of the Alpine countries should have been the first to attack the great peaks, and that Mont Blanc, the Finsteraarhorn, Jungfrau, Wetterhorn, Rheinwaldhorn, Tödi, Piz Bernina, Ortler, Gross Venediger and Gross Glockner should all have been climbed by continental mountaineers before the foundation of the Alpine Club. No mountaineers up to 1850 had a better record than the Swiss.

The earliest of all Alpine Journals was the *Alpina* which was edited by Ulysses von Salis, a member of that famous family whose family seat is in the Swiss canton of the Grisons. *Alpina* contained an article on the ascent of the Glockner and reviews of the mountain literature of the period, books such as those by Bourrit and Ebel, but *Alpina* only survived for four years. The failure of *Alpina* was characteristic of a period when brilliant individual exploits created no school. Mountaineering antedated the British pioneers by a century, but it was the British who founded the first mountaineering club, and the first mountaineering journal with a continuous history to this day, and who were the first to organise mountaineering as a sport.

ROSENLAUI GLACIER
John Brett (1856)
(Tate Gallery)

CHAPTER IV

THE BRITISH PIONEERS

Prior to 1850 a few isolated ascents of Mont Blanc were made by Englishmen, and a few glacier passes, notably the Col du Géant, crossed by British mountaineers, but the first British mountaineer to carry out a series of expeditions in the High Alps was a distinguished Scottish scientist, J.D. Forbes.

Forbes, the Father of British Mountaineering

J.D. Forbes was one of the first scientists to take an active interest in glaciers. He visited Agassiz at the "Hôtel des Neuchâtelois" and, if Agassiz is to be believed, managed to extract more than he gave from the genial and expansive Switzer. Be that as it may, when Forbes published his theories of glacier movement, Agassiz accused him of stealing his ideas, and thus forged the first link in a daisy chain of Alpine quarrels, for Tyndall quarrelled with Forbes after which the torch of strife was passed on from the scientific mountaineers to the unscientific; Tyndall quarrelling with Whymper, Whymper with Coolidge, and Coolidge, the Lord of Battles, with almost every contemporary mountaineer who put pen to paper and with many who did not. Whatever may have been the rights of the Agassiz-Forbes dispute, Forbes undoubtedly proved that he had mastered the basic facts of glacier movement by a remarkable prediction.

In 1820 a party of guides and amateurs were overwhelmed by an avalanche on the Grand Plateau, and three of the guides disappeared into a crevasse. Dr. Hamel, who survived, predicted that the bodies of the guides would reappear at the bottom of the glacier in about a thousand years, whereas Forbes' estimate was forty years. Exactly forty-one years after the accident fragments of human bodies emerged near the lower end of the Glacier des Bossons.

Forbes made the fourth ascent of the Jungfrau in 1841, and the first recorded passage of the Col d'Hérens in 1842, in the course of which he climbed the Stockhorn (11,796 ft.), now Wandfluhhorn, this being the first conquest of a virgin peak by a British mountaineer. His book, *Travels through the Alps of Savoy* (1843) was the first book in the English language in which a series of Alpine climbs are described; its only predecessors being a few pamphlets describing ascents of

Mont Blanc. His writings made many converts to mountaineering in England, but his influence, though great, was less great than that of a very different type of mountaineer, Albert Smith.

Albert Smith

As a child Albert Smith had been given *The Peasants of Chamouni* which inspired him to anticipate his future success as a showman.

"Finally, I got up a small moving panorama of the horrors pertaining to Mont Blanc. . . . and this I so painted up and exaggerated in my enthusiasm that my little sister—who was my only audience but an admirable one, for she cared not how often I exhibited—would become quite pale with fright."

Smith, while he was a student in Paris, discovered that his enthusiasm for Mont Blanc was shared by a medical student whom he persuaded to accompany him to Chamonix. They collected twelve pounds apiece, slept at night in the empty diligence, dined off bread and cheese and contrived to return with some of their twelve pounds unspent after visiting Geneva, Chamonix and Milan.

Smith took up practice as a surgeon, wrote for *Punch*, and made a reputation as an entertainer in *The Overland Mail*, written by himself and founded on a journey to Egypt and Constantinople.

In the summer of 1851 Albert Smith's great ambition, to climb Mont Blanc, was fulfilled. Under the absurd regulations imposed by the *Compagnie des Guides* at Chamonix there had to be four guides for each traveller, Smith's party of four were accompanied by sixteen guides and eighteen porters. The provisions included ninety-four bottles of wine, four legs of mutton, four shoulders of mutton and forty-six fowls.

Smith was much alarmed by the Mur de la Côte. "Should the foot or the baton slip", he assures us, "there is no chance for life. You would glide like lightning from one frozen crag to another, and finally be dashed to pieces hundreds of feet below." In point of fact had Smith fallen he might have slipped some distance with no worse consequence than a tedious reascent to the point from which he fell.

Albert Smith's book *The Story of Mont Blanc*, and still more his lecture at the Egyptian Hall, which became very popular and was patronised by the Queen, made many converts to mountaineering. I do not agree with Graham Brown that Smith "ascended Mont Blanc with the object of making a commercial show of it". His motives, like those of other mountaineers, were mixed, but C. E. Mathews was no more than just when he wrote:

34

"He was emphatically a showman from his birth, but it is not true that he ascended the mountain for the purpose of making a show of it. His well-known entertainment resulted from a lifelong interest which he had taken in the great summit, of which he never failed to speak or write with reverence and affection. . . . It is but just to his memory to record that he, too, was a pioneer. Mountaineering was not then a recognised sport for Englishmen. Hitherto, any information about Mont Blanc had to be sought for in isolated publications. Smith brought more or less accurate knowledge of it, as it were, to the hearths and homes of educated Englishmen. . . . Smith's entertainment gave an undoubted impetus to mountaineering."

"Reserved for Foreigners"

"A highly intelligent Swiss guide", wrote Leslie Stephen, "once gazed with me upon the dreary expanse of chimney pots through which the south-eastern railway escapes from this dingy metropolis. I remarked with an appropriate sigh: 'That is not so fine a view as we have seen together from the top of Mont Blanc.' 'Ah, sir', was the pathetic reply, 'it is much finer.'"

It was not the inhabitants of mountain valleys who were the first to discover that mountains are beautiful, and it was not the mountain men, the *Berglers*, who invented the sport of mountaineering but the foreigners. The Berglers had mastered such elementary mountain-craft as was necessary for the chamois hunter or the smuggler, but were far too practical to climb mountains just for the fun of climbing them. They were, of course, glad that rich foreigners should be infected by this bizarre craze for climbing mountains and prepared to pay Berglers to assist them to reach the summit of peaks which nobody but a man with more money than sense would wish to climb.

The tolerant amusement with which these eccentricities were regarded by the realistic Berglers emerges from the story of an unsuccessful attempt on the then unconquered Mönch by a Rumanian Countess, Hélène Kolzow-Massalsky. From the point where it was no longer possible to carry the Countess in a *Tragsessel*, she was propelled upwards by the combined efforts of four guides, one for each arm, one to push from behind, and one to pull from the front. The Countess, who had suffered acutely from mountain sickness during the night spent in a cave, arrived at the foot of the final snowridge of the Mönch in a state of complete exhaustion, and abandoned the ascent at this point.

In her book about her Swiss tour the Countess, who was better known by her pen name of Dora d'Istria, describes her arrival *on the summit* of the Mönch where, so she informs her readers, she kissed the Rumanian flag, and raised her heart to God. She reprints a testimonial signed by the guides in which she is given credit for making the first ascent of the Mönch and praised in fulsome terms for her heroic endurance. The Berglers of Grindelwald no doubt made merry over this testimonial, but there was one guide present on the expedition who refused to put his name to a statement which he knew to be false, a guide destined to become famous, Christian Almer.

In 1857, two years after this unsuccessful attempt on the Mönch, Christian Almer made the first ascent of the Mönch with Dr. Porges of Vienna. Now it is certain that Almer and the other guides who propelled the Countess up to the foot of the final ridge of the Mönch must have realised that they could have completed the ascent on any fine summer's day, if they were unencumbered by incompetent amateurs. Why then did Almer allow two years to pass before completing the ascent of the then unconquered Mönch? Perhaps because, in the first phase of mountaineering history, a Bergler would have lost rather than gained the esteem of his fellows by climbing a peak just for the fun of climbing it. That sort of thing was all very well for eccentric foreigners but not for sensible Berglers. And even when guides began to share the ambitions of their employers and to take pride in making first ascents, it would still have been considered bad form for a party of guides to attack a virgin peak on their own, instead of waiting till a "Herr" could be found who was prepared to pay handsomely for the privilege of making the first ascent of a famous peak. Why spoil the market by reducing the number of virgin peaks without any compensating remuneration from a grateful "Herr", remuneration which was always greater in the case of a virgin peak than of a peak no longer virgin?

Characteristic of the reluctance of a guide to disillusion a "Herr" who believed himself to be making a first ascent was Peter Bohren's attitude on Alfred Wills' ascent of the Wetterhorn. Bohren had certainly climbed the Wetterhorn at least twice and perhaps three times before, and yet he allowed Wills to believe that he was "the first to scale that awful peak".

The perplexing history of the earlier attempts on the Wetterhorn will be discussed in the next section of this chapter, but one argument, advanced by D. F. O. Dangar and T. S. Blakeney to discredit the alleged first ascent from Grindelwald by two Swiss, seems to me to illustrate the danger of crediting the early guides with an attitude to virgin ascents which they only gradually acquired from their employers. "The inexplicable silence of Bohren (in not disclosing his previous ascents to Wills), who might have preferred his own countryman rather than a foreigner", is not in the least inexplicable once we realise that many guides at that period had no great interest in first ascents, excepting in so far as amateurs were prepared to pay more for first than for subsequent ascents. Again, in 1854 national feeling was, and indeed still is, far less strong in Switzerland than regional loyalties. To Bohren, Wills and Fankhauser would both have been foreigners.

36

I remember once reproaching a Swiss for failing to comply with the international rules which required, or at least strongly recommended that a foreigner should always be appointed to referee an international event. "But we did appoint a foreigner", he exclaimed. The "foreigner" was a native of a rival centre on the other side of the valley.

"The (presumed) conspiracy of silence on the part of the people of Grindelwald in 1854, leading Wills to think of his ascent as the first", is easy to understand. The pioneers unconsciously assumed that the natives shared their interest in first ascents. Evidence to the contrary will be cited in connection with the first ascent of the Matterhorn. It would only be a small minority at Grindelwald who either knew or cared whether the Wetterhorn had been climbed, but the foreigners cared, and anything that made them happy was to be encouraged. Bohren probably did no more than leave his employer under an illusion. That Bohren had a less exact sense of truth than Christian Almer we know, for Almer, as we have seen, refused to sign the testimonial stating that the Rumanian Countess had reached the summit of the Mönch, whereas Bohren had no such scruples. If a client wished to believe that he had climbed a peak when the expedition had only reached a shoulder, or had made the first ascent of a mountain already climbed several times, why disturb his illusions, illusions which did nobody any harm, added to the sum total of human happiness, and to the sum total of francs in one's pocket?

If, as has been suggested, Anglo-Swiss rivalry in first ascents had been in those early days a factor of the least importance, the natives of Alpine valleys would not have waited until a "Herr" arrived, they would have deflowered the virgin peaks on their own.

The Wetterhorn Pioneers

The Wetterhorn consists of three peaks of approximately the same height, the Hasli Jungfrau (12,149 ft.) which is the peak conspicuous from Grindelwald, the Mittelhorn (12,166 ft.), the central and highest peak, and the Rosenhorn (12,110 ft.).

Though the Hasli Jungfrau is not the highest peak, it is commonly known as the Wetterhorn and is the only case I know of the ascent of the lower summit of a range ranking as more important than the conquest of the highest point.

The first of the Wetterhörner to be ascended was the Rosenhorn which was climbed by Desor on August 28th, 1844, three days before his guides climbed the Hasli Jungfrau or Wetterhorn proper. The highest summit of the Wetterhorn, the Mittelhorn, was climbed by Stanhope Templeman Speer on July 9th, 1845, with Johann Jaun of the Grimsel, Kaspar Abplanalp and Jonathan Michel.

The early history of the Wetterhörner is controversial, and has in recent years been the theme of three scholarly articles, the first of which by Sir Gavin de Beer and R. Morrison appeared in *Die Alpen* (1949, pp. 46–50 and 118–120), the second by D. F. O. Dangar and T. S. Blakeney in *The Alpine Journal*, November 1952, and the third by T. Graham Brown in *The Alpine Journal*, November 1953. I wish that I had space in which to summarise a fascinating controversy but I must—alas!—confine myself to a bleak summary of my own conclusions.

The second ascent of any of the Wetterhorn peaks was the ascent of the Hasli Jungfrau on August 31st, 1844, by Grimsel guides, engaged by Desor to explore the route. Their names were M. Bannholzer and J. Jaun. On July 7th, 1845, two Swiss, Gottfried Roth, a doctor at Interlaken, and F. Fankhauser, a forester, with the guides Christian Michel, Johann and Peter Bohren of Grindelwald, are said to have climbed the Hasli Jungfrau and thus to have made the first ascent from Grindelwald, but the authors of the two articles in *The Alpine Journal* mentioned above have cast very grave doubts on this expedition. On July 31st, 1845, Agassiz with friends and guides climbed the Hasli Jungfrau from the Grimsel.

After a long interval of nine years an Englishman, Eardley J. Blackwell, with Peter Bohren and Christian Bleurer attacked the Wetterhorn from Grindelwald on June 14th, 1854, and according to his own entry, in the Führerbuch of one of his guides, "made the ascent of the Wetterhorn in a storm and planted a flag on the highest point". It has been suggested that the peak which Blackwell climbed was the Mittelhorn, or alternatively that he did not reach the actual summit of the Wetterhorn, but I agree with Carl Egger[1] that it is unreasonable to suppose that Blackwell did not reach the summit seeing that Wills found 10 ft. from the summit the iron flag which Blackwell had planted. To the objection that Blackwell's party stopped short because of the cornice, Egger points out that it is by no means certain that there was a cornice as early as June, when Blackwell made his ascent. Graham Brown (*A. J.* LIX, p. 179), though he maintains that Blackwell did not reach the summit on his first attempt, has no doubt that the summit which he did climb was the Hasli Jungfrau. Anyhow, whether he reached the Hasli Jungfrau on his *first* attempt from Grindelwald it is all but certain that on that occasion he made the first ascent from Grindelwald to the pass where the route from Grindelwald joins the route from Rosenlaui and that, in the course of his two ascents, he climbed every foot of the ascent from Grindelwald to the summit. If then the Roth-Fankhauser ascent be disallowed, it is Blackwell, not Wills, who must be given the credit for making the first ascent of the Wetterhorn proper from Grindelwald.

---

[1] *Pioniere der Alpen*, p. 136.

On September 17th, 1854, Alfred Wills with the guides Peter Bohren of Grindelwald, Ulrich Lauener of Lauterbrunnen, and Auguste Balmat and Auguste Simond of Chamonix climbed the Wetterhorn from Grindelwald. Some distance below the summit they suddenly saw two other climbers, one of whom carried on his back a young fir tree, "making all haste they could and determined to be the first on the summit. . . . A great shouting now took place between the two parties, the result of which was that the piratical adventurers promised to wait for us on the rocks above." The "piratical adventurers" were Christian Almer, who had left Grindelwald in the night with Ulrich Kaufmann, determined to plant a small fir tree side by side with the iron "Flagge" which the Wills's guides were taking to the summit.

Alfred Wills described his climb in his book *Wanderings among the High Alps* (1856), the influence of which in popularising mountaineering was beyond doubt very great, but I agree with Egger that the importance of his climb has been greatly exaggerated, "das grosse Wesen, das um die Besteigung Wills gemacht wurde und noch gemacht wird, ist nicht gerechtfertigt".

In 1904 Alfred Wills in a letter to Lady Monkswell told her how delighted he had been to hear his ascent of the Wetterhorn described at an Alpine Club dinner as "the origin of modern mountaineering", and as late as 1927 further currency was given, in the preface to the volume on Mountaineering in the Lonsdale Library, to the preposterous claim that Wills' ascent of the Wetterhorn was the first sporting climb. According to Gavin de Beer the first attack on this legend is to be found in a little book, *The Alps*, which I published in 1914.

Carl Egger reminds us that Ulrich Lauener and Peter Bohren had lent their names to the bogus certificate issued to Dora d'Istria and that similar motives probably explain their decision to leave Wills under the illusion that he was making a first ascent of the Wetterhorn.[1]

If the importance of Alfred Wills' ascent has been exaggerated, the great influence of Speer's ascent of the Mittelhorn in 1845 has been largely forgotten. In this connection Graham Brown's comments are very much to the point:

> "Speer's narrative of the clim̄. probably played a greater part in the beginnings of mountaineering as a sport than the part usually attributed to Sir Alfred Wills' ascent of the Hasli Jungfrau peak from Grindelwald in 1854. Speer's narrative received immediate and wide publicity, which did not wane quickly; Wills' ascent was given little or no publicity at the time, and his earliest published account of it (in his *Wanderings among the High Alps*) did not appear until mid summer, 1856, too

---

[1] Ohne Zweifel muss dabei Absicht im Spiel gewesen sein, die Besteigung Wills aufzubauschen. Es ist zu bemerken, dass Peter Bohren und Ulrich Lauener unter den fünf Führern waren, die ein Jahr darauf die Dora d'Istria anschwindelten. Op. cit. p. 136.

late to attract recruits before 1857 to the sport which had already been established. Wills brought in early recruits to the young sport; Speer's service was to prepare the way for the sport itself."

The circumstances under which Alfred Wills became a judge were sufficiently unusual to deserve recording. His predecessor had died of heart failure in a brothel. Queen Victoria was so shocked that she sent for the Prime Minister and insisted that the personal character, religion and home life of the various possible candidates should be carefully considered before making an appointment. It was Wills who presided over the trial which ended in the conviction of Oscar Wilde.

Though the inflated claims made for Wills' ascent of the Wetterhorn are clearly untenable, I should be sorry to leave the reader under the impression that this historic ascent was not of considerable importance. Certainly among those who helped to create the tradition of the Alpine Club there were few who had greater influence than Alfred Wills.

CHAPTER V

THE ALPINE CLUB

The first published suggestion that an Alpine Club should be formed is to be found in a letter written on February 1st, 1857, by William Mathews to the Rev. Fenton John Anthony Hort. Mathews was a member of a well-known Worcestershire family, destined to play a great role in the development of mountaineering. Hort, a distinguished theologian, was a Fellow of Trinity, Cambridge who had been a friend of Mathews at Cambridge.

> I want you to consider (said Mathews in his letter of February 1st, 1857) whether it would not be possible to establish an Alpine Club, the members of which might dine together once a year, say in London, and give each other what information they could. Each member, at the close of any Alpine tour in Switzerland or elsewhere, should be required to furnish, to the President, a short account of all the undescribed excursions he had made, with a view to the publication of an annual or bi-annual volume. We should thus get a good deal of useful information in a form available to the members.

Hort welcomed the proposal but urged that the dining bills should be kept within reasonable limits.

In the summer of that same year E. S. Kennedy (not to be confused with T. S. Kennedy) met at Guttannen William Mathews and his cousin St. John Mathews and discussed with them two projects, the ascent of the Finsteraarhorn and the formation of some kind of club for mountaineers. They parted, but met again at Grindelwald on August 5th where they joined the Reverend John Hardy and J. C. W. Ellis, and together made the first British ascent of the Finsteraarhorn. This success strengthened their resolve to found a mountaineers' club.

The Foundation of the Alpine Club

On November 6th, 1857, William Mathews senior gave a dinner party at his home, The Leasowes, on the outskirts of Birmingham, to discuss the formation of an Alpine Club. His guests were E. S. Kennedy, three members of the Mathews clan, his son St. John and his two nephews W. and C. E. Mathews. At this dinner a list was compiled of those who might be approached to become original members. Some of those who were invited showed no interest, but those who accepted the invitation met at Ashley's Hotel, Covent Garden, on December 22nd, 1857, and, with E. S. Kennedy in the Chair, founded the first of all Alpine Clubs.

Rule XII, as originally drafted, laid down that no candidate should be elected until he had ascended a peak of at least 13,000 ft. in height, but this rule was soon dropped, and the technical qualifications were left to the Committee to decide. Those qualifications were, at first, anything but exacting; Sir Richard Burton was elected, though he did not take up his membership, his qualification being "General Travel; mountain ranges in all parts of the world". Matthew Arnold was elected in 1859, his only qualification being one very easy glacier expedition, the Théodule Pass.

The technical qualifications of a candidate were considered by the Committee, and the names of those approved were submitted to a ballot of the members. Originally one blackball in five excluded but this was subsequently altered to one blackball in ten, thereby making it even easier for small and unrepresentative cliques to blackball mountaineers of the stature of Mummery.

The first dinner of the Club was held on February 3rd, 1858, in the Thatched House Tavern; scarcely a dozen members attended.

William Longman, later President of the Club, was one of the first to realise that accounts of Alpine ascents would interest a large public. His firm, Longmans Green and Company, published not only *Peaks, Passes, and Glaciers* and *The Alpine Journal* but also many of the earlier Alpine classics such as Charles Hudson's and Kennedy's *Where There's a Will There's a Way*, an account of the guideless ascent of Mont Blanc by a new route, and Thomas Hinchliff's *Summer Months among the Alps*.

Longman, who was present at this first dinner of the Club, sums up what were then the modest hopes of these pioneers:

> "It was at first assumed that the Club would take the character rather of a social gathering of a few mountaineers than of a really important society, at the meetings of which papers were to be read, and contributions made to the geographical and topographical knowledge of mountain regions, and it certainly never entered the mind of any of its founders to conceive that it would be the parent of fruitful children, some of them more prolific than itself."

At the March meeting of 1858 John Ball was offered and accepted the Presidency. John Ball was a man of means and thereby enabled to gratify many tastes and many ambitions. He had been called to the Irish Bar, entered Parliament and became Under-Secretary for the Colonies in Palmerston's administration in spite of the fact that he was a prominent Catholic. He was from the first far more interested in science than in the law. Nobody could have been better qualified to be president of a club, the sub-title of whose official journal was "A Record of Mountain Adventure and Scientific Observation", for he was as interested in scientific observation of mountains as in their exploration. He fell in love with the Alps when he saw them as a boy, at the age of nine, from the Col de la Faucille, and he loved them in later life not only for their beauty and for their challenge to the spirit of adventure, but also for their scientific interest. He was fascinated by everything connected with mountains, their geology, their flora and their fauna. And he had other qualifications, his administrative ability, which had been proved as an Under-secretary, and his retirement from politics which enabled him to devote his abundant leisure to mountain exploration and to mountain literature.

It was John Ball who, in the autumn of 1858, first suggested to Longman the publication of an annual volume, consisting of the mountaineering experiences of members of The Alpine Club. The three volumes of *Peaks, Passes, and Glaciers*, the first of which was published in 1859, was the result. Of even greater influence on the development of mountaineering was the publication of Ball's *Alpine Guide*, the first volume of which, the *Guide to the Western Alps*, appeared in 1863. The revised editions of Ball's Guides, for which W. A. B. Coolidge, A. Valentine Richards and George Broke were responsible, are, even today, of great interest and value. When the first volume appeared Ball had already crossed the main Alpine chain by thirty-two different passes and also traversed a hundred lateral passes.

The first number of *The Alpine Journal*, the world's oldest mountaineering journal, appeared in 1863 under the editorship of the Reverend Hereford Brooke George, a Fellow of New College, whom I first met when he was presiding over the Oxford Alpine Club which he founded. The year in which *The Alpine Journal* made its bow was also the birth year of the Swiss Alpine Club, its only predecessor being the Alpine Club (1857) and the Austrian Alpine Club (1862).

The First Recruits

I published some years ago a careful analysis of the members who joined The Alpine Club between its foundation in 1857 and 1863, based on Mumm's invaluable Alpine Club Register. It was often difficult to decide in the case of members who had more than one profession to which profession they should be assigned. In the case of clerical dons I classified as clergy those whose career before or after their connection with School or University suggests that their main interest was the Church.

Of the first 281 members, 57 were barristers and 23 solicitors; 34 were clergymen, 15 dons and 7 schoolmasters, some of whom took orders. There were 5 scientists, 4 professional authors, 4 artists, 2 architects, 2 librarians and 1 lecturer. The Civil Service was represented by 12, the Army by 7 and the Royal Navy by 2 members, medicine by 4 and surgery by 4 members. There were 2 publishers, 5 engineers, 6 printers, stationers and engravers, 8 bankers, 4 insurance agents, 2 railway directors, 2 estate agents, 5 stockbrokers, 18 merchants. The club included 3 professional politicians, 13 rentiers, 19 landed gentry, 4 foreign members and 7 whose professions cannot be ascertained.

Of the first 281 members not more than 3 belonged by birth to the old aristocracy. The social structure of the club was predominantly middle or upper-middle class. Most of its recruits came from city dwellers, perhaps because the rapid development of mountaineering in the second half of the nineteenth century was in effect the response of man to a new need, the rediscovery of those spiritual values which were clouded by the smoke and grime of the industrial revolution. The country squire in close touch with nature did not feel the same need for an antidote to a megalapolitan civilisation.

More than a quarter of those who replied favourably to Kennedy's circular suggesting the foundation of The Alpine Club were clergymen, and Ronald Clark in his valuable book, admirably illustrated by period photographs, *The Victorian Mountaineers*, reminds us that the original membership included Hort and Lightfoot, outstanding Biblical scholars, that among the pioneers, Hudson the greatest amateur of his day, Hardy, Llewellyn Davies, the brothers Smyth, who with Hudson made the first ascent of Monte Rosa, and the first, second and fourth editors of *The Alpine Journal* were all in Holy Orders.

Science was represented both by amateur scientists like F. F. Tuckett, and professional scientists notably Forbes and John Tyndall.

Francis Fox Tuckett, a Quaker and a successful Bristol businessman, was one of the outstanding pioneers. Between 1856 and 1874 he climbed 165 peaks, of which 84 were of some importance, and made 57 new expeditions, among them the Aletschhorn. Forbes had urged him to make mountaineering "not merely a recreation but also a scientific recreation."

> "He was a sight to see (said Hort in 1861), being hung from head to foot with 'notions' in the strictest sense of the word, several of them being inventions of his own. Besides such commonplace things as a great axe-head and a huge rope and thermometers, he had two barometers, a sypsieometer, and a wonderful apparatus, pot within pot, for boiling water at great heights, first for scientific and then for culinary purposes."

John Tyndall was one of the outstanding mountaineers of the Golden Age. He made the first ascent of the Weisshorn and a solitary ascent of Monte Rosa, a remarkable achievement. He was the son of an Irish shoemaker, but such was the prestige of science in the class-conscious Victorian age that the Duke of Abercorn's sister was delighted when he married her daughter. Tyndall was

44

never rich and often poor, but such was his fantastic disinterestedness in money matters that he offered to settle five hundred a year on a friend of his who fell ill, and when this was declined gave him a hundred pounds. He invested the net profit of his first lecture tour in America, £2500, to found Tyndall fellowships, but though generous in money matters he was ungenerous in controversy, and even his great friend and beneficiary, Hirst, confessed to "exasperation on his want of charity".

His controversy with Whymper after Tyndall's defeat on the Matterhorn was full of mis-statements and an insinuation in a later reference to the Matterhorn accident is, in Lord Schuster's view, indefensible.[1] Tyndall not only quarrelled with fellow-mountaineers but also with fellow-scientists. His bitter and wholly unjustified attack on Forbes, the eminent glaciologist, and first honorary member of the Alpine Club, shocked the leaders of the Alpine Club, notably the gentle and judicial Alfred Wills. Forbes' reply was completely convincing, but Tyndall refused either to withdraw his charges or to prove them. Like many aggressive controversialists he took refuge, when cornered, in a smug protest against controversy as such. "I have abstained from answering my distinguished censor, not from inability to do so, but because I thought and think that, within the limits of the case, it is better to submit to misconception than to make science the field of personal controversy." Tyndall was persuaded to withdraw a resignation which he threatened, when his attack on Forbes lost him the presidency of the Alpine Club, but two years later he resigned as a protest against some jesting remarks by Leslie Stephen at the winter dinner of the Alpine Club, remarks which, in his opinion, "reflected upon the value of science in connection with mountain-eering". The substance of these jests was later reproduced in Stephen's *The Playground of Europe*. "'And what philosophical observations did you make?' will be the enquiry of one of those fanatics who, by a reasoning process to me utterly unscrutable, have somehow irrevocably associated alpine travelling with science. To them I answer that the temperature on the summit of the Zinal Rothorn was approximately (I had no thermometer) 212 (Fahrenheit) below freezing point. As for ozone, if any existed in the atmosphere, it was a greater fool than I take it for."

"A Form of Worship as well as Sport"

There are many passages in the mountain literature of the Golden Age which were written under the influence of the emotion described by a reviewer in the *Oxford Magazine* as "the strange mysticism which sets mountaineering apart from

[1] Lord Schuster, a former president of the Alpine Club, contributed a chapter on Tyndall as a mountaineer to the *Life and Work of John Tyndall*, by Professor A. S. Eve, F. R. S., and C. H. Creasey, O. B. E., Macmillan & Co.

all other sports". For men who have no sympathy with and even men who are actively hostile to institutional religion have felt the influence of mountain mysticism. Geoffrey Young, for instance, refers to the "mystical attractions of mountaineering", to the "religious fervour" of its first devotees and to the fact that its history has "the character and many of the phases of a religious movement". (*Spectator*, September 23rd, 1949.) Leo Amery described mountaineering "as a form of worship as well as a sport ... a communion with the innermost heart of things". Even Tyndall's scepticism melted in the prescence of the mountains. "Some people", he said to Newman Hall, "give me little credit for religious feeling. I assure you that when I walk here and gaze at these mountains I am filled with adoration." Tyndall was often regarded as an exponent of scientific materialism but in his 1874 address to the British Association he insisted that "it was not in hours of clearness or self vigour that this doctrine commends itself to my mind". On the contrary the doctrines of materialism dissolved "in the presence of stronger and healthier thought as offering no solution to the mystery in which we dwell". It may well have been the mountains which provided the antidote of "healthier thought" in which materialism dissolved.

Few of the pioneers were professional writers and it is therefore not surprising that much of what they wrote has no great literary merit. One may concede this, and yet maintain that John Richard Green was altogether too severe when he wrote:

> "What is it which makes men in Alpine travel-books write as men never write elsewhere? What is the origin of a style unique in literature, which misses both the sublime and the ridiculous, and constantly hops from tall-talk to a mirth feeble and inane."[1]

Green was no mountaineer, and therefore irresponsive to the charm of many Alpine essays of no great literary value, but which are worth reading because the pioneers did not keep their emotions to themselves but were writing for fellow mountaineers who were interested not only in their climbs but also in their sentiments. Elliott, for instance, who made the second ascent of the Matterhorn from Zermatt, confessed that it was his own fault if the beauties of the Alps did not raise his "heart in deeper thankfulness and truer affection to the great and loving Father whose hand is visible everywhere", and here is Alfred Wills' description of his first moments on the Wetterhorn:

> I am not ashamed to own that I experienced as this sublime and wonderful prospect burst upon my view, a profound and almost irrepressible emotion...
> We felt as in the more immediate presence of Him who had reared this tremendous pinnacle, and beneath the "majestical roof" of whose deep blue Heaven we stood.

[1] From *Stray Studies*.

46

That there was a religious element in the adoration of mountain beauty is undeniable, but it seems to me very far-fetched to attempt to explain what Ronald Clark calls the "jet propelled speed" of the advance of mountaineering by the "impingement of science on religion". I enjoyed his excellent book *The Victorian Mountaineers*, but it is as difficult to make any comments of value on the ecclesiastical climate of the Victorian age without reading the relevant sources, as it would be to write about the Victorian mountaineers without opening *Peaks, Passes, and Glaciers*. Clark's suggestion that the Victorian "clergy were doing their best to maintain a belief in the cosmology which the awkward scientists were destroying with unnerving ease" is derived from the folklore of Victorian Freethinkers. If Ronald Clark were to dip into the biographies of the great Victorian divines he would soon discover that they were wholly unperturbed by and in the main uninterested in the alleged conflict between science and religion, and that none of them regarded Archbishop Usher's chronology as the rock upon which their faith was built. The controversies which seemed to them important were not scientific but issues such as those which divided the Anglo-Catholics from the Evangelicals or the Anglicans from the Catholics. There was, *pace* Mr. Clark, "no connection between the impingement of science on religion", and the advance of mountaineering, and only an occasional echo in Alpine literature of the controversies which so excited the Victorian secularists. What you do find, however, in the writings of the mountaineers, are fugitive hints not of the beliefs which divided the Victorians but of the beliefs which unite all those who accept the Platonic distinction between the beauty which is temporal and the beauty which is timeless and eternal. It was love of adventure which drew most of the pioneers to the Alps, but many of them felt the urge to confess, even if they were conscious of an inability to explain, that need to worship of which even Tyndall the sceptic was conscious in the presence of the mountains, a sense of adoration which was, as he rightly implied, a form of "religious feeling".

The Achievement of the Pioneers

The panorama from the Gornergrat is a visible reminder of British achievement during the Golden Age of mountaineering. Let us begin our circuit of the horseshoe ring of peaks which overshadow the Zermatt valley with the Mischabelhörner. From the Gornergrat we can see the Dom, the highest peak wholly in Switzerland, and the Täschhorn, and as we follow the range round we see the Alphubel, Allalinhorn, Rimpfischhorn, and Strahlhorn, all of which were first climbed by the British, as were also the highest peak, and Nord End of Monte Rosa, the Lyskamm and Castor. The other twin, Pollux, was first climbed by a French-Swiss, J. Jacot, and the next peak, the Breithorn, by a French traveller,

M. Henri Maynard, as far back as 1813, but these are the only breaks in the monotonous succession of British successes which we recall as our eyes travel round from the Matterhorn past the Gabelhorn and Zinal Rothorn to the glorious Weisshorn.

According to Coolidge, of the thirty-nine major peaks climbed during the Golden Age, thirty-one were first ascended by British amateurs and guides, most of whom were Swiss. A Swiss mountaineer can console himself for the little mark his countrymen made in the mountains which tower above the Gornergrat by letting his eyes range along the distant Bernese Oberland which occupies the northern sky, for though of the peaks visible from the Gornergrat, Blümlisalphorn, Balmhorn, Tschingelhorn, Nesthorn, Bietschhorn, Aletschhorn, Fiescherhorn and Eiger were first climbed by the British, the Wetterhorn, Jungfrau and Finsteraarhorn, monarch of the range, were climbed by the Swiss before the British invasion began, and even during the period of British ascendancy E. von Fellenberg, a distinguished Swiss mountaineer, had a better record of first ascents in this range than most Englishmen. These included the first ascents of the Weisse Frau, Doldenhorn, Lauterbrunnen Breithorn, and with Karl Baedeker of Germany, the Silberhorn.

Gottlieb Studer, who made the first ascent of the peak which bears his name, the Studerhorn, and also of the Gross Wannehorn, was one of the first, as he was undoubtedly the greatest of the Swiss pioneers. He was born in 1804 and between 1823 and 1883 he made no fewer than six hundred and forty-three ascents. He engraved seven hundred and ten panoramas. His classic book *Über Eis und Schnee* is an invaluable source for the Alpine historian, and his position in Swiss mountaineering may be compared to that of John Ball.

Mountaineering Then and Now

The age of specialisation did not begin until the Golden Age had come to an end. The acrobatic talent necessary to lead a severe rock climb was not developed until much later. The pioneers should be compared with explorers, and should be thought of as the precursors of Everest expeditions rather than of the acrobatic rock climbers of to-day.

The difficulties with which they had to contend were not only physical but also mental. The tradition of inaccessibility daunted all but the boldest. The pioneers began to climb when there were few maps of the glacier regions, and when such maps as existed were grossly misleading. There were no Alpine club huts, and very few paths above the higher pastures, and no experienced guides. The great guides who made their reputations during the Golden Age began as shepherds or chamois hunters or smugglers, and many of them learned as much from their employers as they taught them. The relations between the greatest of the pioneers and the greatest of the guides was indeed a genuine partnership in which amateur and professional gradually developed and perfected the technique of mountaineering.

On many first ascents it was the amateur, not the guide, who was the real leader. A case in point was the first ascent of the Eiger on August 11th, 1858, by Richard Barrington. Barrington was, what many of the British pioneers were not, a natural athlete. He had previously ridden the winner of the 'Irish Grand National', a more exacting test of courage and skill than his first ascent of the Eiger. His first peak was the Jungfrau. "I met some Alpine men whose footsteps I had tracked down the glacier. Talking about climbing, I said to them I did not think much of the work I had done, and was answered: 'Try the Eiger or the Matterhorn.' 'All right', I said. . . . Started at 3.30 a.m. on August 11th for the Eiger. We took a flag from the hotel. When we came to the point where one descends into a small hollow, I looked well with my glass over the face of the Eiger next us, and made up my mind to try the rocks in front. . . . Almer and Bohren said it was no use, and declined to come the way I wished. 'All right', I said, 'you may stay; I will try.' So off I went for about 300 or 400 yards over some smooth rocks to the part which was almost perpendicular. I then shouted and waved the flag for them to come on, and after five minutes they followed and came up to me. They said it was impossible. I said: 'I will try.' So with the rope coiled over my shoulders, I scrambled up, sticking like a cat to the rocks, which cut my fingers, and at last got up say 50 to 60 ft. I then lowered the rope, and the guides followed with its assistance."

It was some years before the guides mastered the proper use of the rope. The Rev. J. F. Hardy could not persuade Auguste Simond, one of the best of the Chamonix guides, to use the rope on the Finsteraarhorn. He replied that the rope would be worse than useless for "the weight of any unfortunate who slipped would certainly drag the others down. 'Non, Monsieur', said he, 'ici chacun pour soi-même." Eustace Anderson who made the first ascent of the Klein Schreckhorn with Christian Almer and Peter Bohren, was not roped. "As we were not tied", writes Anderson, "a slip would have proved fatal." It was not an uncommon habit for good guides to remove the rope in dangerous places and hold a coil in one hand. John Stogdon, in a letter to me, described old Peter Taugwalder unroping on the top of the Tête Blanche. Peter Knubel was undoubtedly one of the best guides in the Visptal, but the Rev. Julius Elliott whom he led on the second ascent of the Matterhorn from Zermatt complained that "he held the rope and would not tie it when I bade him, saying it was safer so, which, of course, was false; and I had not the moral courage then to insist on it, fearing that he might turn sulky and refuse to go on, and seeing at that time no particular need for it".

Elliott was killed on the Schreckhorn in 1869 and his guide reported that he had insisted against their advice on unroping, and had fallen to his death. In view of Elliott's strong objection to Knubel unroping one cannot help wondering whether the initiative to unrope came from Elliott.

Such then were the difficulties, human no less than physical, with which the pioneers had to contend, and I agree with Lord Schuster that "but for these men in whiskers, long trousers and gigantic ice-axes, climbing for Englishmen would, if it had ever existed, have been long delayed".

The Alpine Club was born in that Victorian age which it is no longer fashionable to denigrate. "The higher culture", writes Mr. George Trevelyan O.M., "of nineteenth century England was varied, solid and widespread over a large proportion of the community. The world is not likely to see again so fine and broad a culture for many years to come." From this culture came the pioneers of the Alpine Club and I will bring this chapter to an end by quoting a noble tribute to them from the pen of Lord Schuster:

> "They passed, leaving a tradition which was vigorous and yet urbane. They did not suppose that all was for the best in the best possible world. On the contrary they were dissatisfied, full of curiosity, anxious to reach the pass and to enjoy the prospect which, as they were certain, would then lie open to their view, and to go down on the other side and up the village street in the cool of the evening and so home in the gathering darkness under the cold far-distant stars to the bright light of the inn door. Their muscles, they thought, would have been well exercised and attuned to the gentle languor succeeding toil. Their minds, they thought, would be at rest, tormented as they had been through the long day with the constant effort to subdue their bodies to their wills. All through the hours of darkness through which they passed when they first set forth, through the heat of noon, through the gathering in of evening as they came down over the meadows, there had gleamed these visions, first of the peak and its attainment, and then of rest.
>
> Rest could not come to them or to their children. The problems which they sought to solve of icefalls and routes and ridges have long ago been solved. But the eternal problem which troubled them and their generation, the perfectibility of man, remains unsolved and, perhaps, insoluble. Catastrophes, such as they never imagined, have since then fallen upon the human race and threaten to destroy it. For those sorrows and perplexities they might have been as unskilled as we are to find either cure or anodyne. But it is something more than idle fancy to suppose that, as in their quest they kept alight the spirit of bodily adventure in a generation which looked too much to mere comfort on the one hand and to pure speculation on the other, so in their deliberate yet temperate approach to conquest and to peril, they helped to make people who can endure and conquer."

50

CHAPTER VI

WHYMPER AND LESLIE STEPHEN

It would, of course, be easy to devote not only a chapter but a book to brief biographies of the pioneers who were active during the Golden Age of mountaineering, but I prefer to devote more space to fewer people and if I confine myself in this chapter to Edward Whymper and Leslie Stephen I do so because they were outstanding mountaineering personalities of the period.

Edward Whymper, whose life is the theme of Frank Smythe's interesting biography, was born on April 27th, 1840. Edward's grandfather was a brewer; his father, Josiah, a wood engraver and a painter. At the age of fourteen Edward was taken away from school and apprenticed to his father's business. A year later, Edward began a diary, long extracts from which are reproduced by Smythe. The diary is a valuable social document with a sure appeal to all who are interested in the Victorian age. It is the work of a clever boy with considerable gifts for expression. There are many passages in Whymper's diary which remind us of the class-consciousness of the mid-Victorian Age.

Whymper's own position in the social hierarchy is difficult to define. He was not a gentleman, as that term was understood by the Victorian, and as a lecturer he "was troubled", so Frank Smythe tells us, "by a tendency to drop his aitches. This worried him, and round about 1905 to 1908 he got his nephew, Robert Whymper, to attend many of his lectures and call attention to every omission by snapping his fingers".

His father, a talented man, was a member of the Royal Society of Painters in Water-Colours, and his pupils included Frederick Walker, A.R.A., and Keene, the well known contributor to *Punch*. He had eleven children, a fact to which Whymper indirectly owed his career, for if the family had been smaller Whymper might have been sent to a better school and educated for a more ambitious career than that of wood-engraving. It was the fact that Edward began to master the craft of wood-engraving at an early age which gave him his splendid chance. His work attracted the attention of William Longman, the publisher, who was in need of illustrations for a book on the Alps and who commissioned Edward Whymper for this purpose.

Whymper was twenty years of age when he left England for the Alps. He crossed the Channel on July 23rd, 1860, visited Kandersteg, crossed the Gemmi to Leuk, explored the Saas valley and sketched the view from the Fee Alp, one of the few Alpine views which excited his enthusiastic appreciation. From Saas Fee he went to Zermatt.

Smythe makes an excellent point when he contrasts Whymper's first impressions of the Matterhorn, as recorded in his diary, with the sentiments which he put on record for the public:

> "Saw, of course, the Matterhorn repeatedly; what precious stuff Ruskin has written about this, as well as about many other things. When one has a fair view of the mountain as I had, it may be compared to a sugar loaf set up on a table; the sugar loaf should have its head knocked on one side. Grand it is, but beautiful I think it is not."

And this is what he wrote, when he was writing for the public. The quotation is from *Scrambles Amongst the Alps*:

> "Ages hence generations unborn will gaze upon its awful precipices and wonder at its unique form. However exalted may be their ideas, and however exaggerated their expectations, none will come to return disappointed!"

Whymper was a superb salesman. He sold the Matterhorn to the British public, and—like other salesmen—his private opinion of the commodity which he marketed did not always coincide with his publicity pronouncements. Few mountaineers had less appreciation of mountain beauty, or a greater appreciation of mountain adventure.

He returned to the Oberland, went up the Lauterbrunnen valley, and disliked the Staubbach even more than he had expected to. "I had previously expected to be disappointed, but felt quite sold, and would not stop to look at it."

Whymper returned to the Alps in 1861, made the first British ascent of the Pelvoux and, emboldened by this success, attempted the Matterhorn from Italy.

His seven unsuccessful attempts on the Matterhorn (1861–1865) were all directed against the Italian side of the mountain. His persistent neglect of what is now the normal route from Zermatt is difficult to explain. The three brothers, Alfred, Charles and Sandbach Parker, had attacked the Matterhorn by this route, a year before Whymper made his first attempt on the mountain, and *without guides* had reached a height of 12,000 ft., on the eastern face. They were driven back by storm, but reported that the eastern face appeared practicable for many hundred feet above the point from which they had retreated.

Many of Whymper's attempts on the Matterhorn were made with the great Italian guide, J. A. Carrel. Carrel, an ardent patriot who had fought in the Italian

52

wars of liberation, was determined to make the first ascent from Italy by the Italian ridge, and—if possible—to lead an Italian party to the summit. Carrel, like Whymper, had something of the undisciplined nature of the mountain he loved. Like Whymper, he was a born leader, and, like Whymper, he did not readily consent to play second fiddle. It is not surprising that Whymper and Carrel did not form a successful partnership.

Whereas of the peaks visible from Zermatt the Matterhorn was the only virgin peak climbed by Whymper, he made many first ascents in other ranges, the Ecrins in the Dauphiny; and the Aiguille Verte, Aiguille d'Argentière, Grandes Jorasses (lower peak) and Mont Dolent in the Mont Blanc range. But the Matterhorn was the magnet which drew him back again and again to the Valais.

On one occasion climbing alone he reached a point higher than any of his predecessors, and did not turn back until he had attained the height of 13,500 ft. On his return, he slipped while attempting to turn a corner on the Tête du Lion. He shot down an ice slope, somersaulted, and was thrown against the side of the gully where it narrowed. His fall was finally checked, 200 ft. below the point where he had slipped. He plastered up the many wounds in his head before scrambling up to a place of safety where he fainted. He managed to make his way down to Breuil unaided, and within a week he had returned to the attack. A little later he had the satisfaction of seeing Professor John Tyndall, the famous scientist and conqueror of the Weisshorn, fail shortly after reaching the minor summit which still bears his name, Pic Tyndall. Tyndall had engaged the two Carrels and had also brought with him his Swiss guides Bennen and Anton Walter. When the Carrels were appealed to for their opinion they replied: "We are porters, ask your guides."

In this same year, 1863, some leading Italian mountaineers, among them two distinguished scientists, Felice Giordano and Quintino Sella, founded the Italian Alpine Club in Turin. They resolved that as English climbers had robbed them of Monte Viso, prince of Piedmontese peaks, Italians should have the honour of making the first ascent of the Matterhorn.

Whymper knew nothing of these plans when he arrived in Breuil on July 8th, 1865, hoping to persuade Carrel to join him in an attack on the east face of the mountain.

Carrel told Whymper that he had been engaged to travel "with a family of distinction in the valley of Aosta". "You are going to leave me", exclaimed Whymper, "to travel with a party of ladies. The work is not fit for you." Carrel smiled grimly, for he knew that the task which had been assigned to him was more fitted for him than for any other man. It was only after Carrel had left for the Matterhorn that Whymper discovered that he had been "bamboozled and humbugged".

On the 7th July, Giordano had written to Sella:

"Let us, then, set out to attack this Devil's mountain; and let us see that we succeed, if only Whymper has not been beforehand."

On the 11th he wrote again:

"We immediately sent off our advance guard with Carrel at its head. In order not to excite remark, we took the rope and other materials to Avouil, a hamlet which is very remote and close to the Matterhorn; and this is to be our lower base.... I have tried to keep everything secret; but that fellow whose life seems to depend on the Matterhorn, is here suspiciously prying into everything. I have taken all the best men away from him; and yet he is so enamoured of the mountain that he may go with others and make a scene. He is here in the hotel and I try to avoid speaking to him."

Whymper decided to cross the Théodule to Zermatt and engage the first competent guide that he could find for an attack on the mountain from Switzerland. At this point Lord Francis Douglas, who had just made the second ascent of the Gabelhorn, and the first from Zinal, arrived from Zermatt. He confided to Whymper that Peter Taugwalder had prospected the east face of the Matterhorn and was confident that it could be climbed. Graham Brown writing in *The Alpine Journal* gives his reasons for supposing that Douglas had come to Breuil to engage Carrel and that Whymper gate-crashed into his expedition. "There is therefore", he writes, "something magnificent in Whymper's words about Douglas: 'Before long it was determined that he should take part in the expedition.'"

On the 12th they crossed to Zermatt and discovered that the Rev. Charles Hudson had just arrived and was proposing with Michel Croz, a great Chamonix guide, to attempt the Matterhorn. Hudson, who, according to Leslie Stephen, was "as simple and noble a character as ever carried out the precepts of muscular Christianity without talking its cant", was the greatest amateur of the day, a pioneer of guideless climbing who had led a guideless party up Mont Blanc by a new route. He did not waste time attempting the more difficult Italian route but realised from the first the weak points in the eastern face.

Hudson's friend, Douglas Hadow, a young man of nineteen who had just left Harrow, was included in the party. According to Hudson, he "had done Mont Blanc in less time than most men", but though a strong walker he was an inexperienced climber, and was destined to die on the Matterhorn.

They left Zermatt on July 13th, 1865. On July 14th Giordano wrote to Sella: "At 2 p.m. to-day I saw Carrel and Co. on the top of the Matterhorn." But it was not Carrel whom he saw, and a sad disillusion awaited those who had celebrated too soon an Italian victory. "Although every man did his duty", wrote Giordano on the 15th, "it is a lost battle, and I am in great grief."[1]

Whymper's party camped at a height of about 11,000 ft., and were delighted next day to find that the east face up to "the Shoulder" was so straightforward that they did not even bother to rope. Difficulties only began when they turned over on to the northern face, but the "solitary difficult part was of no great extent".

All through the climb false alarms had been raised of men on the top, but no footsteps could be seen when at last they reached the summit ridge. They peered over the ridge and far below they caught sight of the Italians. They shouted until they were hoarse, and then hurled stones down the cliffs—not, of course, on to the Italians but near enough to arouse their attention.

It is interesting to compare Whymper's account of what Carrel said on returning: "The old legends are true—there are spirits on the top of the Matterhorn. We saw them ourselves—they hurled stones at us"—with what Carrel actually reported to Giordano. He did not mistake Whymper for a demon. On the contrary he recognised him by his white trousers.

In the course of the descent, a little below the summit, Hadow slipped, and the rope broke between Taugwalder and Douglas. Whymper and the two Taugwalders alone survived. They spent a miserable night on the east face, and on the following day descended to Zermatt.

On Sunday morning Whymper set out with the Rev. John M'Cormick to recover the bodies. The parish priest of Zermatt, according to Whymper, threatened with excommunication any guide who left without hearing Mass. Priests have no power of excommunication, and no Catholic has ever been excommunicated for failing to hear Mass. The obligation to hear Mass is always subject to commonsense qualifications. What the priest probably did was to suggest that, as the victims were certainly dead, the search party should attend an early Mass, at 6 a.m., before leaving Zermatt. The parish priests in neighbouring villages were less exacting, and though Zermatt was not represented on the search party, there were guides from Täsch.

The accident caused a profound sensation. For three weeks Whymper remained silent and then, in reply to a dignified appeal from Mr. Justice Wills, President of the Alpine Club, Whymper wrote a letter to *The Times*.

There were malicious rumours to the effect that the rope had been cut. It might well be to the advantage of a climber to cut the rope if his companion fell into a concealed crevasse from which it was impossible, as it probably would be if the party consisted of only two mountaineers, to extricate him, but on a rock

[1] The Italian story of the early attempts on the Matterhorn is described in Guido Rey's classic *Il Cervino*, admirably translated by J. E. C. Eaton.

face on which there are, as there are on the Matterhorn, abundant foot and hand holds, there are no conceivable circumstances in which anything could be gained by cutting the rope.

When Hadow slipped there were three possibilities: (1) that the rope would not break and that Taugwalder would succeed in checking the fall without being dragged off the rocks; in that case nobody would have been killed; (2) that the entire party would be dragged off the rocks; or (3) that the rope would break leaving the Taugwalders and Whymper on the face of the mountain.

It is interesting to compare Whymper's account in *The Times* (August 8th, 1865) with the story as retold in *Scrambles Amongst the Alps*. Some of the differences are mere stylistic improvements. Thus: "We were happy that night in camp and feared no evil", is certainly to be preferred to: "We were happy that night in camp and did not dream of calamity."

In his letter to *The Times* he attributes to Croz a remark flattering to Whymper: "I would rather go down with you and another guide alone than with those who are going", but this was omitted from the book, perhaps because the relations of those who died resented the implied slur on their mountaineering ability. In an unpublished letter to Sir Edward Davidson, which I consulted at the Alpine Club, and which was written in 1909, Whymper quotes this remark attributed to Croz, and complacently takes great credit for never having given publicity to it for fear of distressing the relatives. Many picturesque details in the book are not in the letter, such as the attempt to attract Carrel's attention by throwing stones down the cliff. The "sharp-eyed" lad who thought he saw an avalanche on the Matterhorn, and the crosses in the sky, which Whymper imagined that he saw after the accident, also make their first appearance in the book.

Whymper greatly exaggerated the interest with which the natives followed the climb. In 1865 mountaineering was still regarded by most Zermatters as an eccentric and foolish amusement of foreigners with more money than good sense. Herr Karl Lehner, the Postmaster of Zermatt, who has made a study of local traditions tells me that an old lady who was a girl at that time heard somebody say that men had been seen on the top of the Matterhorn, and remembered that those to whom this information had been imparted showed no interest. Alexander Seiler, of course, was interested, but when he rushed into the dining room to announce that there were men on the Matterhorn, half the guests refused to leave the table and continued placidly eating.

Whymper defended Taugwalder from the charge that he had cut the rope, and substituted three accusations of his own:

(1) Whymper suggested that the imperfect rope which broke might have been deliberately selected by Taugwalder as a protection in case of accident.

56

(2) He asserted that the Taugwalders invited him to make a statement to the effect that they had not been paid, the effect of which would arouse sympathy and increase their clientele.

(3) In a private memorandum addressed to the Secretary of the Alpine Club, Whymper stated that he passed a miserable night on the mountain fearing that the Taugwalders might murder him.

As to the first point, Whymper and Hudson were in command of the party and primarily responsible for the selection of ropes.

In his story of the climb Whymper writes:

"Many false alarms of 'men on the summit' had been raised. The higher we rose, the more intense became the excitement. What if we should be beaten at the last moment? The slope eased off, at length we could be detached, and Croz and I, dashing away, ran a neck-and-neck race, which ended in a dead-heat. At 1.40 p.m. the world was at our feet, and the Matterhorn was conquered. Hurrah! Not a footstep could be seen."

In 1949 a friend of mine in the Alpine Club, the late Geoffrey Howard, repeated a story I had heard as a boy. Whymper after a good dinner remarked to A. E. W. Mason: "Thinking it over, I believe that I did cut the rope behind me so that I could more easily race Croz to the top."

If this was so, bad rope may have been used because the better rope was cut by Whymper and, in fairness to a great guide, this relevant evidence should not have been suppressed.

With regard to the second point, Whymper knew no German and the only means of communication between him and the Taugwalders was French. Now in an article which I contributed to *The Alpine Journal* (May, 1946) I have shown that Whymper's knowledge of French was almost non-existent and that Taugwalder had probably only acquired a rudimentary knowledge of the French patois spoken in the Valtournanche to which he had once paid a long visit. My own guess is that the Taugwalders *did* make some reference to the *Führerbuch*, in which mountaineers are expected to record their appreciation of the services rendered by their guides, and that what they wanted was some statement clearing them of responsibility for the accident. Nobody with any real knowledge of the outlook of a mountain peasant could credit the Taugwalders with offering to forgo immediate payment for services rendered in the far-fetched hope of recouping themselves later, thanks to the sympathy thus aroused.

It is odd that only one member of the Alpine Club publicly defended Taugwalder against these reckless charges. Leslie Stephen, in a review of Whymper's book which appeared in *Macmillan's* (August, 1871) and which was completely forgotten until I discovered and republished it, wrote as follows:

"Knowing the carelessness too often displayed on such occasions, the confidence which guides will show in weak ropes, and the probable state of excitement of the whole party, which would easily account for such an oversight, I think the hypothesis of deliberate intention on Taugwalder's part is in the highest degree improbable; and that there is not a particle of direct evidence in its favour. The presumption would be that Croz was almost equally responsible; and, at any rate, such accusations should have some more tangible ground than a vague possibility."

It is an interesting example of the secretiveness of mountain people that no guide or other native of Zermatt seems to have ever mentioned to any member of the Alpine Club the resentment which Whymper's attack provoked in the valley. It was only after my article appeared that Otto Furrer went out of his way to thank me, adding: "You were the first to say a good word for the Taugwalders." Not the first, but unfortunately Stephen's article never reached Zermatt.

No native of Zermatt, in spite of Whymper's assertion to the contrary, ever believed that Taugwalder had cut the rope.

Again, the suggestion that Taugwalder emigrated to America because he was under a cloud in his native valley is yet another example of Whymper's inventive powers where some picturesque detail is needed to round off a story. Taugwalder was persuaded to emigrate by the example of many Zermatters at a time when emigration suddenly seemed attractive, and like many of those who did emigrate he returned to Zermatt.

It was, I suppose, inevitable that people should try to romanticize Whymper's attitude to the tragedy and to his lost companions. Alexander Seiler, for instance, described the Matterhorn as Whymper's "*grösster Unglücksberg*", but the Matterhorn, so far from being Whymper's "unluckiest mountain", promoted this young man of twenty-five from a climber known only to the small fraternity of mountaineers into a world-wide celebrity, a position which he proceeded to exploit with hard-headed realism by his pen and by lecturing, his only sources of income.

Whymper was always the guest of the Seilers when he stayed at the Monte Rosa but the family drew the line at writing off his bill for wine and whisky. Once when Whymper reluctantly paid his drink bill he said, "What would Zermatt be but for me?", to which one of Seiler's daughters replied, "And what would Whymper be but for the Matterhorn?"

It is equally absurd to suggest that Whymper was so shocked by the accident that he never climbed again. Whymper loved the challenge of virgin peaks, but he does not seem to have had much love for mountains as such. The true mountain-lover will repeat ascents, not only those that others have made, but that he himself has made, whereas Whymper only climbed five peaks which he knew for certain were no longer virgin when he climbed them. He had announced that his Alpine career would end if and when he climbed the Matterhorn, but he did, in fact, repeat the ascent once, and later led mountaineering expeditions in the Andes and the Rockies. A mountaineer would no more be tempted to give up climbing because he saw his companions killed than a professional soldier to send in his papers at the first opportunity because his best friends had fallen beside him in battle.

That the accident was a shock we can well believe, but neither Hudson nor Douglas was a friend of Whymper's, and he certainly wasted no emotion mourning Hudson. He knew that he had attached himself to Hudson's expedition, and this seems to have rankled with him and eventually, as the Editor of *The Alpine Journal* pointed out, "he allowed his bitterness against Hudson to appear in an unfair attack".

Whymper was a pathetic and friendless man. His climbing partnerships might be compared to *mariages de convenance*. Few men climbed with Whymper for more than one season. His guides, with the exception perhaps of Croz and Almer, disliked him. He quarrelled with the Carrels whom he took to the Andes, and with Christian Klucker in the Rockies. "*Er war nicht beliebt im Tal*", was Joseph Knubel's verdict. ("He was not beloved in the valley.")

The impression which emerges from Graham Brown's analysis of Whymper's attitude to Hudson is reinforced by an article in the same issue by T. S. Blakeney. He writes:

> "The Alpine Club has been presented with Whymper's own copy of Mummery's *My Climbs in the Alps and Caucasus*. Against Freshfield's tribute quoted in the preface, 'his untimely death is a grievous loss to the Club', Whymper wrote, 'I do not agree'. In *The Sphere*, January 30th, 1909, Whymper reviewed the book and described it as a 'vicious' book. A memorandum pasted inside the volume shows that in the event of his review provoking comment he intended 'to try and belittle Mummery by quoting my times across the Col Dolent against his across the Col des Courtes, and my times on the Aig. Verte against his times.' He then speculates on the conditions in which Mummery's body is likely to be should traces of it be found. 'It will be', he says, 'in the shape of a dislocated skeleton, one bone here and another there. The stomach and heart will be nowhere.' Mrs. Mummery, be it noted, was alive when this review appeared. He concludes his review by postulating that in certain important matters Mummery was insane."

As a young man I met Whymper at a meeting of the Alpine Club. He was standing alone, some little distance from a group of Alpine Club members exchanging reminiscences. He was detached and aloof, like the great peak which he conquered. I was introduced, and he made some commonplace remarks and drifted away.

He was not a lovable nor, apart from mountaineering, an admirable man, but it is impossible to deny him the unmistakable imprint of greatness. He had something of the indomitable character of the mountain which he conquered, with the result that we tend, as Geoffrey Winthrop Young rightly says, to identify him in our memory with the greatness of the Matterhorn. "Through the attitudes of the protagonists" (of mountaineering), writes Young, "he crashed with a rude personal vehemence that remains hopelessly individual." Whymper was certainly a great individualist. He neither rejected nor made any attempt to conform to the social standards and conventions of his contempories. His nephew describes him lunching at Anderton's Hotel in Fleet Street "in a sweater that showed his bare bull-like neck to perfection; he seldom wore anything under the sweater". He smoked the strongest possible shag, and the carpets, tablecloths, upholstered chairs, etc., in his vicinity were frequently burnt full of holes. He invariably smoked in bed, "and not only were his bed clothes soon riddled with holes but his own chest became scarred by hot ashes too".

Whymper remained to the end amazingly tough. At the age of sixty-two he walked from Edinburgh to London, averaging fifty-five miles a day.

In spite of his uncertain aspirates he seems to have had no difficulty in getting into the Alpine Club, from which Mummery was subsequently blackballed. On the other hand his mountaineering partnerships did not last. Whymper was at no time a clubable man, and there may be some truth in Coolidge's malicious gloss on a certain incident described in *Scrambles*. "You will remember, my dear Lunn", said the sage of Grindelwald, "that after climbing the Ecrins, Whymper and Moore spent the night under different rocks. Whymper tells us that he left Moore because he and Croz thought they would try for a roof before finally abandoning all hope of reaching civilisation. The truth is that Moore remained behind because Whymper had got on his nerves. You see, Whymper was pretty uncouth, whereas Moore was a distinguished Civil Servant. He was appointed political and secret secretary to the India Office just before he died. He was a bit of a swell and Whymper grated on him."

For only two women, and indeed for only two human beings, did he feel a strong affection, his mother and Miss Charlotte Hanbury, whom he met when he was fifty-nine years of age and who died a year after they first met. His disastrous marriage at the age of sixty-six to a girl of twenty only lasted four years. There was one child by this marriage, a daughter, Ethel, now Mrs. Blandy, who has carried out many fine climbs in the Zermatt district. He made no lasting friendships among either the amateurs or guides with whom he climbed. He regarded his guides, as Smythe tells us, not as partners in a joint enterprise, but as employees, and he insisted on "unquestioning obedience to all orders", an attitude which led to serious trouble when the guides were men of forceful independence such as Klucker or the Carrels. "Whymper", writes Smythe, "was a hard taskmaster to himself and his guides, and the gulf between them was absolute."

I find it difficult to write dispassionately of his famous book *Scrambles Amongst the Alps*, for this was the first book which I spelt out for myself and the famous wood engravings were the first which fired me with the ambition to become a mountaineer. It is odd how few lovers of that book realise that Whymper only provided "slight memoranda", his own phrase, and did not draw a single one of the illustrations himself on wood. Fifty of these illustrations were drawn on wood by James Mahoney. "I can't understand", Martin Conway once remarked to me, "why Mahoney is only known to us because of *Scrambles*. His *'Cannonade on the Matterhorn'* is a remarkably effective bit of work." Conway was the only mountaineer whom I have met who did not unconsciously give Whymper credit not only for the engravings but also for the drawings.

Whymper had no gift for describing mountain scenery, but no book made more converts to mountaineering than the famous *Scrambles*, and few mountaineers have been more successful in interpreting the romance of mountaineering adventure. His writing is flavoured with dry humour, all the more attractive in contrast to the facetiousness which was so common in the Alpine literature of the period. His writing is effective when it is sincere, and unconvincing when pretentious. He spoils the ending of the immortal chapter on the Matterhorn tragedy by a dreadful peroration which begins:

> "See yonder height! 'Tis far away—unbidden comes the word 'impossible'. 'Not so', says the mountaineer. 'The way is long, I know; it's difficult—it may be dangerous. It's possible, I'm sure; I'll seek the way; take counsel of my brother mountaineers.'"

But at its best Whymper's writing has a simplicity and directness which again recalls the Greeks. There is indeed something of Greek simplicity and Greek irony in the story of the Matterhorn triumph and tragedy:

> "Long after dusk the cliffs above echoed with our laughter and with the songs of our guides; for we were happy that night in camp, and feared no evil."

Whymper died on September 16th, 1911, at Chamonix.

Sir Leslie Stephen

Few of the pioneers had a longer list of first ascents than Leslie Stephen. He was the first to climb the Schreckhorn, Blümlisalp, Bietschhorn, Rimpfischhorn, Zinal Rothorn, Monte della Disgrazia and Mont Mallet, and the first to cross the

61

Fiescherjoch, Eigerjoch, Jungfraujoch and Col des Hirondelles. He was president of the Alpine Club and editor of *The Alpine Journal*.

The Victorians are coming into fashion again and it is no accident that a distinguished modern critic, Mr. Noel Annan, should have chosen Leslie Stephen for a discerning study: *Leslie Stephen. His Thought and Character in Relation to his Time*. A book which is an intriguing contrast to Frederick William Maitland's biography published in 1906.

Whereas Whymper's origins were humble, Stephen was by birth a member of that aristocracy of intellect which did so much to shape the intellectual climate of Victorian England. In this aristocracy of intellect there are two important connections, the first of which centres in the four families of Trevelyan, Macaulay, Huxley and Arnold, and the second is the Stephen connection. Leslie Stephen was the brother of Sir James Fitzjames Stephen, the eminent jurist, and uncle of the parodist J. K. Stephen and of Katherine Stephen, Principal of Newnham College. Leslie Stephen married first a daughter of Thackeray and secondly Julia Jackson, who had Vaughans and Prinseps for uncles, and was a niece of Mrs. Cameron, the famous photographer, and an aunt of H. A. L. Fisher, the Warden of New College, and of Mrs. F. W. Maitland, the historian's wife, who later married Sir Francis Darwin. The daughters of Stephen's second marriage were Vanessa, wife of Clive Bell, and Virginia, the wife of Leonard Woolf. His son Adrian married Karin Costelloe, a niece of Logan Pearsall Smith and of Alys, first wife of Bertrand Russell; she was also the step-daughter of Bernard Berenson.

Both the Macaulays and the Stephens are the descendants of those wealthy evangelicals whom Sydney Smith derisively called "The Clapham Sect", but even those who have no sympathy for the *ethos* of the Clapham sect must respect the solid achievements of evangelical humanitarianism which inspired Wilberforce in his campaign for the abolition of slavery, Shaftesbury in his fight for the Factory Acts and also Florence Nightingale, a descendant of a member of the sect, even though she herself drifted far from the climate of Clapham.

Leslie Stephen was born on November 28th, 1832, and was educated at Eton and at Trinity Hall, Cambridge. He was placed twentieth in the list of Wranglers and was elected a Fellow in 1854. This award was of the type which required the holder to take Holy Orders, which Stephen did in the following year.

Leslie Stephen as a young man was a keen radical, ambitious to be elected to the Apostles, that exclusive society of liberal-minded intellectuals which continues to this day. "Something of his personality grated on his intellectual equals and made them feel that he was not of their own flesh and blood", and he never became an Apostle.

Leslie Stephen was, as Mr. Annan remarks, ashamed of his sensibility and boyish ill-health. He despised weakness and determined to overcome his own weakness. So he went in for the river, and though he rowed very badly and never rose higher than the second boat, he achieved great triumphs as a coach when Trinity Hall went head of the river in 1859, and again in 1862.

"Clad in a filthy shirt and grey flannel trousers with a large purple patch in the seat, and damning the eyes of any cox on the river who did not give way, the Rev. Leslie Stephen was a sight to make Victorian eyes blink."

I agree with Mr. Annan that Stephen, rather than Charles Kingsley, should be regarded as the founder of muscular Christianity, and this in spite of the fact that in his essay on Charles Kingsley he writes: "He is more or less responsible for those offensive persons, the Viking and the muscular Christian."

A muscular Christian has been defined as a man who feared God and had walked a hundred miles in a hundred hours. Stephen, as we shall see, evolved into a muscular agnostic who might be defined as a man who had ceased to fear God, and who could climb ten peaks in ten days.

In 1862, Stephen abandoned Christianity and thereby was forced to resign his Fellowship, for in those days only Anglicans could hold Fellowships.

Stephen inherited from his father a small private income which he had no difficulty in supplementing by literary work. He visited the United States during the Civil War, in which he was a keen partisan of the North; established enduring friendships with J. R. Lowell and Charles Eliot Norton, edited the *Cornhill*, wrote *An Agnostic's Apology*, several books of literary criticism, and launched the *Dictionary of National Biography*, of which he was the first editor. Apart from his work as a literary critic and as a mountaineer, perhaps his most important book was *English Thought in the Eighteenth Century*, a book which the present writer read while at Harrow, and which provided him with an invaluable background when he was writing a life of John Wesley. Mr. Annan praises the style in which this book is written: "How his style shames that of our own generation, how pellucid and natural, how solid without being heavy, ironical without being flashy, how it coaxes the reader from point to point on an easy gentle rein!"

And the same is true of his literary criticism. His literary essays are excellent if judged by the standard of the *Dictionary of National Biography*. They give the essential facts in a pleasant readable style, flavoured with an astringent irony wholly free from malice. Where Stephen fails as a critic is in his defective appreciation of poetry. Poetry appealed to Stephen if it could be linked to ethics or mountains. His interest in ethics emerges in the titles of such essays as *Wordsworth's Ethics* and *Pope as a Moralist*. Almost the only lines of Tennyson which he quotes with real appreciation are the famous quatrain describing the

63

dawn on Monte Rosa, the exquisite lines from *Tithonus* which he applies so aptly to sunrise on the Jungfrau, and the lines from *The Lotus Eaters* which were inspired by the valley of Lauterbrunnen. Most of the essays on the poets are potted biographies mainly concerned with their religious, ethical, or political views. Thus he can write an entire essay about Coleridge with hardly a mention of his poetry, and find in his political and metaphysical fantasies a key to the "strange charm" of *The Ancient Mariner*, while explicitly disclaiming any attempt to discuss "its purely literary merits".

Stephen was a competent critic of a man's writings in relation to his ethical or political doctrines, but you have only to contrast his essay on Sir Thomas Browne with Lytton Strachey's or his essay on Tennyson with Kingsmill's to realise the contrast between competent and inspired criticism.

The nineteenth century was an age of robust confidence in the inevitability of progress, whereas ours is an age of growing disillusion; and great art does not flower in the soil of disenchantment. Matthew Arnold's poetry is as superior to modern poetry as his literary criticism is inferior to the best criticism of this century, and Leslie Stephen certainly wrote no biography as accomplished or as intriguing as Mr. Annan's biography of Leslie Stephen. Even authors whose own positive beliefs are uneroded by modern disillusion are influenced by the climate of opinion, with the result that a great novelist like Evelyn Waugh is more successful in his destructive satires, notably in *The Loved One*, than in his positive interpretation of his own beliefs, as for instance in *Brideshead Revisited*.

One great quality must be conceded to Stephen as a critic—integrity, his only affectation being his pose of the plain bluff Englishman with a profound distrust of high-falutin sentiment and talk. But perhaps "pose" is too strong a word for an attitude which had some roots in reality, for Stephen was a fascinating blend of aesthete and philistine. It was the aesthete who appreciated the subtlest effects of mountain beauty and interpreted those effects in exquisite prose. It was the philistine who paraded his lack of interest in art, and who could not disguise the fact that poetry seldom interested him for its aesthetic value, but only for the message which it conveyed.

The conflict between the aesthete and the philistine is apparent in his mountain writings. There is nothing in Alpine literature lovelier than Leslie Stephen's chapter on the Alps in winter, but the philistine intrudes in the final passage with the tiresome interjection, "but I am verging on the poetical". The conflict between aesthete and philistine also emerges in his references to Ruskin. Stephen had one thing in common with Ruskin, a passion for the mountains, and he seems to have been both fascinated, and also faintly irritated, by Ruskin's mountain writings. "I could not be at ease with him", writes Stephen to C. E. Norton in 1876, "an art in which I am not very skilful. I was afraid of

GEPATSCH GLACIER

Edward Theodore Compton (1887)

contradicting him lest it should annoy him, and of agreeing lest I should be lying, and indeed inclined to treat him as a dangerous compound which might explode in any direction without notice. To bring about any real approximation between people who move in such different spheres, and one of whom is so eccentric, while the other is so matter-of-fact"—the philistine pose once again— "must be in any case a matter of time, and I fear we are not likely to be brought together enough to get over the obvious obstacles." His mixed reaction to Ruskin's mountain prose is evident in many references, as for instance:

"Mr. Ruskin has covered the Matterhorn, for example, with a whole web of poetical associations which, to a severe taste, is perhaps a trifle too fine, though he has done it with an eloquence which his bitterest antagonists must freely acknowledge. Yet most humble writers will feel that if they try to imitate Mr. Ruskin's eloquence they will pay the penalty of becoming ridiculous. It is not everyone who can with impunity compare Alps to archangels. Tall talk is luckily an object of suspicion to Englishmen."

Or again:

"When long ago the Alps cast their spell on me, it was woven in a great degree by the eloquence of *Modern Painters*. I might have followed him from the mountains to picture galleries, and spent among the stones of Venice hours which I devoted to attacking hitherto unascended peaks, and so losing my last chance of becoming an art critic. I became a fair judge of an Alpine guide, but I do not even know how to make a judicious allusion to Botticelli or Tintoretto. I can't say I feel the smallest remorse. I had a good time and at least escaped one temptation of talking nonsense."

But if he had known a little more about art he would not have talked nonsense about the Alpine Club's contribution to mountaineering art. "It will readily be admitted", he wrote in a review of Whymper's *Scrambles Amongst the Alps*, "especially by members of the Alpine Club, that if the Alpine Club has done nothing else it has taught us for the first time really to see mountains." Stephen made this remark with special reference to Whymper's engravings and therefore by implication was comparing the Alpine Club contribution to mountain art with the earlier artists. There are some admirable mountain paintings by Holbein and Durer and Van Eyck. Lory and Linck and Calame, early nineteenth century mountain artists, are as superior to Whymper as Whymper's work is superior to the wretched illustrations in *Peaks, Passes, and Glaciers*.

The truth is that Stephen was invincibly insular. The opening chapters of *The Playground of Europe*, in which Stephen discusses the old and the new school of mountain appreciation, have been extravagantly over-praised. He is effective about the changes of taste so far as the English are concerned, but what are we to think of an author who can omit from such a discussion all mention of Petrarch, the first of the romantic mountaineers, or the sixteenth century Gesner, who not only climbed Pilatus but wrote enthusiastically of the joys of mountain walks, and Placidus à Spescha, who has some claim to be considered the first of the purely sporting mountaineers?

In the seven volumes of literary criticism *(Hours in the Library* and *Studies of a Biographer)* there are very few essays on foreign authors.

Again, nothing is more insular than his attitude to Darwin. I cannot recall any passage in Leslie Stephen's writings which does justice to the great French predecessors of Darwin, the true pioneers of the evolutionary doctrine, Buffon and Lamarck, but I recall many passages in which Stephen acquiesces without protest in the conspiracy to represent Darwin as the first prophet of evolution.

Instead of examining the basic difficulty of Darwinism—the fact that the survival of the fittest is no explanation of the arrival of the fittest—Stephen, as Mr. Annan remarks, "was apt to go off into agnostic bombast". There is, as Mr. Annan rightly insists, "no logical connection at all between moral standards and the evolutionary process . . . evolutionary ethics are fraudulent, they solve the main problems by evading them". Stephen was trying, as Mr. Annan remarks, to make the social sciences do the work of religion. Evolution replaces God. "The power of religion over the very minds which denied it is nowhere more subtly instanced than in Stephen's evolutionary ethics."

Leslie Stephen, who was descended from evangelical Christians, was an evangelical agnostic stubbornly loyal to Christian morality in spite of his rejection of the Christian creed:

> There was an old man of Moldavia,
> Who did not believe in his Saviour,
> But who erected instead,
> With himself as the head,
> The religion of decorous behaviour.

Moldavianism was a short-lived creed, and certainly Moldavianism appealed as little to Stephen's children as the doctrines of the Clapham sect had appealed to their father.

It must be conceded that Leslie Stephen was rather trying as a father. Virginia Woolf has left us an unflattering portrait of Stephen in the "Mr. Ramsay" of her novel *To the Lighthouse,* and Stephen partly confirmed the accuracy of this portrait in the self-accusing journal which he wrote for his children. But if Maitland's "Stephen had a low flashpoint" is a typical Victorian meiosis, Virginia Woolf's article on her father, which appeared in *The Times* on the centenary of his birth, is a more genuine appraisal of Stephen in the family than "Mr. Ramsay".

66

Admittedly Stephen and his daughter had very little in common. Virginia Woolf was one of the creators of the group of intellectuals who are generically classified as "Bloomsbury". Stephen Spender in his interesting autobiography, *World Within World*, has summed up with discernment the special characteristics of this group:

> "Not to regard the French impressionist and post-impressionist painters as sacrosanct, not to be an agnostic and in politics a Liberal with Socialist leanings was to put one outside Bloomsbury ... like a watered-down aristocracy they made moderate but distinct claims on society ... their standard of five hundred pounds a year" (pre-1914 pounds) "and a room of one's own" (Virginia Woolf's formula in a well-known essay) made them decidedly unwilling to sacrifice their independence to the cause of the working class struggle. They were class conscious ... Despite their left-wing sympathies the atmosphere of Bloomsbury was nevertheless snobbish. They were tolerant in their attitude to sexual morals, scrupulous in their personal relations with each other."

None of Stephen's children inherited his passion for mountains, a passion which Bloomsbury regarded as faintly absurd. Lytton Strachey, a member of the original Bloomsbury circle, refers disparagingly to "imbecile mountains". The glorious peaks of the Coolin meant nothing to him. "I thought them simply absurd." Raymond Mortimer, another member of the Bloomsbury group, writes of Stephen as "substituting long walks for long prayers and Alps for sanctuaries, but as severe as Pusey in his attitude to pleasure and in his earnestness equally remote from the eighteenth-century Lytton Strachey".

While I was still at Oxford, Mr. H. A. L. Fisher gave me an introduction to Virginia Woolf, who very kindly asked me to lunch. I think perhaps Vanessa Bell was present and a young man who was perhaps a relation. As I was unenthusiastic about the French post-impressionists and on the contrary regarded "imbecile mountains" as the most important things in the universe, and was a little callow in my uncritical reverence for Leslie Stephen, the lunch was not a great success. They were very courteous, but from time to time I intercepted the exchange of faintly quizzical glances between the high priestess of Bloomsbury and her sister.

Stephen said that his place would be at the most a footnote in history, and this modest estimate may be justified, for his literary criticism is hardly read to-day, but there is one field of literature in which his prestige has been undimmed by time.

There is nothing in the *Playground of Europe* as dramatic as the triumph and tragedy of the first ascent of the Matterhorn, and the contrast between *The Playground of Europe* and *Scrambles Amongst the Alps* is all the greater because Whymper consistently over-wrote his adventures and—one might add—overdrew them. The famous gap on the Ecrins ridge, the engraving of which provides

Scrambles with a frontispiece, only existed in Whymper's imagination. On the other hand, Stephen's attitude, to his own climbs, was one of ironic belittlement.

> "I utterly repudiate the doctrine (he writes) that Alpine travellers are or ought to be the heroes of Alpine adventures. The true way at least to describe all my Alpine ascents is that Michel or Anderegg or Lauener succeeded in performing a feat requiring skill, strength and courage, the difficulty of which was much increased by the difficulty of taking with him his knapsack and his employer. If any passages in the succeeding pages convey the impression that I claim any credit except that of following better men than myself with decent ability, I disavow them in advance and do penance for them in my heart."

We turn to Whymper for mountain drama, to Stephen for an interpretation of mountain beauty and mountain adoration. The word painting of scenery is never easy for whereas the painter in oil or water colour has an infinite range of colour and line at his disposal, the meagre palette of the word painter compels him to supplement factual epithets by metaphor, analogy and simile. All peaks are high and most valleys are profound, and snow usually gleams in the sun and flushes red at dawn, and the writer who attempts to *differentiate* one mountain scene from another must search for the felicitous analogy or metaphor which alone can suggest the characteristics *peculiar* to the view which he is describing. Virgil's

> et jam summa procul villarum culmina fumant
> majoresque cadunt altis de montibus umbris

delights us in the original, but is banal in a translation. It is the form not the content of the lines which appeals to us. "And now afar off the smoke ascends from the cottage roofs and from the high mountains the shadows fall." Nothing here to differentiate one particular sunset from another. Whereas Stephen's description of the sunset from Mont Blanc is a masterpiece of word painting evoking not sunsets in general but one mountain sunset in particular. Or again consider his description of the view from the Schreckhorn and note how he achieves his effect by such felicitous choice of apparently casual similes and metaphors.

> "The charm of such views—little as they are generally appreciated by professed admirers of the picturesque—is to my taste unique, though not easily explained to unbelievers. They have a certain soothing influence like slow and stately music, or one of the strange opium dreams described by De Quincey. If his journey in the mail-coach could have led him through an Alpine pass instead of the quiet Cumberland hills, he would have seen visions still more poetical than that of the minster in the 'dream fugue'. Unable as I am to bend his bow, I can only say that there is something almost unearthly in the sight of enormous spaces of hill and plain, apparently unsubstantial as a mountain mist, glimmering away to the indistinct

68

horizon, and as it were spell-bound by an absolute and eternal silence. The sentiment may be very different when a storm is raging and nothing is visible but the black ribs of the mountains glaring at you through rents in the clouds; but on that perfect day on the top of the Schreckhorn, where not a wreath of vapour was to be seen under the whole vast canopy of the sky, a delicious lazy sense of calm repose was the appropriate frame of mine. One felt as if some immortal being, with no particular duties upon his hands, might be calmly sitting upon those desolate rocks and watching the little shadowy wrinkles of the plain, that were really mountain ranges, rise and fall through slow geological epochs."

Stephen was revered not only as a writer in Alpine circles, but as a man. It was characteristic of him that he should have been the only member of the Alpine Club to protest against Whymper's scandalous attacks on the Taugwalders. The last of the Moldavians was certainly a very noble character. As Mr. Annan says:

"Revenge or malice were beneath him; he despised personal gain and all devious ways of influence or persuasion; and if this magnanimity took him a pace or two out of the world, it invested his character with a noble simplicity."

There is one aspect of Stephen's literary achievement to which neither of his biographers have drawn attention, the contrast between the inspiration of the best passages in the *Playground* and the lack of inspiration which is as noticeable as the high level of competence in most of his literary criticism, a contrast which bears witness to the influence of mountain beauty on his mind.

The beauty which is not wholly of this world broke through the crust of Stephen's near-philistinism, and it may well be that the "shadowy personality" which Stephen tells us that he felt compelled to attribute to the mountains "in spite of all reason" may have provoked salutary doubts as to the validity of his negative creed.

CHAPTER VII

THE GUIDES OF THE GOLDEN AGE

It is impossible to do justice in one chapter to the great guides of the Golden Age of mountaineering, and I refer the reader who feels the need for more information than I can hope to provide within the limitations of the available space, to three excellent books, *The Pioneers of the Alps*, by C. D. Cunningham and Captain W. de W. Abney (1888), *Pioniere der Alpen*, by Carl Egger (1945), and *The Early Alpine Guides*, by Ronald Clark (1949).

First-class guides have always been, and still are the exception. As Ronald Clark rightly says: "The claim that there are not more than a few dozen first-class guides in the whole of the Alps runs like an unbroken sigh through the climbing literature of the sixties and seventies", while C. E. Mathews insisted in his great monograph on Mont Blanc "that of the three hundred men now (1898) on the Chamonix roll those who could be relied on in a grave emergency may be counted almost on the fingers of one hand."

One of the first, perhaps the first guide who was outstanding not only for his mastery of mountain craft but also for his character was Auguste Balmat of Chamonix.

Auguste Balmat (1808–1862)

Auguste Balmat was the great-nephew of Jacques Balmat, who made the first ascent of Mont Blanc, but no men could be less alike in their characters. Balmat's "great fear", said an anonymous writer, believed to be a great-grandson of De Saussure, was "to share not glory but money with others. He was always greedy of gain." But of Auguste, Stephen d'Arve wrote: "L'argent n'avait aucun empire sur cette âme si droite. Tout salaire l'humiliait, et les remerciements qui se traduisaient en souvenirs de livres ou d'objets d'art étaient les seuls qu'il acceptât avec la plus grande reconnaissance."

His association with Professor James Forbes began in 1842. Balmat co-operated for many years in the experiments which formed the basis of Forbes' theory of glacier motion. A number of metal stakes were driven into the glacier and their positions noted from month to month. These observations were controlled by Balmat during the winter and it was characteristic of the man that he would accept no payment for he maintained that he was sufficiently rewarded by the interest which he derived from the experiments. He had the tastes and the aptitudes of a born scientist, a fact which was recognised by the geologists and other scientists to whom he had been introduced by Forbes. "He would carry any weight", wrote Alfred Wills, "and go to any distance to do a service to any traveller he had undertaken to guide, and never betrayed the smallest sense that such drudgery was beneath the notice of a man who corresponded with half the men of science of Europe."

Until Balmat met Alfred Wills his services had been monopolised by scientists, and it was with Wills that he made the second recorded passage of the Adler Pass, the second passage of the Fenêtre de Saleinaz and the famous ascent of the Wetterhorn which has been described in Chapter V of this book.

It was Balmat who suggested to Tyndall that a self-registering thermometer should be placed on the summit of Mont Blanc. Unfortunately the iron ladle which was to have been used to dig a hole had been forgotten, and Balmat dug the hole in the snow with his own hands only protected from the intense cold by a single pair of woollen gloves. Balmat was lucky to escape with the loss of six finger nails. His only comment was that even if he had lost his fingers he would have consoled himself with the reflection that the loss had been sustained in the cause of science.

The Royal Society, on the recommendation of Tyndall, subsequently voted Balmat twenty-five guineas, the equivalent in modern purchasing power of at least a hundred pounds, as a token of appreciation of his services to science.

Balmat died after a long and painful illness at Wills' Alpine home "The Eagle's Nest" at Sixt. Balmat had no expensive tastes. He never drank wine, his only extravagances were those of generosity such as his refusal again and again to accept money for services to science. Alfred Wills once reproached him with his inability to decline requests for help. "If I could but teach you", said Wills, "one monosyllable 'Non', I should render you the greatest of earthly services."

During his illness he suddenly realised that he was penniless, "which so preyed upon a sensitive and remorseful nature that he literally died of a broken heart at the age of 54, stricken to death before one trace of old age could be detected or one physical or mental power had begun to fail."

Melchior Anderegg (1827–1914)

Melchior Anderegg who was born at Zaun, the terrace on the left side of the Aar above Meiringen, was the greatest of the many great guides who were natives of the Haslital, guides such as Johann Jaun, Melchior Bannholzer, Andreas and Hans Fischer, and Andreas and Kaspar Maurer, and Melchior's cousin Jakob.

As a boy Melchior helped his father tend cattle, hunted chamois and mastered the art of wood-carving. At the age of twenty he began to work at the little inn on the Grimsel where he helped his cousin Johann Frutiger.

The first reference to Melchior in Alpine literature is to be found in Thomas Hinchliff's *Summer Months Among the Alps*. Hinchliff asked the innkeeper at the Grimsel to provide two guides with whom he crossed the Strahlegg to Grindelwald. Of these guides Melchior Anderegg was one and Johann Huggler the other; Huggler's name, by the way, is mis-spelt Höckler by Hinchliff, a mistake which was in *all* subsequent English references to Huggler.

Hinchliff's next meeting with Melchior was in the Schwarenbach Hotel between Kandersteg and the Gemmi. A crowd of tourists were examining wood carvings of chamois and bears and the man who carved them was none other than Hinchliff's guide over the Strahlegg. Melchior, who had accepted a position at the Schwarenbach, where he was free both to guide and to sell his carvings, had undoubted artistic talents. Some of the statuettes of his friends were exhibited in London galleries and a self-portrait carved in wood was on exhibition in the Dudley Gallery. Hinchliff promptly engaged him for an ascent of the Altels.

It was in the Schwarenbach that Melchior met the Walkers. Miss Lucy Walker was twenty-four when she first began to climb with Melchior. As a mountaineer she had few predecessors of her own sex. Maria Paradis, a Chamonix maid servant, had climbed Mont Blanc in 1808, and Henriette d'Angeville made the ascent in 1838, but Lucy Walker was the first lady mountaineer with a long and distinguished mountaineering career. For twenty years she climbed with Melchior, and it was in his company that she, her father and her brother made the first ascent of the Balmhorn. She was also the first woman to ascend the Matterhorn, the climb taking place in 1871 with her father, Frank Walker, who was then sixty-three years of age. Once when she was asked why she had never married she replied: "I love mountains and Melchior, and Melchior already has a wife."

Melchior was the favourite guide of Leslie Stephen and Charles Mathews. With Stephen he made the first ascents of the Rimpfischhorn, Oberaarhorn, Blümlisalphorn, Disgrazia, Zinal Rothorn and Mont Mallet. His first ascents with other climbers included the Dent d'Hérens and the highest peak of the Jorasses.

In 1861 Stephen invited him to England; he arrived at London Bridge in a thick fog. Stephen and Hinchliff led Melchior on foot through the murky streets. A few days later they found themselves again at London Bridge Station. "Now, Melchior", said Hinchliff, "you will lead us home." And Melchior, who till then

72

had never seen a larger town than Berne, led them unerringly with only one pause, as if to check landmarks at the foot of Chancery Lane. It was Melchior of whom Leslie Stephen wrote: "A highly intelligent Swiss guide once gazed with me upon the dreary expanse of chimney pots through which the South Western Railway escapes from this dingy metropolis. Fancying that I rightly interpreted his looks as symptomatic of the proverbial homesickness of mountaineers, I remarked with an appropriate sigh: 'That is not so fine a view as we have seen together from the top of Mont Blanc.' 'Ah, Sir!' was his pathetic reply, 'it is far finer.'"

Melchior was pre-eminent not only for his superb craftsmanship, but also for his refusal to accept unjustifiable risks. Charles Mathews quotes a characteristic remark: "'Es geht! Melchior', said a fine climber once in my hearing when we came to a dangerous spot. 'Ja', replied Melchior, 'es geht, aber *ich* gehe nicht.'" According to another version of the same story this was Melchior's reaction when Edward Davidson and C. E. Mathews were discussing the problem of the then unclimbed Zmutt Ridge of the Matterhorn, but whichever version is correct, Melchior's "*It* goes but *I* don't" became proverbial. Melchior's cousin Jakob was less inclined to stress the virtue of prudence. In his account of the first ascent of Mont Blanc by the Brenva ice ridge A. W. Moore writes: "I have always considered it a providential circumstance that, at this moment (when they first struck the ice ridge) Jakob and not Melchior was leading the party . . . In Jakob, with courage as faultless as Melchior's and physical powers even superior, the virtue of prudence is conspicuous chiefly by its absence."

To Melchior's pre-eminence as a mountaineer Whymper paid a notable tribute. "The name of Melchior is as well known (in the Alps) as the name of Napoleon. Melchior too is an emperor in his way, and a very prince among guides. His empire is among the 'eternal snows', his sceptre is an ice-axe." Melchior was a superb ice man, and it may be that the accuracy and speed with which he cut steps was related to his skill as a wood carver. He was pre-eminent not only among mountaineers but also among men. "In the case of all other guides that I have known", wrote Charles Mathews, "there has been some drawback, some self-assertion, some want of courtesy, some defect of temper, some lack of consideration for the feeling of others. No one ever could, or ever did find fault with Melchior Anderegg." And elsewhere Mathews added: "He was my guide for forty-two years and I never heard him use an expression to which the gentlest woman might not have listened."

Melchior's integrity and sense of justice emerges in a story with which this brief study of a great guide may fittingly close. During the Boer war the sympathies of the Swiss were in the main with the Boers, and a meeting was organised in Meiringen to collect subscriptions on their behalf. Melchior listened without comment to many eloquent speeches, and then rose in his place and made a speech as effective as it was short. "I am in favour of opening a subscription to help the Boers but only after we have repaid the British all the money they subscribed to help us after the disastrous fire in Meiringen." There were no further speeches that night.

Christian Almer (1826–1898)

Christian Almer, who was born in Grindelwald on March 18th, 1826, spent his early summers as a shepherd on the Zäsenberg Alp. He married at the age of twenty and a year later took part as a volunteer in the Sonderbund, a *very* civil war between the Protestant and Catholic cantons, which only lasted for three weeks, and in which the casualties in the Federal Army did not exceed seventy-one killed.

Almer was one of the guides who helped to hoist Dora d'Istria up to the base of the final ridge of the Mönch and it is to Almer's credit that he did not sign the bogus certificate giving her credit for completing the ascent (see page 36).

Almer first began to attract attention as the result of his intrusion into Wills' ascent of the Wetterhorn, described in Chapter IV. In 1857 he made the first ascent of the Mönch with Dr. Porges of Vienna and in the following year the first ascent of the Eiger, which has already been described (see page 49). His reputation was now firmly established and there were few outstanding climbers of the Golden Age who did not at some time or another secure his services. "His numerous employers", wrote Edward Whymper, "concur in saying that there is not a truer heart or a surer foot to be found amongst the Alps." This tribute was elicited by Almer's leadership on what was perhaps the most brilliant campaign of the Golden Age, the three weeks in the course of which the following virgin expeditions were successfully completed: Grand Cornier, Grandes Jorasses (west peak), Col Dolent, the Aiguille Verte, the Col de Talèfre, the Ruinette and in addition the third ascent of the Dent Blanche.

From 1868 to 1884 he climbed with W.A.B.Coolidge. His first ascents in addition to the already mentioned included the Ecrins in 1864, the Jungfrau from Wengernalp, the Weisshorn from the Bies Glacier, the Gross Fiescherhorn, the Nesthorn, the Grande Ruine, Pic Coolidge and a record number of first crossings of famous passes, among them the Sesiajoch, Mischabeljoch, Jungfraujoch, Col du Tour Noir, Col de la Pilatte, Brèche de la Meije, Moming Pass, Schallijoch, Ebnefluhjoch, Schmadrijoch, Agassizjoch and Col de Béranger.

Almer played a prominent role in the early phase of winter mountaineering for he was Coolidge's guide on the first winter ascents of the Wetterhorn, Schreckhorn and Jungfrau.

74

On January 7th, 1885, Almer climbed the Jungfrau with the famous guide Christian Jossi and W. W. Graham. The party were caught in a storm as a result of which Almer was frostbitten, and lost a number of toes, but this did not bring his climbing career to an end. At the age of seventy he climbed the Meije and, in the following year, the Wetterhorn.

From 1892 onwards I spent most of my summer holidays in Grindelwald and one of my earlier and more vivid memories is that of meeting Almer and his wife, Margharitha, starting from Grindelwald to celebrate their Golden Wedding on the summit of the Wetterhorn. Frau Almer, who was 72, had never climbed a big peak before. They spent the night and the whole of the following day resting at the Gleckstein Hut which they left shortly after midnight reaching the summit of the Wetterhorn six hours later, on June 20th, 1896.

He died on May 17th, 1898, in his seventy-third year, some six months after crossing the Lauteraarsattel, his last Alpine expedition.

Ulrich Lauener (1821–1900)

Ulrich Lauener was born in the Lauterbrunnen Valley in 1821. His brothers Christian, Jakob and Johann, killed by an avalanche on the Jungfrau in 1853, were all well known guides.

Ulrich in his old age often recalled with pride that he had, as a young guide, handed his heavy sack to a shepherd on the Zäsenberg who, in return for a consideration, carried it for him until they reached the glacier. That shepherd was Christian Almer, destined within a few years to surpass Ulrich. Ulrich's career began before Melchior and Almer had established their reputation and for some years Ulrich and his brother Christian had more engagements outside the Chamonix district than any other guides.

Ulrich took part in Alfred Wills' famous ascent of the Wetterhorn in 1854, but that was by no means the first or the most important of his climbs. Shortly before the Wetterhorn ascent he led the brothers Smyth, the Reverend Christopher and James Grenville on the first ascent of the east peak of Monte Rosa. In the following year he was the leading guide on the first ascent of the highest peak of Monte Rosa, the Dufourspitze (15,217 ft.). By a felicitous coincidence this peak, the highest point in Switzerland, was climbed on the Swiss national fête day. The party consisted of the brothers Smyth, the Reverend Charles Hudson, later killed on the Matterhorn, J. Birkbeck, E. J. W. Stevenson, Ulrich Lauener, Johannes and Matthäus Zumtaugwald and two Zermatt guides. By another coincidence the Monte Rosa Hotel was opened by Alexander Seiler, the true creator of Zermatt as a tourist centre, in the very year (1855) that Monte Rosa was first ascended. Ulrich Lauener is one of the guides who figures in Whymper's engraving of a group of famous climbers outside the Monte Rosa Hotel.

Ulrich Lauener was one of Leslie Stephen's guides on the first crossing of the Eigerjoch. On August 7th, 1859, Leslie Stephen, William and George Mathews left the Wengernalp accompanied by Ulrich Lauener and the two Chamonix men, Jean-Baptiste Croz and Charlet.

> "The Mathews (writes Stephen) were accompanied by two Chamonix men, Jean-Baptiste Croz and Charlet, whilst I had secured the gigantic Ulrich Lauener, the most picturesque of guides. Tall, spare, blue-eyed, long-limbed and square-shouldered, with a jovial laugh and a not ungraceful swagger, he is the very model of a true mountaineer; and, except that his rule is apt to be rather autocratic, I would not wish for a pleasanter companion. He has, however, certain views as to the superiority of the Teutonic over the Latin races, which rather interfered with the harmony of the party at a later date."

The climbers were doing their best to extricate themselves from a maze of crevasses and séracs, and the Chamonix guides warned them not to speak for fear of bringing down one of the nicely poised ice-masses on their heads.

> "On my translating this well-meant piece of advice to Lauener, he immediately selected the most dangerous-looking pinnacle in sight, and mounting to the top of it sent forth a series of screams, loud enough, I should have thought, to bring down the top of the Mönch."

Lauener rose brilliantly to the occasion when it was necessary to cut steps for hour after hour up to the Eigerjoch. The pass was safely crossed but the party were benighted.

> "Lauener carefully warned us not to go to sleep. Lauener himself rose once into exuberant spirits. His good temper and fun seemed to rise with the occasion; and after telling us a variety of anecdotes, beginning with chamois-hunting and ending (of all things in the world) with examinations—for it seems that Swiss guides share with under-graduates, this particular form of misery—he retired to the nook which the Chamonix guides had selected, and, to the best of my belief, passed the rest of the night in chaffing them."

But though Ulrich proved himself a brilliant leader on the Eigerjoch, he lacked the enterprise which would have enabled him to maintain the prominent position which he once enjoyed, and which he lost to Almer and Anderegg. He flatly refused to attempt the unconquered Schreckhorn with Leslie Stephen. "He was", writes Carl Egger, "without initiative and the importance which the English at that period attached to new expeditions provoked in him no response."

But though his only new expeditions of outstanding importance were Monte Rosa, Eigerjoch and the first descent of the Gabelhorn over the north-west face with Whitwell, he continued guiding to an advanced age, and at the age of sixty cut no less than seven hundreds steps on a traverse of the Schmadrijoch to Ried.

Michel Croz (1830–1865)

Michel Croz was born in the little village of Le Tour in the valley of Chamonix on April 22nd, 1830, and it was not until his thirtieth year that he first attracted attention. In 1859 he led William Mathews, one of the greatest amateurs of the day, on an ascent of Mont Blanc, and Mathews, impressed by the ability of a man whom he described as "being only happy when upwards of 10,000 ft. high", engaged him for the following year.

During the five years that followed Croz only climbed with the outstanding pioneers of the period: Mathews, Moore, Tuckett and Whymper. Whymper was a hard man and Croz was one of the very few people who evoked from him not only respect but affection.

> "Of all the guides with whom I travelled (wrote Whymper), Michel Croz was the man who was most after my own heart. He did not work like a blunt razor, and take to his toil unkindly. He did not need urging, or to be told a second time to do anything. You had only to say *what* was to be done, and *how* it was to be done and the work *was* done, if it was possible. Such men are not common and when they are known they are valued. Michel was not widely known, but those who did know him came again and again. The inscription that is placed on his tomb truthfully records that he was beloved by his comrades and esteemed by travellers."

Croz' most outstanding qualities as a mountaineer were first his superb ice-manship and secondly his talent as a route finder.

> "I cannot close this chapter (writes Whymper) without paying a tribute to the ability with which Croz led us through a dense mist, down the remainder of the Glacier de Pilatte. As an exhibition of strength and skill, it has notably never been surpassed in the Alps or elsewhere. On this almost unknown and very steep glacier he was perfectly at home even in the mists. Never able to see fifty feet ahead, he still went on with the utmost certainty, and without having to retrace a single step."

Whereas many guides only co-operated unwillingly with guides from another country, "the combination of Croz and Almer was", writes Whymper, "a perfect one. . . . It is pleasant to remember how they worked together, and how each one confided to you that he liked the other *so* much because he worked *so* well." Croz and Almer were the guides on the famous first ascent of the Ecrins. Among the more important first ascents on which Croz took part may be mentioned the Aiguille d'Argentière, the Viso, the first crossing of the Col des Ecrins, the Brèche de la Meije, the Moming Pass, the Grande Casse, Castor, Mont Dolent, Grand Cornier, Jorasses (west peak) and, by himself, Mont Pourri.

The climax of Croz' career was the day when he led the victorious party on the first ascent of the Matterhorn. Croz is buried at Zermatt at the foot of the great peak which was the scene of his greatest triumph and of his death.

Jean-Antoine Carrel (1829–1890)

Jean-Antoine Carrel was born in 1829 in the little village of Valtournanche, five miles below Breuil, at the foot of the Matterhorn. He was working as a stonemason when he was enrolled in the army and fought in the Italian wars of liberation, returning to his native valley in 1857.

In one respect Jean-Antoine stands out from most if not from all the guides of his period. His outlook was that of the genuine amateur. The only first ascent of any importance during the Golden Age by guides unaccompanied by amateurs was the first ascent of the Wetterhorn, and even this is not an exception to the general rule for guides were paid by Desor to find the route to the summit.

Carrel did not wait until some English amateurs arrived before attacking the great peak which dominated his native valley and which had cast its spell on him long before it attracted the attention of the mountaineering world. On a midsummer morning in 1857 Jean-Antoine and Jean-Jacques Carrel, a mighty hunter, and a young man of twenty, Aimé Gorret, later a priest, met before dawn at the chalet of Avouilles. They reached a point now known as the Tête du Lion (12,188 ft.) and studied the Matterhorn with quiet assurance. The great peak would not run away. Some day they would return and settle the issue.

On August 28th, 1861, Whymper arrived at Breuil with an Oberland guide and met Carrel, "a resolute looking fellow, with a certain defiant air, who was rather taking". Carrel agreed to accompany Whymper but insisted on his comrade being taken. Whymper demurred and negotiations broke down. Whymper tried in vain to get another man but the men approached either refused or asked a prohibitive price. "This it may be said once and for all was the reason why so many futile attempts were made on the Matterhorn. One guide after another was brought up to the Matterhorn and patted on the back but all declined business."

Whymper and his guide bivouacked in a cowshed and as night approached saw "stealing up the mountain-side Jean-Antoine Carrel and the comrade". The comrade turned out to be Jean-Antoine's uncle, Jean-Jacques Carrel, who had been on the mountain the year before with Mr. Vaughan Hawkins, Professor Tyndall and the guide Bennen. Next day Whymper reached the "chimney" and climbed the *mauvais pas*, but his guide refused to follow. The Carrels reached a point about 300 ft. higher. "Jean-Antoine Carrel", wrote Whymper, "was the finest rock climber I have ever seen. He was the only man who persistently refused to accept defeat and who continued to believe in spite of all discouragements that the mountain was not inaccessible, and that it could be ascended from the side of his native valley."

The two supreme moments of his life were those in which he heard the shouts of victory at the battle of Colle di Santiarno, and the cries of triumph when he completed the first ascent of the Italian ridge of the Matterhorn. The bitterest moment in his life, we may be sure, was when he saw from high up on the Italian ridge Whymper and his companions on the summit of the great peak which it had been his ambition to be the first to conquer.

Carrel had always hoped not only to be the first to climb the Matterhorn but to *lead* the first ascent by way of the Italian ridge. The Matterhorn was his mountain. He resented Whymper's attempt in 1862 with Swiss guides. "Carrel", writes Whymper, "clearly considered the mountain as a kind of preserve and regarded our attempts as an act of poaching." Tyndall returned to the attack in 1862 and gave the command of the expedition to the Swiss, Bennen sometimes spelt Benet, and engaged the Carrels in a subordinate position, and when Tyndall turned to the Carrels for advice they replied: "We are porters, ask your guides."

In 1863 Giuseppe Torelli, a young Italian politician, sought out Carrel and confided in him that he was the emissary of the Italians who had met in Turin to found an Italian Alpine Club, and that the first item on the agenda of this club was the conquest of the Matterhorn. This was what Carrel wanted, to lead Italians up the Italian ridge of the great peak. He lost no time in travelling to Biella where he met Quintino Sella, the statesman of whom it was said that he "gave Rome to Italy and founded the Italian Alpine Club". The results of that interview have already been briefly described in Chapter V and here it is only necessary to insist that Carrel cannot fairly be accused of deceiving Whymper. He was under no obligation to explain to Whymper that the "family of distinction" who had engaged him were not, as Whymper supposed, English, but Whymper's Italian rivals. The conquest of the Italian ridge a few days after Whymper's first ascent was, one fears, a poor consolation prize.

In 1879 Carrel accompanied Whymper to the Andes and led on the ascents of Chimborazo and Cotopaxi.

Carrel was in his sixty-second year when he started for his last climb. On August 23rd, 1890, Leone Sinigaglia had engaged him to traverse the Matterhorn to Zermatt. They were caught by bad weather in the Italian hut where they spent two nights. That Carrel was far from well was clear but the provisions were running out, and it was decided to descend. The rocks were either buried in snow or, where exposed, covered by verglas. Carrel insisted on leading, and fought his way downwards undaunted by blinding snow storms through which he led them unerringly. Fourteen hours after leaving the hut they were still on the rocks, but Carrel still refused to allow the other guides to relieve him until he had piloted his party into safety, but they had no sooner reached easy ground than Carrel collapsed. "We tried to lift him", writes Sinigaglia, "but it was impossible. He was getting stiff. We stooped down and asked him if he wished to commend his soul to God. With a last effort he answered 'yes', and then fell on his back, dead, upon the snow."

Among the guides of Breuil there were some who had resented his un-challenged supremacy, but there were none who did not acknowledge his greatness. Some years after he died a climber stopped in front of Carrel's cross, and remarked to the son of his greatest rival: "So that is where Carrel fell."

"Carrel did not fall", came the indignant reply, "Carrel died."

I wish that my available space permitted me to do more than pay a brief tribute to many another great guide of the Golden Age. Christian Michel, for instance, who led Stephen up the Schreckhorn; Franz Andenmatten (*not*, as usually spelt in the works of English writers, Andermatten) of Almagel in the Saas Valley whose first ascents included the Zinal Rothorn from Zermatt and the Laquinhorn and Nadelhorn; Johann Joseph Benet (*or* Bennen) who led Tyndall up the Weisshorn and who was killed on the Haut-de-Cry; the brothers Zumtaugwald who, with Peter Taugwalder of the Matterhorn, were the first genuine high Alpine guides of their valley, their predecessors being mere guides over easy passes such as Théodule and Weisstor. Matthäus Zumtaugwald took part in the first ascent of Monte Rosa, his brother Johann led in the first ascents of the Dom and Täschhorn. Franz Biner of Zermatt made his name at the very end of the Golden Age. He was one of Whymper's guides but according to Whymper acted "more as a porter than guide" during the subsequent ascents of the Grand Cornier, Grandes Jorasses, Aiguille Verte, Ruinette and the passage of the Col Dolent.

The fact that I have confined myself in this chapter to the guides who became famous during the Golden Age explains the absence of all reference to such great masters of the craft as Alexander Burgener of Saas, Aloys Pollinger of St. Niklaus or Christian Klucker of the Fextal, but I would like to conclude this chapter by quoting one of the noblest tributes ever paid to a guide, Captain J. P. Farrar's tribute to Daniel Maquignaz, with whom he made the second ascent of Mont Blanc by the Peuterey Ridge in 1893. No writer has summed up more felicitously the bond which unites a great amateur to a great guide.

WEISSHORN

Albert Gos (ca. 1900)

(Swiss Foundation)

"To some I may seem to have portrayed in too glowing colours a man who in life was a simple Piedmontese peasant. Still, there are many among my contemporaries who will understand the feeling of more than ordinary friendship that binds one to a man like this whom one has learned to know and to judge in that school of stern, though voluntary, discipline and not infrequent danger that is of the essence of serious mountaineering. I lose in him one from whom I learned much—from whom I never ceased to learn—my leader on many a glorious day of triumph—one whose memory will in my mind for ever be entwined with some of the most unsullied and serene joys that enter into the life of man.

May you rest in peace, mon Daniel, sans peur et sans reproche, in the shadow of your marvellous mountain that none knew—in all its moods and by all its ways—so well as you. You have played the man in your generation. You are not forgotten, in memory you live."

CHAPTER VIII

THE SILVER AGE OF MOUNTAINEERING

The Golden Age of mountaineering is deemed to have begun with Wills' ascent of the Wetterhorn and to have ended with the ascent of the Matterhorn. The Silver Age of mountaineering is a convenient term for the period which begins after the conquest of the Matterhorn, and ends with the conquest of the Dent du Géant. The Dent du Géant, a peak in the Mont Blanc range, consists of twin summits of approximately the same height, there being only thirteen feet difference between the highest point (13,166 ft.) and the lower summit (13,153 ft.).

On July 29th, 1882, Alessandro, Alfonso, Corradino and Gaudenzio Sella with the guides Jean-Joseph, Baptiste and Daniel Maquignaz made the first ascent of one of the twin summits of the Dent du Géant. A few days later, on August 20th, 1882, W.W.Graham with the guides Alphonse Payot and Auguste Cupelin climbed the higher of the two summits.

The conquest[1] of the Dent du Géant was important for two reasons. Its ascent closed an epoch and inaugurated a revolution, the beginning of artificial climbing. The Dent du Géant was the last great Alpine peak to be conquered which was named and famous *before* it was climbed. There is a radical distinction between mountains which were climbed because they were famous, of which the most striking example is the Matterhorn, and mountains which only became famous after they had been climbed, such as some of the Chamonix Aiguilles, the Grand Capucin for instance.

It was only in the Eastern Alps that any peaks of importance remained virgin after the Silver Age of mountaineering had ended, but pinnacles such as the Winklerturm which was climbed in 1887, though difficult, could not be described as "great" for these Dolomite towers are for the most under 3000 m. in height. The Dent du Géant, on the other hand, is not only a *great* peak, a distinguished member of that hierarchy of 4000-metre peaks which correspond in the Alps to Himalayan 8000-metre giants, but it is also an autonomous mountain, not a satellite or buttress of some greater peak such as the Aiguille Blanche de Peuterey.

---

[1] It has, I know, suddenly become unfashionable to write of "conquest" in connection with mountains, but where a single word ("conquest") can be made to do the work of two words ("first ascent") I am resigned to being unmodish. There are respectable precedents for the use of "conquest" in this connection. Whymper, for instance, writes of the Matterhorn, "It proved to be a stubborn foe ... like a terrible enemy—conquered but not crushed—it took a terrible vengance."

With the conquest of the Dent du Géant a chapter in Alpine history ends, for it was the last of the great virgin peaks to be climbed, and thereafter pioneers in search of novelty had to concentrate on the virgin ridges, and faces of peaks no longer virgin, or to specialise in those minor pinnacles or satellites of greater peaks which were only given a name *after* they had been climbed.

But the ascent of the Dent du Géant was important not only because it closed a great epoch of Alpine exploration but also because of the revolutionary methods which were used to reach the summit. The brothers Maquignaz had spent four days hammering pitons into the rocks, and hanging fixed ropes on the more difficult pitches before the Sellas made the ascent. This new technique provoked the first outbreak of a fierce controversy between the supporters and opponents of artificial climbing, a controversy which continues to this day.

The modern conviction that no rock is too steep or too smooth to be climbed, if not by free at least by artificial climbing, can be traced back to the Sellas' ascent of the Dent du Géant. Throughout the Silver Age of mountaineering the interest in difficult rock climbs had steadily increased. The pioneers in general felt happier on ice than on difficult rocks. Leslie Stephen's party, for instance, on reaching the Lower Eigerjoch discovered that the ridge could not be crossed at that point and that the only alternative to defeat was to cut steps for hours up the ice slope leading to the Upper Eigerjoch. The few rocky pinnacles on the ridge which joins the Lower and Upper Eigerjoch seemed to them a far more formidable obstacle than the long ice slope leading to the Upper Eigerjoch. By way of contrast it is interesting to recall the performance of a modern skier, Miss Angela Stormonth-Darling, who, starting from the Jungfraujoch, crossed the Mönchjoch, reached the Upper Eigerjoch on ski and carried her ski along this ridge to the Lower Eigerjoch, whence Miss Stormonth-Darling and her sole companion, the guide Oskar Gertsch, skied down to the Scheidegg.

That the standard of rock climbing in the Golden Age was not particularly high would seem to be a reasonable deduction from A. W. Moore's comment on his ascent of the Wetterhorn which he climbed, not by the normal route, but by a shallow gully to the north of the Willsgrätli, a straightforward and easy scramble, as I discovered in the course of a solitary ascent. "I still think", wrote Moore, "that some parts of the climb were as awkward as anything I have done." On the other hand the standard of ice-craft in the Golden Age was very high.

On July 15th, 1865, Moore, who thought the Wetterhorn a difficult climb, G. S. Mathews, F. and H. Walker, with the guides Jakob and Melchior Anderegg, made the first ascent of Mont Blanc by the Brenva Ridge which still ranks as a first class ice expedition. Captain J. P. Farrar wrote that this climb "involved the most continuous step-cutting in hard steep ice I have ever seen". The first descent of this route by R. W. Lloyd was considered a fine achievement as late as 1911.

One of the great guideless partnerships in Alpine history, Claude Wilson, J. H. Wicks and E. H. F. Bradby, found that this climb fully extended their powers.

Judged by modern standards the equipment of mountaineers even at the end of the Silver Age was still rudimentary, the ice-axe alone being approximately the same as the modern axe. At the beginning of the Golden Age the guides often carried the kind of household axe which they used for chopping wood. In the Savoy Alps an axe head fitted to a long shaft came into early use. On many expeditions only the leading guide carried an axe, the amateurs contenting themselves with alpenstocks. Even with primitive ice-axes some remarkable feats of step-cutting were accomplished, 1300 steps, for instance, were cut in the course of an early ascent of the Jungfrau from the Rottal. In 1864 the Alpine Club appointed, on Leslie Stephen's suggestion, a committee to consider and advise on the most practicable form of ice-axe, rope and sleeping-bag.

There were few changes in the rock climber's equipment during the Silver Age. Mummery, for instance, climbed in nailed boots, or exceptionally in socks as for instance on the ascent of the Charmoz. It was in the Eastern Alps that espadrilles, roped soled boots, were first substituted for nailed boots, but the fashion was slow in spreading to the Western Alps. Geoffrey Young's great climbs, the Mer de Glace Face of the Grépon among others, were accomplished in nailed boots.

British Mountaineers during the Silver Age

It was during the Silver Age that members of the Alpine Club began to turn their attention to more distant ranges, such as the Caucasus, and that continental mountaineers began to claim their fair share of new routes in the Alps. The Meije, the conquest of which was perhaps the greatest achievement of the Silver Age, was first climbed by a Frenchman but most of the important climbs of this period were accomplished by British mountaineers. As for instance, the first ascents of the highest point of the Grandes Jorasses on June 30th, 1868, by Horace Walker with the guides Melchior Anderegg, Johann Jaun and Julien Grange, of the Grand Dru in 1878 by Clinton Dent and J. Walker Hartley with the guides Alexander Burgener and Kaspar Maurer, of the Grépon on August 5th, 1881, by A. F. Mummery with the guides Benedikt Venetz, who led the Mummery crack, and Alexander Burgener.

Among the many new routes on peaks no longer virgin which were attempted during this period, none was more important than the following climbs. The Zmutt Ridge of the Matterhorn was climbed on the same day, September 3rd, 1879, by two parties, Mummery with the guides Alexander Burgener, Johann Petrus and Augustin Gentinetta, and William Penhall with the guides Ferdinand Imseng and Louis Zurbriggen. The Italian face of Monte Rosa was first ascended

84

by R. and W. M. Pendlebury and Charles Taylor with the guide Ferdinand Imseng on July 22nd, 1872. An interesting variant of this route was made on July 31st, 1889, by Abbé Achille Ratti, who later became Pope Pius XI, with Abbé Louis Graselli and the guides Joseph Gadin and Alexis Promont. On September 5th, 1872, Clinton Dent and G. A. Passingham made the first ascent of the Zinal Rothorn from Zermatt. On August 13th, 1879, Passingham with the guides Ferdinand Imseng and Louis Zurbriggen made the first ascent of the west face of the Weisshorn.

One of the most remarkable climbs of the period was the first ascent of the south face of Mont Blanc by the glaciers of Brouillard and Frêney on July 31st, 1877, by J. Eccles with the guides Michel-Clément and Alphonse Payot. In the eighty years that have elapsed since this first ascent this tremendous climb has only been twice repeated.

On August 11th, 1882, a few days before the Silver Age ended, J. Stafford Anderson and G. P. Baker with the guides Ulrich Almer and Aloys Pollinger made the first ascent of the famous Viereselsgrat of the Dent Blanche, and finally the last great climb which brings this period to an end was accomplished when W. W. Graham reached the higher of the twin summits of the Dent du Géant.

The Alpine Club and Guideless Climbing

The only blemish on the record of the Alpine Club during the Silver Age was the disapproval of guideless climbing, officially recorded at a meeting of the Club in 1870 when F. C. Grove read a paper provoked by the publication of *The High Alps without Guides*, by the Rev. A. G. Girdlestone. Girdlestone was a plucky and enterprising but somewhat incompetent mountaineer, and his misadventures on easy expeditions were no advertisement for guideless climbing. At the conclusion of the paper "it was agreed without a single dissentient that it is highly desirable that it should be known to be the settled opinion of the Alpine Club, that, whilst the danger may be reduced to an insignificant amount by proper care, the neglect to take guides on difficult expeditions, and especially the neglect to take them when the party is not exclusively composed of practised mountaineers, is totally unjustifiable and calculated to produce the most lamentable results."

This resolution was a temporary aberration, all the more difficult to understand in view of the fact that many members of the Alpine Club had already initiated guideless climbing and achieved far greater success than Girdlestone. Hudson, E. S. Kennedy, C. Ainslie, and C. and J. G. Smyth had made guideless ascents of the Klein Matterhorn and Breithorn and the first guideless ascent of Mont Blanc (also the first ascent from St. Gervais) as early as 1855. Even more remarkable were the guideless ascents of the three brothers A. T., S. S., and C. S. Parker. In

1860 they crossed the Strahlegg and Schwarzberg-Weisstor, and made the first attempt on the Matterhorn from Zermatt. In 1865 they climbed the Wildstrubel, crossed the Triftjoch and made the first guideless ascent of the Finsteraarhorn. In 1858 Tyndall made a solitary ascent of Monte Rosa.

In 1872, two years after the Alpine Club had done their best to conceal, by a deplorable resolution, the fact that the pioneers of guideless climbing were members of the Club, John Stogdon, a famous Harrow master, and the Rev. Arthur Fairbanks made guideless ascents of the Gross Nesthorn and Aletschhorn, but did not risk provoking the censure of the orthodox by publishing any record of these expeditions. In 1876 Cust, Cawood and Colgrove climbed the Matterhorn without guides. "Cricket", wrote Arthur Cust, "is a sport which is admitted by all to need acquired skill. A man can buy his mountaineering as he can buy his yachting. None the less, there are yachtsmen and yachtsmen."

Human motives are often mixed. Among those responsible for the conservative attitude of the Club the majority were, no doubt, only influenced by a genuine concern for the good name of mountaineering, but there were others who were affected, if only unconsciously, by the realisation that a standard was being set which was higher than that to which they could attain.

"You have little idea", Mr. Stogdon once remarked to me, "of the awe with which climbers were regarded in the seventies. The prestige of even a mediocre mountaineer in those days was scarcely less than that of a golf champion today."

Mountaineers, of course, were often attacked in the press for their incredible foolhardiness, but even the most sensitive of men can accept with Christian resignation the charge of reckless courage. "The profession of soldiers and sailors", said Samuel Johnson, "has the dignity of danger", and sports which have this "dignity of danger" inevitably rank higher in public estimation than those which involve risk neither to life nor to limb. It is therefore easy to understand the attraction of mountaineering for intellectuals who lacked the qualities necessary for success in competitive sports, but who had the enterprise to perceive the possibilities of this new sport, and the stamina and courage necessary for mountaineering. It was, perhaps, both a new and not unwelcome experience for scholars who had been derided as "saps" while at school to be chided by their female friends for their insensate foolhardiness in facing the manifold perils of the Alps. And, human nature being what human nature is, it was inevitable that those who could not have led a guideless party up a second-class peak would not welcome a development which threatened to divide mountaineers into the guideless élite and a guided proletariat. As late as 1892 Clinton Dent could write in the Badminton volume on Mountaineering which he edited:

"It is on rocks alone that an amateur can and must exercise his own powers, and not be wholly dependant on his guides. On snow the amateur is but an impediment, an extra burden, as has often been said, to his guides; they have to hack out huge steps for his benefit; he is entirely dependant on them for steering clear of avalanches, rotten snow bridges and the like."

Two men exercised a decisive influence on overcoming the prejudice against guideless climbing, Mummery, whose personality and achievements are discussed in the next chapter, and Charles Pilkington who was president of the Alpine Club from 1896 to 1898. With his brother Lawrence and Frederick Gardiner he carried out, during the years 1878, 1879 and 1881, a remarkable series of guideless climbs which included the Matterhorn, Ecrins, Meije, Finsteraarhorn and Zinal Rothorn. Wilhelm Lehner quotes with indignation a statement by the editor of *The Alpine Journal* to the effect that these guideless climbs were "without parallel in alpine history" and comments that the editor neither knew nor wanted to know ("nichts wusste oder nichts wissen wollte") of the solitary ascents of Hermann Barth and J. J. Weilenmann (which are referred to later in this chapter). But it is not reasonable to compare short and difficult rock ascents with moun-taineering on a big scale, and neither Barth nor Weilenmann exercised an influence comparable to that of Charles Pilkington. I agree with Lady Chorley who contributes an interesting study of Pilkington to *Les Alpinistes Célèbres*, that Pilkington "was the first to prove"—certainly the first to convince the Alpine Club—"by a series of successes that if one prepares oneself seriously it is possible and even reasonable to climb without guides".

French Mountaineering during the Silver Age

It would be an overstatement to insist that the Meije bears the same relation to the Silver Age as the Matterhorn does to the Golden Age, but it was perhaps the most important climb of the period, and as it was first conquered by a French-man it is fitting that this section should begin with an attempt to sketch in outline the careers of some few of the more prominent French climbers of the period.

One of the first of all Alpine pioneers was a French captain, A. A. Durand, who had the enterprise to attack the Pelvoux on July 30th, 1828. In company with two chamois hunters he reached the lower summit of the Pelvoux which now bears his name, the Pointe Durand (12,900 ft.). It is possible that he also attained the highest peak of the Pelvoux, but the first undoubted ascent of the Pointe Puiseux (12,947 ft.) was that which was made by Victor Puiseux, a young pro-fessor at Besançon, on August 9th, 1848.

Puiseux's companion, one of the chamois hunters who had helped to guide Durand to the Pelvoux, was old and tired, and stopped half way up the mountain leaving the young professor to complete the ascent alone. Victor Puiseux had satisfied himself that a man from the plains could find his own way to the summit of a great peak without professional assistance, and he communicated his confidence to his son, Pierre, who made over three hundred guideless climbs, including a solitary ascent of Mont Blanc by the Aiguille du Goûter.

Victor and Pierre Puiseux were among the founders of the French Alpine Club in 1874, but their greatest claim to honour is the fact that they were the founders of guideless climbing. It is therefore difficult to explain the comparatively small impression they have made on so many historians. Lehner, in the German history of mountaineering certainly mentions them, but he can write of the Abbé Bayle, who undoubtedly made some fine ascents in the Grandes Rousses between 1876 and 1878, a quarter of a century after Puiseux's ascent of the Pelvoux, that Bayle was the first Frenchman to achieve high ascents in the Dauphiny Alps. Even Mlle Claire Engel, a Frenchwoman, can claim for Boileau de Castelnau that "he was the first Frenchman who conquered a great peak", and this though his ascent of the Meije took place twenty-nine years after Puiseux had conquered the Pelvoux which is only a few metres lower than the Meije. It is, perhaps, ungracious to mention this slip for Mlle Engel has placed all those who are interested in Alpine history in her debt by her excellent chapter on Boileau de Castelnau in her book *They Came to the Hills*. Very little was known about the conqueror of the Meije until Mlle Engel got in touch with the family and obtained from them not only the use of unpublished documents but also a great deal of personal information.

Baron Boileau de Castelnau belonged to an ancient French family. He was the eighteenth descendant in the direct line of the Chief Provost of St. Louis. The family had been one of the first of the noble families of France to embrace Protestantism, and many of them left France at the time of the Huguenot exodus. Emmanuel Boileau de Castelnau, the conqueror of the Meije, was born in 1857. At the age of thirteen he was taken to Luchon in the Pyrenees and given a guide who took him up the Pic de Néthou and the Maladetta, and fired him with an enthusiasm for mountaineering. His father not only acquiesced in his determination to become a climber, but gave him the most amazing amount of freedom while he was still a boy. Even before Emmanuel had reached the age of sixteen he travelled by himself, planned his own mountaineering campaigns, chose his own guides and paid his own hotel bills. Before he was twenty he had climbed the Jungfrau, Finsteraarhorn, Matterhorn and Dent Blanche, and Mont Blanc four times.

The Meije was the object of a long siege. In 1870 Coolidge and Miss Brevoort had climbed the Pic Central, but the highest and most difficult summit, the Grand Pic (13,081 ft.) resisted with success a series of attacks by British, French, German and Italian climbers. Amongst those who tried and failed were famous mountaineers such as Eccles and Middlemore, Lord Wentworth, Coolidge and Henri Duhamel.[1]

Finally on August 16th, 1877, Emmanuel Boileau de Castelnau made the first ascent of the Meije, with the guides Pierre Gaspard and son.

Shortly afterwards he ceased to climb, and his pioneering ambitions found satisfaction in a succession of new sports. He was one of the first cyclists in France, and in 1898 finished second in the Paris-Tours bicycle race. Later at the age of thirty-eight he finished fifth in the first Tour de France Automobile race, and a little later took to flying, at first in balloons and then in primitive 'planes. In his later years he devoted himself almost exclusively to his estate. "He developed", writes Mlle Engel, "a genius for agriculture, making his vineyards the finest in the district", but he was wholly out of touch with the mountaineering world and, but for Mlle. Engel's industry, we should know very little about that brief but brilliant period of his life when his main enthusiasm was mountaineering.

It would be improper to summarise, however briefly, French achievements during the Silver Age without some mention of Henri Cordier (1856–1877). On July 31st, 1876, Cordier, Thomas Middlemore and J. Oakley Maund with three Meiringen guides, Jakob Anderegg, Johann Jaun and Andreas Mauer made the first ascent of the Aiguille Verte from the glacier d'Argentière, and on the 4th and 7th of August in the same year the first ascents of Les Courtes and Les Droites.

Nearly half a century passed before the second ascent of the Cordier Couloir on the Verte was accomplished, the climbers being three famous members of the Groupe de Haute Montagne, Henry de Ségogne, J. Lagarde and Tom de Lépiney. They repeated Cordier's route on August 7th, 1924.

Henri Cordier was killed at the age of twenty-one on descent from Le Plaret of which he had just completed the first ascent.

I have already commented on the fact that the natives of Alpine valleys made no first ascents during the Golden Age unless they were employed to lead amateurs to the summit or, as in the case of the first ascent of the Wetterhorn, paid to explore the route to the summit. The first ascent of the Petit Dru on August 29th, 1879, was notable not only because it was a difficult climb but also because it was accomplished by three guides, Jean Charlet, Prosper Payot and Frédéric Folliguet. Charlet had been the leading guide of an English woman, Miss Isabelle Straton, on the first winter ascent of Mont Blanc (January 31st, 1876). A few months later they were married at Argentière.

---

[1] Henri Duhamel was the first Frenchman to introduce ski-ing into France. He began in 1879 at Grenoble. See my *History of Ski-ing*, page 29.

The Development of Guideless climbing in Austria and Germany

Perhaps the greatest pioneer in the Eastern Alps was the Viennese, Paul Grohman (1838–1908), whose first ascents included the Gross Zinne, the Cristallo, the Marmolata, the Langkofel, the three points of the Tofana and many other Dolomite peaks. It was perhaps inevitable that the Germans and Austrians should have achieved their first successes in their own mountains, but before long their best climbers invaded the Western Alps. Dr. Paul Güssfeldt for instance, who was born in Berlin and later was a Professor at the Berlin University, distinguished himself in the Engadine where he made in 1877 the first ascent of the Piz Scerscen, and in 1878 was the first to climb the Bernina by the ridge which connects that peak with the Piz Bianco. His greatest achievement was the first ascent of the Peuterey Arête of Mont Blanc (August 14–17th, 1893) with Emile Rey, Christian Klucker and César Ollier.

The greatest contribution of the Austrians and Germans to mountaineering during and immediately after the Silver Age was the impetus which they gave to the development of guideless climbing. Even before the Golden Age had opened Stephan Steinberger had made a solitary ascent of one of the lesser summits of the Gross Venediger, and in 1861 a solitary and first ascent of the Königsspitze. Solitary climbing would seem to have had more attraction for the Germanic than for any other mountaineers. Between 1859 and 1862 J. J. Weilenmann, a Swiss, made many solitary ascents in the Ötztal Alps; Hermann von Barth (1845–1879), a member of one of the oldest Bavarian families, was also unaccompanied during his brilliant pioneer climbs in the northern limestone ranges such as the Karwendel and Wetterstein, and at a later period Georg Winkler's sensational career consisted exclusively of solitary climbs. Born in 1869 he was only fifteen when he made the first ascent of the Totensessel and climbed the formidable Totenkirchl. He was small, just under five feet in height, but to some extent neutralised the disadvantage of his lack of height by carrying with him an iron claw attached to a rope. It was his habit to fling the claw upwards until it obtained purchase, and help himself up with the attached rope. At the age of eighteen he made a solitary and first ascent of the Winklerturm, the most difficult of the Vajolet towers. At the age of nineteen he climbed the Zinal Rothorn and vanished two days later in a solitary attempt on the Weisshorn. An old shepherd on a lofty alp saw him pass, "Plus la trace lumineuse du météore s'efface."[1]

Hermann von Barth's saying, "Wer mit mir geht, der sei zu sterben bereit" ("Who goes with me must be ready to die"), would have provoked in English mountaineering circles a mixture of embarrassment, derision and disapproval, and was only saved from the charge of foolish rhetoric by the fact that it was an

---

[1] In 1956 his body emerged from the ice.

attitude which von Barth was ready to translate into action. This saying of von Barth's, which is quoted without comment by Lehner, is rightly described by him as a "Kampfruf" (war cry), for these younger Germanic climbers created a tradition, which persists to this day, a tradition which sometimes seems to equate mountaineering with war, and to asquiesce in casualties not much less than those incurred in battle.

Far saner in their outlook and even more successful in their achievements were the greatest guideless trio of the nineteenth century, Ludwig Purtscheller (1849–1900) and the brothers Otto and Emil Zsigmondy. No mountaineer has equalled Purtscheller's Alpine record, 1700 peaks of which forty were over 4000 m. His climbing was not confined to the Alps, for in 1889 with Hans Meyer he made the first ascent of Kilimanjaro (19,334 ft.) in Kenya. He died as the result of a fall into a crevasse.[1]

Emil Zsigmondy (1861–1885) was born in Vienna, and by profession a doctor. Perhaps his finest expedition was the complete traverse of the Meije from the Pic Central to the Grand Pic, with his brother and Purtscheller. He was the author of a book on the dangers of mountaineering which was translated into French, and which would require very little re-writing to bring it completely up to date. He was killed in an attempt on the south face of the Meije, a desperate cliff which was not conquered until 1912 by the brilliant Dolomite guide Angelo Dibona. "And what have we left but hope?" were the last words he spoke before he fell.

Herr Wilhelm Lehner, in his monumental work, *Die Eroberung der Alpen*, is not content merely to record first ascents. His book owes much of its interest to the fact that Herr Lehner has made a real effort to understand and to explain the influence of national characteristics on the development of mountaineering in difficult country. I am impressed, for instance, by his explanation of the fact that the Germans and Austrians were in advance of the British in the development of guideless climbing.

> "Mountaineering among the English", he writes, "was almost exclusively the monopoly of the well-to-do, which no doubt explains their indifference to the charms of guideless climbing. They were able to secure the assistance of the best guides and to make their *début* with first-class tours which a guideless climber could only undertake after a long apprenticeship. Among the Germans, on the contrary, mountaineering was more democratic. It is essentially the sport of the middle classes and, above all, of the young university students. Guideless climbing developed all the more rapidly because few Germans could afford to pay for guides. Here, at least, lack of money was no disadvantage to the development of the sport.
> And there is another factor which must be taken into consideration. The Englishmen came to the Alps as fully developed master men *(fertige Herrenmenschen)*.

[1] He broke his arm in two places and died six months later.

They were financially independent and in a position to develop their personalities by free choice of a career. The German, on the other hand, came from a narrow circle, and was forced to devote himself throughout life to a restricted calling. The German had little opportunity to become a complete man or fully to develop his own personal tastes and characteristics. To the young German then, as now, the mountains appealed primarily as an avenue of escape from restrictions. Among the mountains he sought to develop his own personality, which was impossible in the routine of his middle-class life. Fully conscious of his 'Herrentum', the Anglo-Saxon could afford to disregard his dependence on guides. The German was attracted by guideless climbing because he found in it the freedom which he missed elsewhere and the awakening of his dormant sense of mastery."

Many of the pioneers thought of guides much as an African explorer thought of natives. It was the function of the explorer to plan the expedition and to decide on its objective. It was the function of the native to relieve him of all unnecessary labour. "I do not myself cut steps", wrote Leslie Stephen, "when I can get a guide to do it for me, first because a guide can do it much better; and secondly because he is paid to do it." Douglas Freshfield, famous for his explorations in the Caucasus and Himalaya, carried this attitude to extreme lengths. E. J. Garwood once led Freshfield on a guideless ascent of the Bernina. Freshfield complained that the rope was hurting him and Garwood discovered that he had tied himself with a slip-knot. "Well", Freshfield remarked smilingly, "you will have a good joke against the President of the Alpine Club; you see, I am accustomed to climb with guides who always roped me up."

Herr Lehner underestimated the extent to which guideless climbing was practised by the British in the Alps and seemed unaware of the fact that professional guides were unknown in our own mountains and that the exploration of our native rock climbs was carried out exclusively by guideless parties, but it is certainly true that prior to the First World War the proportion of guideless climbers was higher among continental than among British climbers.

"We cannot ignore the fact", said Captain J. P. Farrar in his Valedictory Presidential address (December, 1919), "that mountaineering as practised with the *full* approval of this Club has remained in leading strings longer than any other hard pursuit followed by active Englishmen. Good feeling towards a particular guide, or the difficulty of finding a companion of like powers, tastes and better temper has had much to do with this result.... But this Club is getting old. We must study youth. Caution can be overdone."

Since the First World War few of our younger climbers could afford to employ guides, even if they wished to do so, with the result that the Alpine Club recruits its members largely from guideless climbers.

CHAPTER IX

MUMMERY AND COOLIDGE

Wilfred Noyce has enriched our knowledge of the Everest adventure by his book, *South Col*, in which he not only describes the different phases of the climb but successfully evokes the personalities of the climbers. All such personalia were rigorously banished from mountaineering literature of the nineteenth century. Self-revelation was not uncommon in the writings of the pioneers, but the conventions of the period forbade mountaineers to be expansive about their friends. The names of those members of a climbing party mentioned in a book or article could usually be exchanged without producing any effect of discontinuity for they were mere names on the printed page. Sometimes even the name was suppressed, as for instance in Hereford George's account of the first ascent of the Jungfrau from the Wengernalp, in which his companion Sir George Young, father of Geoffrey Winthrop Young, is referred to as G–.

Fortunately the convention which vetoed any personal description of the *amateur* members of the party was relaxed in the case of guides. Ulrich Lauener comes to life in Leslie Stephen's story of the Eigerjoch from which I have quoted on page 76; J. A. Carrel is anything but a mere name on a page in Whymper's *Scrambles*, and old Sémiond, who led or rather who followed Whymper up the Pelvoux reveals himself in one remark far more vividly than the shadowy personalities of Whymper's climbing companions. "Ah", said old Sémiond, "as to fleas, I don't pretend to be different from anyone else. *I have them*."

The unwritten history of the Alpine Club is an invaluable source for the historian. I am old enough to have met men like Whymper and Hereford George, who made Alpine history in the Golden Age, and to have been on terms of intimate friendship with one great personality of the Silver Age, Martin Conway, and of intermittent friendship with another celebrity of the same period, W. A. B. Coolidge.

Conway and Coolidge enjoyed Alpine gossip, and had an inexhaustible store of unpublished and often unpublishable personalia about the leaders of our Alpine world. Indeed, as I write I can hear the rattle of displaced skeletons released from their cupboards, for Coolidge's reminiscences were often faintly tinged with malice. I am grateful to them and to other survivors from the Silver

Age for a better understanding of Alpine history than I could ever have obtained from books. I devoted a chapter to Whymper and Leslie Stephen not only because they were the dominant personalities of the Golden Age but also because Stephen was the perfect foil to Whymper. For similar reasons I have chosen Mummery and Coolidge as representatives of the Silver Age.

Albert Frederick Mummery (1856—1895)

Mummery, even more than Whymper, has become the symbol of an age. Whymper by his great book made many converts to mountaineering, but he created no school and led no revolt against the accepted orthodoxies of the day. Mummery on the other hand was by temperament a heresiarch and not only in mountaineering. His revolutionary economic theories attracted no attention during his life time but have since been widely accepted. As a mountaineer he was regarded with distrust by the high priests of Alpine orthodoxy whose doctrines were crystalised in Clinton Dent's *Badminton* volume on mountaineering. Mummery repaid distrust with a vigorous polemic which established his position as the leading advocate of the new revelation, and for this reason there is a tendency, even more marked among continental than among British mountaineers, to give Mummery alone credit for the improvement in technique and higher standards of performance for which, as Geoffrey Young rightly says, "his guides and friends and, in fact, the whole accumulating wave of new mountain interest and exploration in which he shared were all equally responsible".

Certainly Mummery's influence was immense and endures to this day, as is clear from the references to him in *Les Alpinistes Célèbres*, published in 1956, as for instance Mme Micheline Morin's tribute:

"The personality of Mummery dominates this period of Alpine history. He was an innovator and the head of a school. He attracted a group of enthusiastic climbers."

Or Alain de Chatellus' verdict in the same volume:

"Mummery's book made many disciples in the succeeding generations, more perhaps on the Continent than in his own country. The great individualists who formed the Alpine élite up to 1930 all more or less derive from him."

All this is true and his great services to mountaineering need no embellishment from myth, such as the statement in Mr. James Ullman's informative and, in general, accurate book *The Age of Mountaineering* : "Mummery's climbs were legion and at one time or another during his career he pioneered new routes in almost every district of the Alps." Mummery in fact resembles Whymper in that both

94

of them made a tremendous reputation on far fewer climbs than many of their less known contemporaries, and so far from pioneering new routes in almost every region of the Alps, his only new expedition outside the immediate neighbourhood of Chamonix or Zermatt was the passage of the easy Schreckjoch from the Lower to the Upper Grindelwald Glacier.

Mummery was, perhaps, more brilliant as a mountain tactician than as a strategist, though I think Geoffrey Young is perhaps a little severe when he writes: "His mountain judgment, his letters show to have been defective, and his route designing and finding of his famous partnership was done in his earlier years by his great guides and in the latter by two of his great colleagues," but Young praises him unreservedly as a tactician. "As a climber he was unsurpassed in his day: a supreme ice man—the equal at least, as Norman Collie wrote to me last year, of the best professionals—a first rate rock climber, of the new order of rock climbing, and, moreover, gifted with a dynamic personality, at once detached, original and electrifying, which rose above the challenge of difficulty or danger with serene humour. It was this personal magnetism which led his expert parties to trust unquestioningly to his tactical leadership upon any ascent or in any crisis."

Mummery's first visit to the Alps was in 1871. At the age of fifteen he crossed the easy Théodule Pass from Breuil to Zermatt and surrendered to the mountain spell. The first of his great climbs to attract attention was the ascent of the Zmutt Ridge of the Matterhorn in 1879. Two years later he made the first ascent of the Grépon, where he set a new standard in rock climbing. In 1888 he visited the Caucasus with a guide from Meiringen, Heinrich Zurflüh, and made the first ascent of Dychtau (17,054 ft.).

In his last three Alpine seasons (1892–1894) Mummery carried out a series of first-class guideless climbs, the Grépon, the first guideless ascent of the Brenva Ridge of Mont Blanc and the Dent du Requin among others. The Requin was the first important virgin peak the conquest of which was made by an all-British guideless party, Mummery, J. N. Collie, G. Hastings and W. C. Slingsby. In 1895 Mummery made an attempt on Nanga Parbat and was last seen on the way to the Diama Pass.

His famous book, *My Climbs in the Alps and Caucasus*, was published in 1895 shortly before his death. It is one of the very few mountaineering books published in the last century which still continues to influence the rock specialists of our own age. The flashes of authentic humour in the book redeem the all too frequent lapses into facetiousness. Humour is timeless but facetiousness dates very quickly. *The Diary of a Nobody*, which was contemporary with Mummery's book, is as enchanting as when this masterpiece of humour was first written, but polysyllabic facetiousness, referring for instance to the Devil as "His satanic majesty", may have raised a smile when Mummery's book first appeared but irritates a modern reader, and the best that can be said about Mummery's arch allusions to swearing is that there is a certain period charm about a passage such as this:

> "It is distinctly unpleasant when a companion, whom you think is enjoying himself suddenly informs you that he is doubtful of his power to stand in the steps. At such times nothing but the fact that one has been brought up surrounded by the best religious influences, prevents the ejaculation of the strongest and most soul-satisfying expletives known to the English tongue."

But in spite of dated mannerisms Mummery's book is one of the greatest which mountaineering has ever inspired. There are men who have loved the beauty of the mountains but have been content to worship them from the valleys and middle heights, and there are rock acrobats for whom the mountains are nothing more than a gymnasium. Mummery's book glows with an intense vitality and conveys as few other mountaineering books convey, the joy of battle, as for instance:

> "But grim and hopeless as the cliffs may sometimes look when ebbing twilight is chased by shrieking wind and snow and the furies are in mad hunt along the ridges, there is ever the feeling that brave companions and a constant spirit will cut the gathering web of peril, 'forsan et haec olim meminisse juvabit'."

Or again:

> "The gaunt, bare slabs, the square, precipitous steps in the ridge, and the black, bulging ice of the gully, are the very breath of life to his being. I do not pretend to be able to analyse this feeling, still less to be able to make it clear to unbelievers. It must be felt to be understood, but it is potent to happiness and sends the blood tingling through the veins destroying every trace of cynicism and striking at the very roots of pessimistic philosophy."

But to Mummery the mountains were far more than an arena for athletic achievement. My choice of Coolidge as the perfect foil to Mummery was determined not only by the contrast between their mountain achievements, Coolidge who never moved without two guides and Mummery the guideless climber, but also by the contrast between their response to mountain beauty. Mummery's book opens with a passage, perhaps the noblest overture in Alpine literature, a passage which glows with the authentic flame of mountain love:

> "At the age of fifteen the crags of the Via Mala and the snows of the Théodule roused a passion within me that has grown with years, and has to no small extent moulded my life and thought. It has led me into regions of such fairy beauty that the fabled wonders of Xanadu seem commonplace beside them; it has brought me

BREITHORN
Ferdinand Hodler (1911)
(Lucerne Kunsthaus)

friends who may be relied on in fair weather and in foul, and it has stored my mind with memories that are treasures, corruptible neither by moth nor rust, sickness nor old age. My boyish delight in the great white peaks towering above the gloom of pines is still awakened when the lumbering diligence rolls through the gorge of the Diosaz or when the Matterhorn rises from out the foliage of Val Tournanche. I remember, as if it were yesterday, my first sight of the great mountain. It was shining in all the calm majesty of a September moon, and in the stillness of an autumn night, it seemed the very embodiment of mystery and a fitting dwelling-place for the spirits with which old legends people its stone-swept slopes."

Contrast this with the opening passage of *Alpine Studies* by the Reverend W. A. B. Coolidge:

"It so happens that the first snowy mountains on which I ever set eyes were those of the Maritime Alps. A very delicate lad, the doctors ordered me away from my native land (U.S.A.) to spend the winter of 1864-5 at Cannes, then comparatively little known. I was accompanied by my mother, my only sister, and my mother's sister (and so my aunt) Miss Brevoort, who later on was to climb many Alpine summits with me. I was ill with typhoid fever (caught in Paris) for the greater part of the winter. But in the spring of 1865 (being then only 14 years of age) I made many excursions in the neighbourhood, though practically none on foot, my favourite spot being the island of St. Honorat, one of the Lérins Islands, just opposite Cannes. Thence, as well as from Cannes itself, I must often have seen the snowy peaks of the Maritime Alps on the horizon. But I paid no attention whatever to them, my mind being absorbed by the scheme (partly carried out) of writing a history of the Lérins Islands."

The boy whose imagination was not fired by the beauty of the Maritime Alps in spring, because he was too pre-occupied with his monograph on the Lérins Islands evolved into the man who treated the Alps as pegs for historical monographs, incredibly tedious, and who described his own expeditions in articles the aridity of which was unrelieved by the slightest hint that he was aware of a beauty which he certainly made no attempt to describe.

Mummery and the Alpine Club

The Victorian conventions which had such a depersonalising effect on the Victorian mountaineers as they emerged from the pages of Alpine literature had a similar effect on the descriptions of the Alpine Club and its early history which appeared from time to time in *The Alpine Journal* and in books such as the Badminton volume on mountaineering. What Geoffrey Young rightly refers to as "a mid-century convention partially perverting the mountain message" has had a dessicating effect on Alpine history. We should not tolerate such a censorship in a history of England.

The achievements of the Club have been so outstanding, and not only in the past, that it is a pity to provide a sceptical reaction among the young by uncritical panegyric, or by the kind of history which concentrates on the objective facts, virgin peaks climbed, with dates and names of the successful climbers. The history of the Alpine Club owes much of its interest to the fact that the Club was a cross-section of upper class England, and that its particular ethos was the creation of many men distinguished in other walks of life.

The Club was not only very English in its outlook, but a mirror of Victorian England. Indeed long after the great Queen had died the Club retained an attractive Victorian flavour. Most of the continental Alpine clubs, the Swiss, for instance, or the French or the Italian, admitted candidates irrespective of mountaineering or social qualifications. Their objective was a large membership and the financial resources which result from a large membership. They are in a position to negotiate special terms for their members and they have rendered immense services to the entire mountaineering community by building innumerable mountain club huts which all climbers irrespective of club membership are free to use.[1]

The membership of the Alpine Club has never exceeded seven hundred, and is restricted to those whose record of mountaineering expeditions is considered adequate by the Committee. Until 1938 the names of those whose mountaineering qualifications had been approved by the Committee were submitted to a secret ballot of all members present at one of the monthly meetings of the Club, one black ball in ten excluding. In practice this meant that a clique of a dozen members could keep anybody out of the Club.

The Alpine Club in its early years attached little importance to social qualifications. Albert Smith was regarded as a little vulgar. T. W. Atkinson (elected 1859) began life as a brick layer. Whymper was lower middle class. Coolidge maintained that it was Sir Edward Davidson who tried to make a social club out of the Alpine Club.

Clubs which make no claim to represent the mountaineers of a particular country should be free to impose any qualification they deem appropriate, a class qualification as in the case of certain continental ski clubs restricted to working men, or even a religious qualification as in the case of the Achille Ratti Club, founded by Bishop Pearson, which has introduced the members of Catholic Boys' Clubs to the rocks of Cumberland and Wales. But everybody who possesses the necessary technical qualifications should be regarded as eligible for the club or association which is regarded as representing in his country the particular sport in which he is interested, be that sport mountaineering or tennis or cricket.

---

[1] Thanks very largely to the efforts of the late J. A. B. Bruce an association of British members of the Swiss Alpine Club was formed which in 1912 built and presented to the Swiss Alpine Club the Britannia Club Hut above Saas Fee.

Technical qualification, yes. Social qualification, no. Only those should be excluded from the Alpine Club whose behaviour above or below the snowline is calculated to bring mountaineering or the Club into disrepute.

It may be of interest to record the fact that the Ski Club of Great Britain began by modelling itself on the Alpine Club, with a technical and social qualification. I was instrumental in abolishing both, with the result that I am the only skier ever to have been excluded from the Ski Club of Great Britain for social reasons.

Whether a social qualification be desirable is a question on which members may legitimately differ, but everybody is now agreed that the secret ballot of all members was a mischievous procedure. This method of election, which was universal in the nineteenth century, has now been abandoned by almost every club of importance, including those whose raison d'être is their social qualification. The irresponsible are seldom elected to club committees to whom may therefore safely be entrusted the election of new members. On the other hand the secret ballot enables a clique of irresponsible members to exclude those whom the overwhelming majority of members desire to see elected. The habitual blackballer who delighted in the secret ballot was a well known club type. He was often a man who had been lucky to be elected, a borderline candidate, and he was almost always a man whose personal status depended less on his own achievements than on the prestige of the club to which he belonged.

Irresponsible blackballing had caused trouble in the Alpine Club from the first. T. S. Kennedy, the conqueror of the Dent Blanche, resigned after two of his candidates had been blackballed for no discoverable reason. Distinguished mountaineers often refused to run the risk of being blackballed and were lost to the Club. Passingham who made the first ascent of the west face of the Weisshorn and of the Zinal Rothorn from Zermatt was a case in point. He taught gymnastics. One of the great pioneers of climbing in Great Britain told me himself that he had often been asked to stand, and declined because he did not wish to give the blackballers a chance. He was, I am glad to say, eventually elected an honorary member.

Mummery, blackballed at his first attempt, is described in the *Alpine Club Register* as "Partner with his brother in a tanning business at Dover and Canterbury". Lord Schuster told me that it was believed at the time that Mummery had a retail shop in Dover, and that it was the prejudice against the retail trade that was responsible for the blackballing.[1] As I have heard a young mountaineer declaim against the snobbery of the Victorian Alpine Club it is fair to add that my informant assured me that the overwhelming majority of the Club were

[1] C. H. Pasteur, who was in a good position to know, maintained that jealousy on Davidson's part was the only cause of the blackballing.

indignant about the blackballing. He also added that there was nothing in Mummery's accent or manner to which the most class-conscious member of the Club could take exception. Envy of Mummery's achievements and the resentment of some of the old guard at his aggressive criticisms of the prevailing orthodoxy were probably contributory factors. He was elected at the second attempt. Coolidge told me that he had taken charge of the ballot box and shifted some balls from the "No" to the "Aye" part of the box.

Coolidge's claim to have faked the ballot was disputed by the late H. E. G. Tyndale and more recently by T. S. Blakeney, and I have commented on their objections in *Switzerland and the English, p. 215* and in *The Alpine Journal 1955, p. 439*. Coolidge's judgments were often warped by his vanity but I do not believe that he would have told a deliberate untruth. His references to Mummery in conversation were consistently friendly, whereas his hatred of Sir Edward Davidson, believed to have been responsible for Mummery's blackballing, and later for mine, was intense, and nothing would have given him greater pleasure than to have faked Mummery into a club from which Davidson had tried to exclude him.

Mummery was not by any means the last case of irresponsible blackballing; two mountaineers whose social qualifications were unexceptionable and who had a distinguished record of new ascents among the Chamonix Aiguilles were blackballed by the same clique. One of them was subsequently elected, the other made no further attempt to join. I too was their victim. Two ex-presidents, Captain J. P. Farrar and Lord Conway, were my sponsors. "You're as good as elected", said Farrar, "nobody will blackball *our* candidate." I knew better, but risks are there to be taken. At the age of sixteen I had been blackballed from the Ski Club of Great Britain, which later elected me president, because my father was a travel agent, and it was therefore assumed that I would have a professional interest in winter sports. When I stood for the Alpine Club I was still a director of the travel agency my father founded and, as in Mummery's case, exception was taken not only to my business connections but also to the vigour with which I had criticised the current orthodoxy, for ski-mountaineering was as suspect at the beginning of this century as Mummery's heresies in the eighties.

I was in Grindelwald when I opened Farrar's telegram. "Defeated by a small clique at an unrepresentative meeting."

To me the Alpine Club was not merely a club. It was the communion of the faithful, the visible expression on earth of that worship of mountain beauty in which I had for so long attempted to find a substitute for the religion which I had lost. The first book which I had spelt out laboriously for myself as a child was *Scrambles Amongst the Alps*. While I was at Harrow I had borrowed *The Alpine Journals* volume by volume from John Stogdon, and read them from the first page to the last. Stephen's *The Playground of Europe* was my breviary.

I put the telegram into my pocket and walked up to the little bench near the Abbach Falls where I rested. I looked across the valley to the noble monument of the Wetterhorn and the Gothic spire of the Schreckhorn, for ever associated in my mind with the Early Fathers of mountain faith, Alfred Wills and Leslie Stephen. I pulled the telegram out of my pocket and reread the announcement of my excommunication from the company of the faithful, and suddenly I remembered the words which my father loved to quote, words scratched into walls of an Inquisition Dungeon: "They cannot cast me out from Thy true Church...."

In 1938 the president, Colonel Strutt, asked me to stand again. "What's the use?" I replied, "A clique of a dozen can keep anybody out of the Club." "I'll guarantee that you'll be elected", replied Strutt. Now it was common knowledge that he had falsified the results of a previous ballot, as indeed he admitted to me some years later. "If I had not done so", he said, "a vice-president and two members of the Committee would have resigned. I was prepared to do the same for you. Fortunately it was not necessary."

I was proposed by Lord Schuster and seconded by Leo Amery. I did not know when I asked Claud Schuster to propose me that he was the Committee's nominee for the presidency. "I told them", he wrote to me after I was elected, "that I would not accept the presidency if you were blackballed." I was deeply moved by this quixotic gesture of friendship, for Schuster knew nothing of Strutt's plans. Many mountaineers would find it easier to refuse the Garter than the presidency of the world's premier Alpine Club.

It was by then clear that when presidents were reduced to falsifying the results of the ballot, the time had come for a drastic change in the rules governing the election of members, and it was not the least of Schuster's many services to the Club that he was responsible for the present rule under which the election of members is vested in the Committee alone. By a curious coincidence the first meeting of the Club which I attended as a member was also the last at which candidates were elected by a ballot of the members. Schuster proposed the new rule and was supported by Raymond Greene, a member of one of the Everest expeditions who made an unmistakable reference to my case and a cheery attack on the blackballers, one of whom was sitting just in front of him. When the new rule had been passed I went up to the president and said: "Congratulations on opening the stable door when the steed is in."

There are, I know, respectable precedents for the intrusion of personal reminiscences into historical writing, as for instance Thucydides' reference to the fact that "He who wrote these things" came to the rescue with six triremes at the battle of Amphipolis, but I am not conscious of any need to justify my brief account of episodes which, rightly considered, are no discredit to the Club, except in so far as the Club adopted a method of election which was once universal in English clubs, and which has now been universally abandoned. Moreover, though many a mountaineer in the past has recalled the reverence with which he regarded the Alpine Club before being elected, and of his pride on being admitted to that august society, no mountaineer has recorded what exclusion from the Club meant to the excommunicated, and this is a lacuna in the history of the Club, which I am in a position to fill. "With a great price I obtained this freedom" and my own experience seems to me worth recounting, if only as evidence of what the Alpine Club meant to mountaineers who grew to manhood at a time when most of the founding fathers were still alive.

William Augustus Brevoort Coolidge (1850–1926)

On his father's side Coolidge was a member of an old Boston family, which has given a president to the United States. His mother was a Brevoort, a family of Dutch origin, which settled in America in 1770.

Coolidge left America at the age of fourteen, and never returned. He graduated from Exeter College, Oxford, and was elected a Fellow of Magdalen in 1875. In 1896 he settled in Grindelwald, and died there in 1926.

Coolidge had never possessed nor needed a passport for, prior to the First World War, one could travel anywhere in Europe, other than in Russia, Turkey or the Balkans, without a passport. He had never bothered to regulate his position and discovered at the outbreak of the First World War that he had no nationality, for he had lost his American without acquiring British nationality. He was indeed one of the first and certainly one of the most distinguished representatives of a group with which modern persecutions have made us all too familiar—the Stateless. The Americans, however, are fully entitled to claim him as the first American mountaineer to achieve fame in the Alps. In the nineteenth century, writes Dr. J. Monroe Thorington, a former president of the American Alpine Club, in his scholarly and interesting *A Survey of Early American Ascents in the Alps in the Nineteenth Century*, "scarcely any Americans not living abroad went to the Alps solely for climbing. Until 1870 we had no tradition in this sphere...." The first Americans to climb Mont Blanc were William Howard and Jeremiah Van Rensselaer, whose ascent, the tenth in all, was made on July 12th, 1819. The Americans who climbed Mont Blanc "accepted it", as Dr. Thorington insists, "as a sporting venture which most of them never expected to repeat".

The first American to climb a virgin peak, and to have climbed in more than one region of the Alps, was James Kent Stone who, with Leslie Stephen, made the first ascent of the Blümlisalphorn. His other climbs were Monte Rosa,

Lysjoch, Altels, Mont Velan and the Strahlhorn. He graduated from Harvard in 1861, became a Catholic, and joined a Religious Order, taking the name Father Fidelis. In a letter to Mr. J. E. C. Eaton, Honorary Secretary of the Alpine Club, Father Fidelis wrote:

"Your favour of the 22nd ult. reached me at the address below, and I would have answered promptly but was disabled by illness, from which I did not expect to recover. However, I am now much better, and if I pull through the winter, may last a while longer. In any case, shall probably remain at this address for the rest of my life.

"My climbing days, for recreation, were ended, of course, long ago, but I spent many years in South America, doing missionary duty there, and several times I had the privilege—it was real happiness—of crossing the Cordilleras, and my mind then went back to those days of early romance, when, in company with honoured and ever-remembered friends of the dear old Alpine Club, I revelled among the Peaks and Passes of Switzerland. Especially have I always held in loyal rememberance one with whose kind friendship I was favoured, Sir Leslie Stephen, who was then plain Leslie Stephen, of Trinity Hall, Cambridge. He staggered me once by saying (I didn't believe him) that I was the 'best walker he had ever seen'.

"I have now entered my eighty-first year, having returned to my old haunts in the North only a year ago.

"Thanking you, dear Sir, for having taken the pains to hunt me up, and for your courtesy in writing to me."

The first American honorary member was the future president, Theodore Roosevelt. At the age of twenty-three he climbed the Matterhorn and the Jungfrau. His qualifications were considered insufficient when he was first proposed but, on the proposal of E. N. Buxton and the future Lord Bryce, he was elected an honorary member of the Club in 1897.

Coolidge's first Alpine season was in 1865. Up till 1876 he climbed with his aunt, Miss Brevoort. After her death he continued climbing till 1898. He was the first to explore the Dauphiny, where his first ascents included the Râteau, Les Bans, Grande Ruine, Pic Coolidge and the Pic Central de la Meije. He made the second ascent of the Meije proper. He was also a pioneer of winter mountaineering and made the first winter ascents of the Wetterhorn, Jungfrau and Schreckhorn.

In all Coolidge made seventeen hundred expeditions[1], of which nine hundred were of a certain importance. "All his expeditions", writes a young French climber, Bernard Denjoy, "are now considered easy. It was, however, his great merit to have discovered the Oisans, and to have made this range known."

[1] By an odd coincidence the precise number of Purtscheller's expeditions. No other mountaineer has equalled this record, Purtscheller's list was equal in quantity but superior in quality.

From 1868 onwards Coolidge's leading guide was Christian Almer. No famous mountaineer has ever been more dependant on his guides. He was unathletic and short-sighted. He could never have led the simplest of rock climbs—he confessed that he far preferred snow climbs to rock peaks—and he would certainly have lost himself had he attempted the easiest of mountains without guides, but he was amazingly tough and deserves full credit as one of the pioneers of winter mountaineering, no sport for the soft.

Nobody would turn to his books in search of literature—I have already quoted a characteristic specimen of his prose style—but he was the greatest of Alpine scholars. Gladstone, who once sat next to him at dinner, remarked that he had greatly enjoyed talking to a mountaineer who was interested not only in the peaks which he had climbed but also in the people who lived in their shadow. His monumental volume on *Josias Simler et les origines de l'Alpinisme jusqu'en 1600* is a great contribution to Alpine scholarship which fully merited the award of the Silver Medal from the French Geographical Society. Of far greater general use was his re-editing and revising of Ball's *Alpine Guide*, and above all the *Climbers' Guides*, initiated by Conway and Coolidge, which have proved of immense value to guideless climbers.

No connoisseur of eccentrics could help feeling a qualified affection for this splendid specimen of the cantankerous scholar. He made some enemies by his polemics, but most mountaineers "steadily declined", as Captain Farrar said, "to be his enemies". Most of us felt, as Farrar felt, that his knowledge of the history of mountaineering "gave him such a claim to general recognition that if he chose to indulge occasionally in violent polemics it was for us to hold our peace, and to wait till the clouds rolled by". His most famous battle was when he impugned (and rightly impugned) the veracity of Whymper's story (and illustration) of Almer's jump across a gap in the Ecrins Ridge, which no subsequent English mountaineer has ever seen. He resigned because he was indignant with the Committee for failing to support his attack on Whymper. He was elected an honorary member in 1904, and resigned again in 1910, as a protest against the proposal of the Committee that Sir Edward Davidson should be elected president. In 1923 he was once again elected an honorary member; and did not live long enough to tender a third resignation.

As a sample of the kind of trivia which provided Coolidge with a succulent feud, the birth of the great Coolidge-Davidson vendetta may, perhaps, merit a passing mention. Davidson fired the first shot. Coolidge had inadvertently omitted the first "*c*" in *Schreckhorn*, in a tribute to his guide Christian Almer, a tribute written in Almer's *Führerbuch*, as the little book is called which the guide produces at the end of an engagement for the comments of his appreciative clients. Davidson noting with pleasure the misspelling of Coolidge, the infallible pedant, added an anonymous comment: "The usual spelling among Germans is Schreckhorn." In the same *Führerbuch* Davidson's climbing partner had spelt Jungfrau without a "*g*", and Davidson had added his signature, thus endorsing the tribute in which Jungfrau was spelt without a "*g*".

In 1896 Almer's *Führerbuch* was reproduced in facsimile. Coolidge recognised Davidson's handwriting, and was infuriated by the public advertisement of his lapse. "I hunted and I hunted", he exclaimed to me, "until at last I found that Davidson had put his name to Jungfrau without a '*g*'." And his little beard fluttered with excitement, as he recalled that fierce moment of anticipatory revenge. Douglas Freshfield, who shared Coolidge's dislike of Davidson, reviewed the *Führerbuch* in *The Alpine Journal* (xviii. 63). Davidson's distinguished handwriting was well known, and by this time most members of the Club were aware that Davidson was the author of the anonymous comment on Coolidge's spelling.

"Few even of the most pedantic critics", wrote Freshfield, "will think the worse of Mr. W. E. Davidson for putting his name under Jungfrau without a '*g*', or of Mr. Coolidge and two other climbers for leaving out the first '*c*' in Schreckhorn.... It is true that an unhappy Alpine snob, to whom even Almer's book was not sacred, has defaced one of its pages by the superfluous gloss, 'the usual spelling among Germans is Schreckhorn'. We cannot affect any sympathy for this specimen of a class well known to all who have turned over old hotel books in the punishment that has overtaken him." To this Davidson replied with great indignation: "I have not written the word in question either with a '*g*', without a '*g*' or in any other way, from one end of the *Führerbuch* to the other." "Mr. Davidson", replied Douglas Freshfield with the dignity which this momentous issue clearly demanded, "can hardly need to be reminded that both in law and literature we are all responsible for what we sign."

A friend of mine who had been an undergraduate at Magdalen, Oxford, of which Coolidge was for some time a Fellow, described his astonishment when he discovered that Coolidge was a great mountaineer. "I remember him", said my friend, "as a tubby, undersized little man, the sort of Don whom one might expect to 'sport his oak' on Bump supper nights to avoid being assaulted by intoxicated toughs."

It was wholly delightful for the Rev. W. A. B. Coolidge to be promoted by his Alpine exploits from the category of a "tubby, undersized little man" to that of an Alpine hero.

Nobody who had received as I had a reprint of his biographical notice from *Who's Who*, surrounded by an embroidered border of edelweiss and gentians, would register surprise on discovering that Coolidge's judgments were so often coloured by vanity. For instance, his ungenerous comment on de Castelnau, who robbed Coolidge of his great ambition, the first ascent of the Meije. "The Meije", wrote Coolidge, "fell by a kind of accident to a young Frenchman who was a chamois hunter rather than a peak hunter." De Castelnau was certainly a good shot and he was also a pioneer balloonist and Coolidge might just as well have written: "which fell by accident to a young Frenchman whose ascents were more often made in balloons than in boots."

Coolidge disapproved of guideless climbing, because he climbed with guides. He had a high opinion of winter mountaineers because he had made many fine ascents in winter. He had a complete contempt for skiers, because he could not ski; and he refused to admit that there was such a thing as ski-mountaineering. He had never climbed outside the Alps and *therefore* "it was difficult", to quote from Freshfield's obituary notice, "to induce him to take interest in any range outside the Alps; even the assault on Mount Everest failed to stir him". He devoted all his leisure to Alpine history, and had a high opinion of the one Alpine historian with whom he had never quarrelled, himself. He could describe neither a climb nor a view, and his prose was excrutiatingly tedious, and he was therefore "intolerant", to quote again from Freshfield, "of any attempts at aesthetic description".

My first contact with Coolidge was in the course of a controversy in *The Field*, in which Colonel Strutt had stated that ski were only of use for reaching Alpine huts and that no ski-runner had equalled Coolidge's winter ascents on foot. This I ventured to doubt, and the lack of reverence, if not of respect with which I referred to these ascents produced a characteristic reply from Coolidge, in which— I quote from memory—he said: "Mr. Lunn tells us in *Oxford Mountaineering Essays* that he was four at the time of the Grindelwald fire. He must therefore be only twenty-one today. He tells us that he climbed his first peak at the age of fifteen. He can therefore only have had six years climbing experience. And yet this young and inexperienced mountaineer ventures to, etc."

The Field used to send me mountaineering books to review, among them two of Coolidge's. I gave him full marks for erudition and for his pioneer work as a winter mountaineer, but hinted that the entertainment value of his books left something to be desired.

Many years later I settled in Grindelwald and was curious to meet the old sage. I therefore wrote to him expressing my gratitude for all the pleasure which his books had given me. He replied: "I am puzzled by your letter. You pay me compliments for which I thank you but can you by any chance be the same Arnold Lunn who in *The Field* wrote ". . . Here he quoted a review . . ." and who in *The Alps* wrote of me as follows:

"'My friends tell me', writes a well-known veteran, 'that I am singular in my strange desire to avoid meeting the never ceasing stream of tourists, and I am beginning to believe that they are right, and that I am differently constituted from other people.' The author of this trite confession has only to study travel literature in general and Alpine literature in particular to discover that quite commonplace people can misquote the remark about the madding crowd, and that even members of the lower middle class have been known to put the sentiment into practice. A sense of humour and a sense for solitude are two things which their true possessors are chary of mentioning."

"Can it be that the Arnold Lunn who pilloried me in this fashion can be the Arnold Lunn who now writes of me with flattering respect?"

The old boy had kept a complete dossier of me and my works, and my allusions to him had all been carefully tabulated. I wrote back at once: "You are right. There are two Arnold Lunns; A. L. the first, an irreverent bumptious youth who recently died, and A. L. the second, who has a proper respect for his elders, and a proper reverence for the works of one of the great pioneers of the Alps."

Mollified by this grovel, the cantankerous sage allowed me to call, and thereafter for some years I used to spend an hour or two with him every week throughout the summer months.

Coolidge varied the monotony of his Alpine battles by an occasional skirmish with the Anglican chaplains at Grindelwald. "I should have become a Roman Catholic", he once confided to me, "but for the dogma of the Immaculate Conception." I wish there had been no such barrier, for Coolidge's skirmishes with the Vatican subsequent to his reception would have provided more amusing material for his biographers than his arguments with low church parsons at Grindelwald. Coolidge was high church in doctrine, and no church in practice.

Shortly before he died Martin Conway came to tea with us in our Grindelwald chalet. "Coolidge", he began, "has told me to forbid you his house." I asked what crime had provoked this interdict. "Well, you know Murray's guide has recently been re-issued, and Coolidge maintains that he ought to have been asked to edit it." "Yes, I know, but what has that to do with me?" "Well, the editor expresses in the preface his indebtedness to you for some information you gave him. You've been thanked in a book which Coolidge ought to have been invited to edit." Conway laughed. "You look surprised, my dear Arnold, but let me assure you that Coolidge has often declared war with far less provocation than that!"

Coolidge died suddenly on May 8th, 1926. Owing to the General Strike my wife and I were the only English mourners. It was curious to see the English church packed by Grindelwalders, few if any of whom had ever attended an English service. They all stood through the prayers, and would apparently have remained standing if the chaplain had not motioned them to sit down while he read the lessons. The effect was strange—the coffin containing the mortal remains of the old Oxford don in the aisle, the English chaplain, and the characteristically Swiss congregation.

After the service we all walked to the Swiss cemetery, and Dr. Dübi spoke with eloquence and with real feeling of his old friend. He referred to their first meeting among the mountains many years ago, to their long partnership in Alpine research, and to Coolidge's great work as the first historian who specialised in the history of mountaineering. He paid him full credit for generosity, and mentioned his royal gifts to the various museums. Then, with a candour as rare as it is refreshing in funeral orations, he stated frankly that his old friend had a difficult side to his nature and was inclined to be a trifle "schroff", especially in the written word.

The Swiss Pfarrer then spoke the final words and the mourners dispersed.

The funeral was in the afternoon. It was one of those warm spring days, full of colour and sound. The avalanches poured down the cliffs of the Mettenberg, and their echoes broke in on Dr. Dübi's speech like the low roll of minute guns.

CHAPTER X

BEYOND THE ALPS (1868—1914)

The inevitable consequence of the exhaustion of Alpine peaks, which were both famous and virgin, was a succession of expeditions by mountaineers of the Alpine Club to other great mountain ranges. The space at my disposal only permits the briefest review of such exploration from 1868, the date of the first British expedition in the Caucasus, to the outbreak of the First World War which interrupted Raeburn's exploration of the same range.

The Caucasus

The first important mountain expedition outside the Alps was the expedition to the Caucasus in 1868. The party, which consisted of Douglas Freshfield, whose career is summarised in the next chapter, A. W. Moore and C. C. Tucker, climbed the slightly lower of the twin summits of Elbruz and also Kasbek at the other end of the 700 mile long range.

The Caucasus were left untroubled by mountaineers for six years, but in 1874 F. C. Grove, author of *The Frosty Caucasus*, F. Gardiner and Horace Walker with the guide Peter Knubel made various ascents, among them the highest summit of Elbruz (18,480 ft.). This ascent was repeated in 1884 by a Hungarian climber, M. de Déchy.

In 1888 Mummery with Zurflüh of Meiringen climbed Dychtau (17,054 ft.), the second highest peak of the range. In the same year J. G. Cockin and Ulrich Almer conquered the north peak of Ushba (15,410 ft.) which has twin peaks of almost the same height. The south peak was not climbed until 1903 by a German-Swiss party.

In 1886 Clinton Dent and W. F. Donkin made the first ascent of Gestola and two years later the same climbers, together with H. Fox, again visited the Caucasus, Donkin and Fox being lost in an attempt on Koshtantau. Hermann Woolley climbed Koshtantau in the following year and, with J. G. Cockin and others, returned to continue his explorations in 1893, 1895 and 1896. W. R. Rickmers was another prominent name in Caucasian travel at the turn of the century and Tom G. Longstaff and L. W. Rolleston, in 1903, ran a most successful guideless expedition that accounted for a number of new climbs. The last

British parties to visit this region before the outbreak of war in 1914 were those of W. N. Ling and Harold Raeburn, in 1912 and 1914.

The publication, in 1896, of D. W. Freshfield's "Exploration of the Caucasus" was an event of great importance in the annals of Caucasian mountaineering.

Sella's work in photographing the Caucasus will be described in the next chapter.

Norway

William Cecil Slingsby (1849–1929) is regarded both by the British and the Norwegians as the "father of Norwegian mountaineering". No mountaineer had a comparable record of Norwegian first ascents. His most remarkable ascent was that of Skagastölstind in 1875. His two Norwegian companions stopped at what is now known as Mohn's Skar, and Slingsby continued alone.

> "I certainly should not have attempted rocks such as those when alone upon any other mountain than Skagastölstind; but it was the particular peak on which I had concentrated my energies, and that solitary climb I shall always look back upon with a feeling of veneration, as it formed an event in my life which can never be forgotten; and although I have climbed a greater number of the higher Norsk mountains than any other person, yet the ascent of none can leave such a vivid impression in my mind as this."

Among his more notable expeditions were the first crossing of a pass across the Justedalsbrae and the first ascent of Rulten in the Lofoten.

Slingsby was a pioneer not only of mountaineering in Norway but also of mountain ski-ing. His early experiences were described in a letter to the *Winter Sports Review* (1911–12):

> "Dear Sir,
> Though I have never yet joined the Winter Sports in Switzerland yet, strange to say, I advocated so long ago as the year 1880, in *Den Norske Turist Forenings Aarbog* for 1880, p. 107, to the Norwegians themselves the sport of ski-running over their wildest mountain country, which I had myself, to a small extent, practised in 1880. At that time the Norsk had not taken to their true highlands in winter. This advocacy I repeated in my book 'Norway, the Northern Playground', p. 200.
> Yours faithfully,   Wm. Cecil Slingsby."

In a subsequent letter Mr. Slingsby adds:

> "The expedition on ski in the year 1880, to which I recently referred, was not, when compared with those undertaken today, a very successful one, solely because the snow was too soft. It was, however, exceedingly difficult, and the Keiser Pass (1550 m.), though it might have been crossed on ski by native reindeer hunters, certainly had not then been tackled by amateur mountaineers or tourists.
> The Morke Koldedal Pass is a very grand one, and even now is seldom traversed in summer, let alone in winter. However, my mountaineering friends in Norway are, rightly or wrongly, good enough to say that my suggestion on page 107 of the *Nor. Tur. For. Aarbog* for 1880 was the earliest known recommendation to mountain lovers to take a run on ski over the wildest mountain region in their country."

Slingsby was not the last Englishman to influence the development of sports native to Norway, mountaineering in his case and downhill ski-ing in the case of an Englishman described by the Norwegian president of the International Ski Association as "the father of modern downhill and slalom racing".

Slingsby spent far more time in Norway than in the Alps but he achieved some splendid Alpine climbs, notably the guideless conquest of the Dent du Requin with Mummery, J. N. Collie and G. Hastings. He was also a pioneer of climbing in Great Britain, where he made the first ascent (1891) of the north face of the Pillar Rock with W. P. Haskett-Smith and G. Hastings, and in 1892 of the Eagle's Nest Ridge of Great Gable with G. P. Baker, W. A. Brigg and G. A. Solly. He was one of the founders of the Climbers' Club in 1898. His daughter married Geoffrey Young.

The Pyrenees

In the early history of Pyrenean climbers two members of the Alpine Club played an outstanding role, Charles Packe and Count Henry Russell-Killough. Russell's father was Irish, his mother French. Packe's *Guide to the Pyrenees* was in the opinion of R. L. G. Irving "much the best till well into the present century".

British Mountains

The first rock climb to be accomplished in Great Britain was that of the Pillar Rock in 1826.

From the 1850's onwards members of the Alpine Club often trained on the Cumberland Fells at first mainly by walking to keep fit.

The first outstanding pioneer of climbing in the British Isles was Walter Parry Haskett-Smith (1861–1946) who began his exploration of the Cumberland Cliffs in 1882 when he made, among other climbs, the first ascent of the Pavey Ark Great Gully. In 1886 he discovered and made a solitary first ascent of the famous Needle on Great Gable. In his early days Haskett-Smith was preoccupied with gullies, and gave an amusing explanation of this bias, which Edward Pyatt quotes in an excellent article on Haskett-Smith in the *Climbers' Club Journal*, 1955.

"It is one great merit of a climb if it clearly defines itself. When A makes a climb, he wants B, C and D to have the benefit of every single obstacle with which he himself met, while B, C and D are equally anxious to say that they followed the exact line that Mr. A found so difficult, and thought it perfectly easy. And this is why so many of our climbs are ghylls. If you climb just to amuse yourself you can wander vaguely over a face of rock; but if you want to describe your climb to others, it saves a lot of time if you can say—'There that's our gully! Stick to it all the way up!'"

Haskett-Smith began to climb in Britain and he was in no way influenced by Alpine climbing.

> "His very substantial contribution", writes Mr. Pyatt, "to the development of British rock climbing was made entirely on his own initiative, after the original impetus had been given by Bowring. As all his early climbing was done solo his role as founder is unchallengeable."

In 1894 Haskett-Smith published the first volume (England) on climbing in the British Isles.

Second only to Haskett-Smith in their influence on the development of climbing in Great Britain were the Keswick brothers, George D. and Ashley P. Abraham. Their photographs, perhaps the best rock climbing photographs of the period, were used to illustrate Owen Glynne Jones' *Rock Climbing in the English Lake District*. After Jones' death—he was killed on the Ferpècle Ridge of the Dent Blanche—the Abraham brothers wrote *Rock Climbing in North Wales*. These books had an immense and beneficial influence on the development of British climbing.

Another great pioneer of climbing in North Wales was J. M. Archer Thomson, whose famous guide book to Welsh crags was published by the Climbers' Club. Other famous pioneers of Welsh climbing were G. W. Young, whose Pen-y-pass parties have acquired a legendary fame, A. W. Andrews and H. V. Reade.

Whereas abroad the national mountaineering clubs are in general control of mountaineering in their particular country, mountaineering clubs in our country have developed on less logical and more individualistic lines. The Alpine Club has never claimed a general suzerainity over the sport as a whole, and rock climbing in Great Britain owes far less to the Alpine Club than to various regional or quasi-regional clubs of which the oldest is the Scottish Mountaineering Club, founded in 1889. The Yorkshire Ramblers was founded in 1892, the Climbers' Club, which has a traditional association with the Oxford and Cambridge Mountaineering Clubs, in 1898; the Rucksack Club, based on Manchester was founded in 1902; the Wayfarers in 1906, the Fell and Rock, the largest of these clubs, in 1906, and the Ladies Alpine Club in 1907. The Pinnacle Club (for ladies) which specialises in severe rock climbing was founded in 1921.

Thanks to these vigorous clubs the standard of rock climbing continued to improve during the period under review (1868–1914). The ascent by S. W. Herford and G. S. Sansom, both killed in the First World War, of the Central Buttress of Scafell in 1914 was long considered to be the most severe rock climb in Great Britain. "It is the only climb of that period", a modern rock climber, Peter Holmes, remarked to me, "which still enjoys immense prestige with the present generation."

The Alaskan mountains of which McKinley is the highest, are arctic mountains, and the glaciers which flow down from their crests are the greatest in the world outside the Polar Ice Cap. The conquest of Mount St. Elias (18,008 ft.) in 1897 by the Duke of the Abruzzi will be described in the next chapter.

Sixteen years later McKinley (20,300 ft.) was conquered and the story of the ascent and of earlier attempts is the theme of an excellent chapter in *The Age of Mountaineering*, by James Ramsey Ullman. In 1906, Dr. Frederic Cook, later notorious for his bogus claim to have reached the North Pole, lectured on his "conquest" of Mount McKinley to learned societies and public gatherings before his claim, which the mountaineering world never accepted, was finally exposed. It was shown that the photographs alleged to be taken from the summit of Mount McKinley were actually taken from an insignificant foothill peak.

Four years later, Mount McKinley was the scene of one of the most eccentric mountaineering expeditions in history. Six prospectors and miners, "the sourdoughs of McKinley", as they were known to mountaineering history, were typical Alaskan frontiersmen. They were convinced that Cook was bogus, and set out to prove that they could succeed where they felt convinced that he had failed. The 500 dollars, their entire capital, was provided by a public-spirited saloon keeper of Fairbanks.

> "There was (writes Mr. Ullman) no leader, no pre-arranged plan of attack, and by the time they reached the base of the mountain half the party had come to blows with the other half and left for home."

The party possessed neither scientific knowledge nor proper equipment but their instincts were sound and their choice of approach—the Muldrow Glacier—was inspired.

The three members of the expedition who were left, Peter Anderson, Billy Taylor and Charley McGonagall, camped at the head of the glacier and, with the foods and equipment that "an average person might take for a picnic lunch", they climbed from 11,000 to 20,000 ft. and back—*all in one day*. And by sheer bad luck they chose the northern of the two peaks, which is 300 ft. lower than the highest peak. "And in another week or so they were safe and sound in Billy McPhee's Fairbanks saloon telling all about it to anyone who would buy them a drink."

Naturally their fantastic story was not believed, but when Archdeacon Hudson Stuck and his companions Harry Karstens, Robert Tatum, Walter Harper and two Indians, named Johnny and Esaias, made the first ascent of the highest summit in 1913, he saw on the southern peak the flagstaff which the sourdoughs had planted "plain prominent and unmistakable", though the American flag had long since been torn to shreds by the arctic winds.

In the spring of 1932 a party consisting of Alfred Lindley, Erling Strom, Harry Liek and Grant Pearson made the second ascent of Mount McKinley. They were the first to climb *both* summits. Lindley was a famous American skier who represented his country on the governing body of international ski-ing. He was killed in an aeroplane accident.

Mount Logan (19,850 ft.) in the Yukon is the highest peak in Canada and the second highest in the North American continent. It was climbed on June 23rd, 1925, by A. H. MacCarthy, a famous Canadian mountaineer, and his companions. At 4.30 p.m. they reached what they believed to be the highest point only to behold the actual summit 3 miles ahead, and this was only attained at 8 p.m. They had no sooner started the descent than the storm broke and they had to burrow in the snow where they remained throughout the twilight of the arctic night. After spending yet a second night in the open they reached their base camp just as the three day blizzard was blowing itself out. For endurance and courage their achievement has rarely been surpassed.

Canadian Rockies

Little was known or mapped of the peaks and glaciers in the Canadian Rockies when Harold Ward Topham and the Rev. William Spotswood Green, C. B., an Irishman, joined a party in 1888 to explore the Selkirks. Of the Alpine Club pioneers in Canada the most successful was Norman Collie who was a distinguished scientist, an artist and a most accomplished writer. He was a close friend of Mummery's and was one of his companions on the guideless party that made the first ascent of the Requin, and a member of the expedition to Nanga Parbat on which Mummery perished.

Collie was a dauntless and often a solitary explorer of Scottish, English and Irish precipices, and of the sea cliffs of our Western coast. "Of these mountain worlds", writes G. W. Young, "he wrote with all the poetry of a Celt, and all the knowledge of a faultless mountaineer in passages of bard-like beauty." As for instance in the following passage:

"... The ledges of rock high up, with the grey lichen on them, will still afford a resting-place from which the long glaciers far down below can be seen as they descend to the green-hued woods and the hazy valleys filled with sunshine. The overhanging cornices high above, for ever on the point of breaking off, will still hang poised in unstable equilibrium. The storms will sweep as frequently as of old across that mountain land, hiding for a brief space all in gloom; the lightning flashes, the roar of the thunder, the driving snow, and the keen biting wind will

114

hunt the too presumptuous climber back to lower altitudes, as they have done often before; and afterwards the sun will again shine, dissolving the clouds, drying the lower slopes, and showing how the old mountains have once more put on a clean garment, which in magnificence, in glittering splendour, is as unmatched or unequalled as the deep, glowing colour of that 'solitary handmaid of eternity', the open ocean, or the glories of the heavens at dawn or at sunset."

Mount Assiniboine (11,870 ft.), which bears some slight resemblance to the Matterhorn, was climbed by the Rev. James Outram and two Canadian Pacific Railway guides in 1901; Mount Robson (12,972 ft.) by the brilliant Canadian climber A. H. MacCarthy and W. W. Foster in 1913 with the famous Austrian guide Conrad Kain.

The Andes

The exploration of the Andes began in Ecuador just south of the Equator where rise some of the loftiest volcanoes in the world. Chimborazo, indeed, was for some time deemed to be the highest mountain in the world, this on the authority of the first scientific expedition to a lofty mountain range, the expedition which between 1736 and 1744 explored the mountains of Ecuador under the leadership of the Frenchmen Bouguer and La Condamine.

In 1802 the German naturalist, Alexander von Humboldt, made attempts on the actual summits of both Chimborazo and Cotapaxi. In 1872 the first great peak in South America to be climbed, Cotopaxi (19,335 ft.), was ascended by a German geologist, Wilhelm Reiss and his companion A. M. Escobar. Eight years later, in 1880, Whymper with the two Carrels, J. A. and Louis, made the fifth ascent of Cotopaxi and the first ascent of Chimborazo (20,550 ft.).

In the winter (summer in the southern hemisphere) of 1896–97 a party, which consisted of Edward A. FitzGerald, who had already made a name in New Zealand, a young Englishman, Stuart Vines and guides headed by the famous Mattias Zurbriggen attacked Aconcagua. On January 14th, 1897, FitzGerald, Vines and Zurbriggen left their high camp for an attack on the summit. Fitzgerald was overcome by sickness and helped down by Vines. Zurbriggen went on alone and planted his ice-axe on the highest point. A few days later the ascent was repeated by Vines and an Italian porter, Nicolas Lanti.

Zurbriggen of Saas, one of the greatest guides of the period, wrote a book about his mountain adventures which enjoyed some success. His end was tragic, he took to drink, spent all his money and shot himself in Geneva.

The ascent of Aconcagua was repeated in the following year by Martin Conway who also made the first ascent of the slightly lower summit of Illimani (21,200 ft.) which towers above La Paz, capital of Bolivia.

Many explorers had penetrated into the recesses of the Himalaya before men began to climb there for sport. First came the surveyors, then the naturalists of whom the most famous was Joseph Hooker who travelled extensively in Nepal and Sikkim in 1848–49.

"W. W. Graham", writes Professor Kenneth Mason in his admirable and invaluable history of Himalayan climbing[1], "was the first traveller to come out from England with the main object of climbing mountains 'more for sport and adventures than for the advancement of scientific knowledge' as he admitted on his return to the Geographical Society in 1884."

Graham's party made some climbs in Sikkim and claimed to have climbed Kabru (24,002 ft.) on October 8th, 1883. His claim was challenged at the time by Sir Martin Conway and though supported with some reservations by Dr. Tom Longstaff is decisively rejected by Professor Kenneth Mason. "The period of Himalayan mountaineering", writes Professor Mason, "that begins about 1885, opens with the journeys of Francis Younghusband, the establishment of the Gilgit Agency and the first exploration of the border states of Hunza and Nagir.

In the brief essays on Conway, Freshfield and the Duke of the Abruzzi in the following chapter mention will be made of their respective expeditions to the Himalaya in 1892, 1899 and 1909.

In 1905 Dr. Tom Longstaff, later president of the Alpine Club, explored the Nanda Devi "ring" and returned two years later to make on June 12th 1907 the first ascent of Trisul (23,360 ft.), the highest peak then attained about whose ascent there was no doubt. His guides were the two Brocherels of Courmayeur and Subadar Karbir. A. L. Mumm, a keen explorer both in the Rockies and Himalaya, had been his companion on an earlier and unsuccessful attempt. In the same year two Norwegians, C. W. Rubenson and Monrad Aas, reached an estimated altitude of 23,900 ft. in an attempt on Kabru.

"Perhaps no climber enjoyed himself more", writes Professor Mason, "among the Sikkim Himalaya than Dr. A. M. Kellas of Glasgow whose first visit to Sikkim was in 1907." In 1910 he climbed Pauhunri (23,180 ft.) and Chomiomo (22,430 ft.). He died on the first expedition to Everest in 1921.

C. F. Meade made three determined attacks on Kamet in 1910, 1912 and 1913, and reached a pass now known as Meade's Col (23,420 ft.), about 2000 ft. below the summit of Kamet. The combined effects of soft snow, sun and altitude robbed him of success.

---

[1] *Abode of Snow*, A History of Himalayan Exploration and Mountaineering by Kenneth Mason, formerly Superintendent, Survey of India and Professor of Geography in the University of Oxford 1932–52.

The last great Himalayan expedition before the outbreak of the First World War was the Italian expedition to the Karakorum under the leadership of Filippo De Filippi. The aims of the expedition were geographical exploration rather than mountain climbing and in point of fact no peaks of any importance were ascended.

The New Zealand Alps

Mount Cook (12,350 ft.) is the highest peak in New Zealand but the snowline is 3000 ft. lower than in the Alps and the weather more uncertain.

In the New Zealand summer of 1881–82 the Rev. W. S. Green, whose explorations in Canada have already been mentioned, reached the final snow cap of Mount Cook with the guides Ulrich Kaufmann and Emil Boss. It was late in the day and they deemed it more prudent not to press on to the actual summit which was first reached by the New Zealanders, T. C. Fyfe, G. Graham, and J. Clarke.

Shortly after Green's ascent of Mount Cook, A. P. Harper, the real father of New Zealand mountaineering, began with C. E. Mannering a series of explorations. A. P. Harper was the founder of the New Zealand Alpine Club and was elected a member of the Alpine Club in 1892 and an honorary member in 1932. His hope that he would live long enough to attend the Centenary Dinner in 1957 was not to be gratified for he died in 1955. His profound respect for the traditions of the Alpine Club sometimes exposed him to criticisms in New Zealand from those who felt that the New Zealand Alpine Club should develop on its own lines while continuing to maintain the close connection with the mother club which indeed has always been more than intimate. I am inclined to believe that for many New Zealanders the triumph of Everest would have been even sweeter had Sir Edmund Hillary's partner been an Englishman from the United Kingdom.

In 1895 E. A. FitzGerald arrived in New Zealand with Mattias Zurbriggen who, as we have seen, later made a solitary ascent of Aconcagua. In a recent booklet *New Zealanders and Everest*, by L. V. Bryant, a special tribute is paid to the influence on New Zealand mountaineers of "the great British climbers of the past". R. L. G. Irving, in his interesting book *A History of British Mountaineering*, quotes with rapturous approval a paragraph from this booklet in which Mr. Bryant contrasts the British school of climbers with the modernists.

"The young thruster", writes Mr. Bryant, "has argued that every safe route has been done and that only the dangerous remain. He has been quite willing, therefore, in order to achieve fame, to spend hour after hour toiling up ice and snow gullies that form the channel for every missile the mountain has to discharge. This school throws to the winds the precautions and safeguards that are fundamental to the 'English School'; adopts techniques which invite disaster, uses mechanical devices which convert the sport into a branch of engineering, and ignores the margin of safety which saves the sport from disrepute and which brings British parties home safely almost invariably."

E. A. FitzGerald's *Climbs in the New Zealand Alps* was the second record in book form of mountaineering in New Zealand, the first being W. S. Green's *The High Alps of New Zealand*. He arrived in New Zealand in January 1895 with Mattias Zurbriggen and made the first ascent of Mount Tasman (11,475 ft.), the second highest peak in New Zealand, and the first crossing of FitzGerald's Pass, a very useful exploration from the Hermitage over the main divide to the west coast. On Mount Sefton they were nearly killed, for FitzGerald was knocked over by a falling boulder, and two of the three strands of the rope were severed by rock, and it was only with the greatest difficulty that Zurbriggen withstood the shock. H. G. Willink, who provided most of the illustrations for the Badminton volume on mountaineering, illustrated FitzGerald's book and made the best use of FitzGerald's account of this incident.

Some of the more pedantic critics made it clear that they would have preferred a less popular style and a more severely scientific treatment both in the texts and in the illustrations. FitzGerald was so angered by this criticism that he resolved that his next book, of which Aconcagua was the theme, should be written in the style of a learned journal. Human figures were almost entirely excluded from the illustrations. Whereas the first book was popular in every sense of the term, the most pedantic of critics could not have damned the second book as a popular presentation of a mountaineering theme. The publisher, who had based his advance royalties on the sales of the first book, was unedified by FitzGerald's concession to the scientific spirit, for the sales of the second book were most disappointing.

CHAPTER XI

FOUR GREAT MOUNTAIN EXPLORERS

From 1868, when the first British mountaineering party explored the Caucasus, to the opening shots of the First World War four mountain explorers have a special claim on the history of mountaineering, Douglas Freshfield, The Duke of the Abruzzi, Martin Conway and Vittorio Sella.

Douglas William Freshfield (1845–1934)

Douglas Freshfield was born in 1845 and was educated at Eton and University College, Oxford. His father had been solicitor to the Bank of England. Douglas Freshfield was called to the Bar but never practised, for he inherited considerable wealth and was thus enabled to devote himself exclusively to mountain exploration and to the encouragement of geographical scholarship. His activities in these allied fields were rewarded with generous recognition. He was president of the Alpine Club and of the Royal Geographical Society, and was offered a knight-hood which he declined, because he felt that he had nothing to gain in public esteem by becoming "Sir Douglas".

Freshfield's was a type of career which is becoming increasingly rare in this age of severe taxation and death duties, for it depended on inherited wealth. In this he resembled another eminent Victorian associated with mountains, John Ruskin.

Freshfield was introduced at an early stage to the mountains, for both his parents were very fond of Switzerland. His mother's book *A Summer in the Grisons* (1862) sent the first wave of English visitors to the Grisons.[1] At Pontresina in those days there was only a rough village inn. Before he left Eton he had climbed the Titlis and Mont Blanc.

Freshfield was primarily an explorer. He preferred, as did so many of the pioneers, snow and ice to rock, on which he was a very mediocre performer. One of his climbing companions, E. J. Garwood, said of him that he was "extremely wiry and a notably fast, untiring walker", but his reputation as a mountaineer rests in the main, as Dr. T. G. Longstaff rightly says, on his "mountain sense",

---

[1] Quoted in Mlle Engel's book *They Came to the Hills* from a letter which she received from Freshfield.

his genius as a route finder and his ability for disentangling the topography of mountain ranges and for giving a clear and objective account of his explorations. He was far less interested in the mountain ranges which had been thoroughly explored than in those where there were still problems of local topography to solve.

His first book, a youthful essay privately printed *Across Country from Thonon to Trent* describes the kind of mountain journey he delighted in, a journey which enabled him to explore the Italian valleys at the head of the lakes of Como and Garda, and also the Dolomites. Other Alpine ranges, which he was among the first to explore, were the Maritimes and, further afield, the Dinaric Alps. In the course of his long climbing career he not only organised expeditions to the Caucasus, mentioned in the last chapter, and a circuit round Kangchenjunga, but also climbed in Algeria and the Pyrenees. At the age of sixty bad weather alone prevented him reaching the summit of Ruwenzori.

From 1863 until he died François Dévouassoud accompanied him as guide in the Caucasus and elsewhere. Douglas Freshfield refers to his "fine manner and literary instinct", which Mlle Engel attributes to the fact that Dévouassoud had attended a Jesuit College in Tanninges. When Freshfield's stirrup broke and he fell, as the party rode into Damascus, Dévouassoud exclaimed: "Ah Monsieur, vous faites bien de suivre l'exemple de saint Paul." Of Dévouassoud, Freshfield wrote: "He has taken tea with dignity with the Armenian patriarch at Etchmiadzin, has handed coffee at Jerusalem to a Turkish Pasha and paid his respects to the Archbishop of Canterbury."

Second only to Freshfield's passion for mountains was his interest in geography. With the help of the Royal Geographical Society he persuaded Oxford and Cambridge to institute honour schools in geography, an example which was soon followed in other universities. Freshfield was also responsible for persuading the Geographical Society to recognise mountaineering as a branch of exploration, and it was on his recommendation that the Royal Geographical Society gave gold medals to Hooker, Whymper, the Duke of the Abruzzi and Conway.

As an interpreter of the mountains Freshfield just failed to reach first rank.

"For Freshfield's ironic, vigorous outlook (writes G.W. Young), his resurgent enterprise and pungent speech could find no outlet in his chosen style—it did not admit even of Stephen's 'poetical or humorous turn'—any more than he himself could ever tolerate association with any one school, or even any one generation of mountaineers for long enough to be recognised as the leading spirit he ought to have become. In our former hall at Savile Row, I watched him on the platform steps, tall and head-tossing, and overlooking us with his genial, Aquiline sneer. He hurried down, caught me by the elbow and said 'Let's sit at the back—there's only those bald and white heads to the fore!' He himself was then well over eighty; but he still revelled in all the intolerant privileges of youth."

Though Freshfield does not rank as a mountain author with the greatest, he was always an accomplished and civilised writer, and once at least wrote something memorable. He led an expedition to the Caucasus to unravel the mystery of the disappearance of Donkin and Fox and their guides Fischer and Jaun. Foul play had been suspected, unjustly as events proved. Here is a passage from his description of the finding of their last bivouac on Dychtau.

"The silence of the upper snows was broken only by the constant ring of the axes and the voices of our comrades, which rose clearly through the thin air as they still laboured in their sad task of seeking all that might be found under the icy coverlet. Their figures were thrown out on the edge of the crags against the surface of the Tiutiun snowfields, as are those of sailors on a masthead against the sea, when seen from some high cliff. The day was cloudless, the air crystalline, space was for a moment annihilated or shown in a scale by which we each seemed to stand, not 6 ft., but 14,000 ft. high! The many passes and heights of the central ridge of the Caucasus lay literally at our feet. We looked over them and past the clustered peaks and vast snow-reservoirs of the Adai Khokh Group to innumerable indefinite distances, amongst which I recognised the horn of Shoda, green heights of Racha, blue mountains of Achalzich, opalescent Armenian ranges fading into a saffron sky, on which hung the far-off amber cloudlets which often mark the position of Ararat. Every detail was distinct as on a mapman's model, yet the whole was vast and vague, wonderful and strange, creating an impression of immeasurable shining space, of the Earth as it might first appear to a visitant from some other planet. The splendour of nature on this day of days seemed not out of harmony with the sadness of our errand. It affected the mind as a solemn and sympathetic Music. While I gazed, four white butterflies circled round the little monument, and again fluttered off. An ancient Greek would have found a symbol in the incident."

Freshfield was not only a classical scholar but he always assumed the same background in his readers and therefore did not think it necessary to explain that the butterfly was the Greek symbol of immortality.

The Duke of the Abruzzi (1873–1933)

The Duke of the Abruzzi was a member of the cadet branch of the Royal House of Savoy. He began to climb in 1892 and in 1894 he made with Mummery an ascent of the Matterhorn by the Zmutt Ridge. He was among the pioneers of winter mountaineering, and made the first winter ascent of Monte Viso in 1897, but it was as an explorer of the great mountain ranges of the world that he became famous.

The Duke organised and led three great expeditions, on the first of which his party made the first ascent of Mount St. Elias (18,012 ft.) in Alaska, on July 31st, 1897; on the second of which he made the first ascent of the highest point of

Ruwenzori (16,795 ft.) in Uganda, on June 18th, 1906; and on the third of which he established a height record in the Karakorum (24,607 ft.) in an attempt on Bride Peak.

Of these expeditions the conquest of Mount St. Elias was by far the most remarkable, involving as it did not only mountaineering but also exploration, arctic in character. The summit was reached after a month's march, and the entire expedition lasted one hundred and fifty-four days. His companions were Vittorio Sella, Filippo De Filippi, U. Cagni, later admiral of the Italian fleet, F. Gonella, Joseph Petigax, J. A. Maquignaz, A. Croux, E. Botta and A. Pélissier. "Though only twenty-four at the time of this expedition he was", writes Count Aldo Bonacossa: "already a leader of men, with the power to attract a team whose devotion to the Duke was life-long. He was sometimes a little exacting in his demands, and he never ceased to be a prince, but how great was his psychological insight into the souls of men, and above all how striking was his personal example in endurance and in dangers!"

In the year following his ascent of Mount St. Elias he explored Spitsbergen with the faithful Cagni, and a little later Siberia in winter. In 1899 he organised an expedition to the yet unattained North Pole, in the course of which two of his frostbitten fingers had to be amputated.

During the First World War he commanded the allied naval units which embarked more than 150 000 Serbs, and transported them across the Adriatic. At the end of the war he returned to Africa as a pioneer, and founded in Somaliland the flourishing village which still bears his name. He died there in 1933, mourned by the natives "comme chef et père". His nephew, the Duke Amedeo d'Aosta told Count Bonacossa that he desired that the portrait of an American lady whom he loved should be buried with him in his tomb. He did not marry because he respected the wishes of his aunt Queen Marguerita of Italy. Count Bonacossa concludes the sketch which he contributed to *Les Alpinistes Célèbres* with a characteristic anecdote of another great mountaineer. "It was sad", Count Bonacossa once remarked to King Albert of the Belgians, "that these lovers were Royal Highnesses." The King paused, glanced at his friend Bonacossa above his spectacles, and a faint smile lingered on his lips. After which they continued their walk.

Lord Conway of Allington (1856–1937)

Martin Conway was born at Rochester on April 12th, 1856, the son of a Canon of Westminster. He was educated at Repton and Trinity College, Cambridge. He made his name as an art critic by *Early Flemish Artists* (1887), which was followed by *Albrecht Dürer* (1889), *Early Tuscan Artists* (1902) and *The Van Eycks*

(1921). Of the many art critics with whose works I am familiar there are few from whom I have learned more than Conway. His great gifts received recognition, first as Professor of Art in Liverpool, and later as Slade Professor at Cambridge, and as Trustee of the National Portrait Gallery and of the Wallace Collection. In 1918 he was elected as a Unionist to represent the Combined English Universities, and in 1931 he was created Baron Conway of Allington. He died on April 19th, 1937.

Conway was elected a member of the Alpine Club in 1877, and president in 1902. Like Freshfield and many other pioneers, he was good on snow and ice but mediocre on rocks, which he avoided as far as possible. He was primarily an explorer. In a series of three papers which he published in *The Alpine Journal* for 1891 he divided mountaineers into centrists and excentrists, and again into gymnasts and mountain climbers. The ideal mountain climber he maintained is one who "loves first and foremost to wander far and wide among the mountains, does not sleep willingly two consecutive nights in the same inn, hates centres, gets tired of a district, always wants to see what is on the other side of any range of hills, prefers passes to peaks but hates not getting to the top of anything he starts for, chooses the easiest and most normal route, likes to know the names of all the peaks in view, and cannot bear to see a group of peaks none of which he has climbed". The ideal mountaineer, by an odd coincidence, closely resembled Martin Conway, but the veiled eulogy of his own type, and strong criticisms of other types was not, so Claude Wilson remarked in his obituary, taken very seriously by the Club.

Conway's fame as a mountaineer rests not on any particular Alpine climb but on his exploration of distant ranges, the Karakorum (1892), Spitsbergen (often misspelt Spitzbergen) (1896 and 1897), the Andes and Tierra del Fuego (1898), and on the long mountain journey which was the theme of his book *The Alps from End to End.*

He was one of the first British to ski, and his early experiences are described in his books *The First Crossing of Spitsbergen* and *With Ski and Sledge over Arctic Glaciers.* When I founded the Alpine Ski Club I was most anxious to secure, as our first president, a man who was a pioneer both of ski-ing and of mountaineering, and great was my satisfaction when I was able to announce to the foundation meeting on March 7th, 1908, that Sir Martin Conway had accepted the presidency.

Conway was a pioneer not only in mountaineering but also in mountain literature. His *Zermatt Pocket Book* (1881) was the first *Climbers' Guide* in any language. It was followed by the two-volume *Pennine Guide*, and then by the "Conway and Coolidge" *Climbers' Guides* which covered the main mountain ranges of the Alps. These books not only recorded the physical details of the different routes to the summit but also the names of all those who pioneered the routes in question. "Some mountaineers", Conway once confided to me, "who professed that they climbed only for the fun of climbing, and who were very severe on what they considered to be the self-advertising of mountaineers who called attention to their own ascents, took very good care to correct me if I had attributed a first ascent which they had made to some other party. I then announced in *The Alpine Journal* that unrecorded first ascents did not count, and after that I had no more trouble."

By thus indirectly drawing attention to what had *not* been climbed Conway gave a great stimulus, as G.W. Young says, to the "new route" movement. "Similarly", writes Young, "his *The Alps from End to End* formed a deliberate challenge to our approaching Alpine centrism and stagnation. I can recall how it shattered through certain Chamonix and Zermatt cobwebs."

Conway's keen eye for the nuances of form and colour which made his reputation as an art critic also established him as one of the great masters of mountain description. "Any goose sees glory" in Matterhorn or Jungfrau, but only a connoisseur of mountain beauty can appreciate the delicate loveliness of the Plaine Morte, to the unobservant nothing but a flat and featureless expanse of snow, and only a master of evocative writing could have described the Plaine Morte as Conway describes it:

"It is so large, so simple, and so secluded. It seems like the portion of some strange world. Its effect of size is increased by the insignificance of the wall that surrounds it, enough to shut out all distant views, and no more. The sense of novelty, of strangeness came upon me, such as I felt when all the Hispar Glacier under its dark roof of cloud first opened on my view. Beautiful too, it was with the beauty of all great snowfields; its large undulations, its rippled surface glinting under the touch of the low risen sun. To add to its mystery there came over the sky a veil of mist which presently reduced the brilliancy of the day, increasing the apparent size of everything and lengthening all distances. Two birds like swallows twittered around, and seemed out of place. The further we went the more profound was the solitude."

Mountaineers are indebted to Conway for many beautiful and appropriate names given by him to unnamed peaks and passes. That there was nothing romantic in the attitude of mountain peasants to the mountain is a conclusion which can be deduced with confidence from the unimaginative mountain names for which they are responsible. The Alps contain innumerable white peaks (Weisshorn, Dent Blanche, Mont Blanc, Monte Bianco), black peaks (Schwarzhorn, Aiguille Noire, Monte Nero), red peaks (Rothorn, Aiguille Rouge), peaks which served as an elementary compass bearing behind which the sun appeared at midday (Mittaghorn, Dent du Midi), peaks called the glacier peak (Gletscherhorn, Monte Rosa, a dialect word for glacier), etc., etc.

Few indeed are the exceptions such as Eiger, Mönch and Jungfrau. If Mischabel really be the Arabic for Lion's whelp we owe the name not to natives but to the invading Saracens, and the Dom (Cathedral) was so called not by a simple mountain peasant but by the priest of Randa. Apart from these few exceptions names with a touch of poetry are the invention of foreigners: Aiguilles Dorées (Forbes), Adler Pass (Alfred Wills) and Col des Hirondelles (Leslie Stephen), Wellenkuppe, Windjoch, Dent du Requin and Le Cardinal (Conway).

"Martin Conway was a personality", writes Geoffrey Young, "appropriate to a renaissance, of scintillating contrasts, a romantic, a sociologist, an art connoisseur, a wordling, an omniscient lecturer and compiler, a busy public character, and a completely casual will-o'-the-wisp". Conway reminds us of the Renaissance not only by his versatility but also by his realistic attitude towards success. He might indeed have taken for his own Cosimo Medici's motto: "The secret of happiness is to aim at finite ends." "The House of Commons", he once confided to me, "is delightful if one has no political ambitions." In the House he was on friendly terms with politicians who amused him or politicians whose friendship might be useful to him irrespective of their political views. Forlorn hopes and lost causes might stir his sympathy but could never engage his active support. He cherished a mild but friendly disdain for the human race, but the stupidities of mankind were never allowed to disturb his tranquillity. Montaigne remarked that it was taking a man's opinions too seriously to burn him alive for them. Conway, who had so much in common with Montaigne, might have added that it was taking a man's stupidities too seriously to burn with indignation because of them.

Conway neither provoked enmity nor formed profound friendships. "Whether in the Alps or in the Himalaya", wrote Claude Wilson, "his companionships seldom remained coherent for very long." He was a good mixer, and his friendly charm spun a web of fragile but useful relationships. It was characteristic of Conway that he should be the first man to be knighted in connection with mountaineering, the main reason for the honour being the map of Karakorum glaciers which Conway surveyed. It was no less characteristic that Conway should have been the first art critic permitted by the Bolsheviks to examine their art museums. His book *Art Treasures of Soviet Russia* (1925) was a by-product of this useful contact.

He was almost the only prominent mountaineer with whom even Coolidge found it impossible to quarrel. Few prominent men can have trodden on fewer corns. My father once sent me round to ask for his signature for a letter to *The Times* on some question of public policy on which Conway's views were similar to those of other distinguished signatories whom my father had collected. "I'd rather not", said Conway, "it might annoy Ramsay Macdonald (then premier) who is thinking of giving me a peerage." Conway's peerage was the theme of a cartoon in *Punch* which he enjoyed enormously, showing him trying on a coronet, and labelled "The Climber".

There was only one enemy whom this disciple of Cosimo de Medici could not charm into surrender, the last enemy death. In his old age Conway took my brother Hugh for a walk near Pontresina. "Suddenly", said my brother, "he paused and said: 'The last time I passed that chalet was forty years ago.' He looked at it with unutterable disgust and muttered crossly: 'It's appalling how quickly time passes.'" He seems, however, to have cherished the hope that even time could be softened by the Conway treatment, and *A Pilgrim's Quest for the Divine* (1936) may be regarded as his philosophical testament. I did not read the book but I remember a conversation in which Conway summed up what he so clearly wanted to believe. "Time", he said, "is an illusion, past time is really not past. It is still here. The past and the present and the future are all one." Conway looked at me and I suppose I appeared unconvinced. "But surely", he continued with a note of pleading in his voice as if he were anxious to find external support for what he so desperately wanted to believe, "surely there must be a sense in which the past and the present and the future are all one phase of the same thing. I am more and more convinced that the past is not really past...."

A consoling reflection if, and only if one's past had been as delightful as Conway's, but the doctrine that the past is not really past would seem less attractive to a man who had survived some years in Belsen or in the slave-labour camps of Siberia.

Claude Wilson in his obituary notice remarked that Conway "was not readily approachable by his juniors", a criticism which surprised me for in my experience his relations with the young were so natural that one's danger was to forget the gulf not only of years but also of achievement, and to talk to him as if he were a gifted but genial contemporary. I remember a wonderful motor tour in his company from the Riviera to Chamonix. No travelling companion could have been more entertaining over a wider range of subjects. To have known him was indeed a liberal education for a young man interested not only in mountaineering but in art.

Vittorio Sella (1859–1943)

Vittorio Sella was born on August 28th, 1859, the son of a textile manufacturer of Biella, and the nephew of Quintino Sella, the great statesman of the Risorgimento whose statue can be seen in Biella. Vittorio's father died when he was young and it was his famous uncle, Quintino, the founder of the Italian Alpine Club, who assumed parental responsibility. Quintino's nephews, Vittorio Sella and Guido Rey, were both fired by his passion for the mountains. "My only merit", Sella was to write to a friend more than half a century later, "is that I have loved the mountains since I climbed them as a boy with my uncle, and that I took photographs of them."

Sella's father, Venanzio, was a pioneer photographer, and had written the first text book on photography to be published in Italy. Vittorio began to experiment with photography and before long was taking his heavy camera with him into the hills. His first success was the panorama from the summit of Mont Mars near Biella. The camera weighed nearly forty pounds, the plates over two pounds each. Every plate had to be sensitized in a flapping tent on a gusty summit before being exposed, and basins, bottles and canvas buckets had to be carried to the summit. His plates measured 30x36 cm. (i. e. about 12x14 inches). Six nights were spent on the summit. The panorama from Mont Blanc to beyond Monte Rosa was an outstanding success.

Sella's only rival as a mountain photographer was William Frederick Donkin who, in the year after Sella photographed the panorama from Mont Mars, exhibited at the Alpine Club a panorama from the Dom.[1]

Towards the end of 1882 Sella decided that even larger plates were needed for alpine photography, and he ordered from Daklmeyers in London a camera to take 30x40 cm. plates (approximately 12x15½ inches). These weighed about two pounds. The total weight of camera, tripod and slides and photographic equipment for a two day journey into the hills was about 70 pounds, and 270 pounds for a three week expedition. It was this camera which Sella used exclusively from 1883 to 1892 in the mountains, not only in the Alps but also in the Caucasus.

Sella made three expeditions to the Caucasus in 1889, 1890 and 1896. He accompanied the Duke of the Abruzzi to Alaska in 1897, and with him made the first ascent of Mount St. Elias. Most of the photographs which he took on this expedition were unfortunately damaged. He was with the Duke on the first ascent of Ruwenzori in 1906, and on the expedition to the Himalaya in 1909. He provided all the illustrations for the books and articles in which these expeditions were described.

The best of many tributes to the excellence of his work came from the pen of a famous American photographer, Ansel Adams, who paid a notable tribute to Sella's work in the *Sierra Club Bulletin*.

"Knowing the physical pressure of time and energy attendant on ambitious mountain expeditions, we are amazed by the mood of calmness and perfection pervading all of Sella's photographs", he wrote. "The exquisitely right moment

[1] Donkin's niece, Miss Hilda Donkin, the daughter of a housemaster at Rugby, gave me when I was a young Harrovian about a thousand Donkin prints which he had rejected as not up to standard. A certain facility for identifying distant mountains I owe in part to the many hours I spent studying Donkin's prints.

of exposure, the awareness of the orientation of the camera and sun, best to reveal the intricacies of the forms of ice and stone, the unmannered viewpoint—these qualities reveal the reverent and intelligent artist. In Sella's photographs there is no faked grandeur: rather is there under-statement, caution, and truthful purpose. Sella has brought to us not only the facts and forms of the far-off splendours of the world, but the essence of experience which finds a spiritual response in the inner recesses of our mind and heart."

Sella's unique photograph library, plates and prints is housed today in the Sella Institute at San Gerolamo, Biella. Mountaineers who are anxious to obtain an enlargement showing the details of a particular ridge will often apply to the Institute for they are sure to obtain an incomparably more satisfactory result from the enlargement of a detail on these big plates than from the films of small cameras carried by modern explorers.

Sella was not only a pioneer of mountain photography but also of winter mountaineering. On March 16th and 17th, 1882, he traversed the Matterhorn from Breuil to Zermatt with Louis, J. A. and Baptiste Carrel, this being the first winter ascent of the great peak. They reached the Great Tower as the dawn broke.

> "The sky was serene", writes Sella, "all the tones were cold, but warm towards the west. A beautiful day was beginning. The prospect of at last conquering this majestic mountain filled me with a sentiment of profound satisfaction and moral energy. I have seldom felt so strong physically or so alert mentally. The comparative absence of snow facilitated the climb up to the Cravate and to the Pic Tyndall. Here we halted for breakfast. . . .
> "At 2 p.m., fifteen hours after leaving Breuil, our party reached the summit of the Matterhorn. The view was magnificent. We revelled in its inconceivable majesty without attempting to analyse each detail. Our emotion, which was almost sacred, cannot be described."

It is said that Quintino Sella when shown his nephew's first mountain narrative warned him to keep his emotions to himself and to confine himself to facts. Strange advice from a great mountaineer who never hesitated to record the profound emotions evoked in him by Alpine majesty. It is all to the good that Vittorio in his narrative of the Matterhorn in winter seems to have ignored his uncle's advice. As for instance in the following passage.

> ". . . When we arrived at the cairn on the Swiss summit, the descent appeared practicable and we immediately started downwards. Soon the sun disappeared from our eyes. The great mass of the Matterhorn projected its shadow on the Gorner Glacier, and lengthened gradually towards the old Weissthor. Very magnificent was this cobalt shadow spread against the background of glacier radiant with light."

On the 26th January, 1884, Sella with the guides J. J. and Daniel Maquignaz made the first winter ascent of Monte Rosa, and on March 22nd, 1885, with his

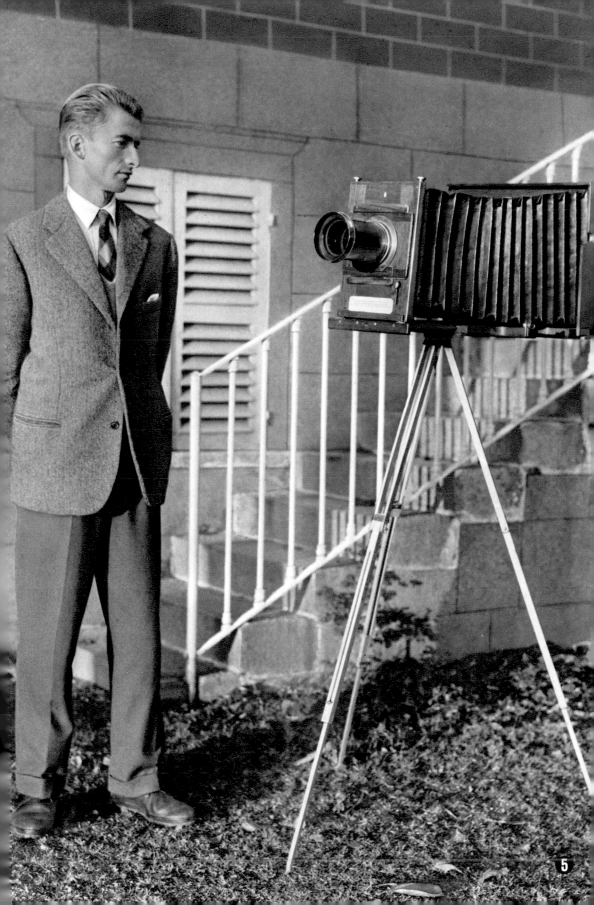

Cousins Corradino and Alfonso and the guides Maquignaz and Guglielmina the first winter ascent of the Lyskamm. On January 4th, 1888, Sella with Corradino and his brothers Gaudenzio and Erminio, and the guides Emile Rey and three Maquignaz brothers made the first winter traverse of Mont Blanc from Courmayeur to Chamonix. His last winter climb was the traverse of Monte Rosa from the Cabane Gnifetti via the Cresta Rey descending by the Monte Rosa Glacier.

Vittorio Sella died in the middle of the Second World War on August 11th, 1943. We had corresponded when I was writing about winter mountaineering, but the first member of the family that I met was his great nephew, Dr. Ludovico Sella, when he was serving as an attaché of the Italian Olympic Committee to the British team at Cortina in 1956. He was a great grandson of Quintino Sella and a great nephew of Vittorio Sella. A few weeks later I spent a delightful ten days at his home and I am indebted to his parents Signor Ernesto and Signora Clotilde Sella for some of the facts in this brief sketch. The facts about the plates which Sella used I found in a very useful and well illustrated book about Vittorio Sella, *The Splendid Hills*, by Ronald Clark.

Many of the British prisoners of war who escaped across the Alps passed near Biella and have every reason to remember with gratitude the Sella clan who live on the hill of San Gerolamo above Biella. These escaping prisoners were fitted out with clothes, boots, etc., by the Sella clan and this at considerable risk, for though the Italian Government was then fighting on the side of the allies, the die-hard fascists were in league with the Germans. An English officer who met my hostess when she was in her holiday home on the Riviera, said to her: "You're from Biella, I believe. Well, I'd like you to know I'm one of many British who owe a great debt to a lady called Mrs. Black of Biella." "Mrs. Black" was a cover name assumed by Mrs. Ghita Halenke, whose mother was a Sella by birth who adopted this name because a copy of the Black Madonna of the famous shrine of Oropa occupied a niche in front of her house.

CHAPTER XII

THE ALPS (1882—1914)

The Sella brothers, as one of them later admitted, had a certain sense of guilt when they decided to countenance the preliminary engineering which rendered possible their ascent of the Dent du Géant. Indeed the classic tradition of free climbing was still dominant during the forty-two years which separated the ending of the Silver Age of mountaineering from the pistol shot of Sarajevo which rang down the curtain on the old Europe. Joseph Knubel told me that in all his long and famous association with G. W. Young only two pitons were used, both, if I remember aright, as belays on the first descent of the east ridge of the Grandes Jorasses to the Col des Hirondelles. Of the forty-two years under review it will only be possible to mention the outstanding climbs and climbers.

The Aiguille Blanche de Peuterey (13,482 ft.) was conquered on July 31st, 1885, by Seymour King with the guides Emile Rey, Ambros Supersaxo and Aloys Anthamatten. Rey, who was born near Courmayeur in 1846, had previously led Lord Wentworth on the first ascent of the Aiguille Noire de Peuterey (12,402 ft.) and was to accompany Paul Güssfeldt on the first ascent of the Peuterey Ridge of Mont Blanc in 1893 (see page 90). In 1895 Rey was killed on reaching easy ground after descending the Dent du Géant.

In 1893 the Dent du Requin was conquered by an all British guideless party (Mummery, Collie, Hastings and Slingsby, see page 95).

I wish that my available space allowed me to do more than make a passing reference to many famous mountaineers of this period. The leading Austrians were the Zsigmondy brothers and Purtscheller whose achievements are referred to in Chapter VIII, Pfannl, Preuss, Lammer, Fiechtle and Karl Blodig.

Heinrich Pfannl (1870–1929) was the first to make a "free" ascent of the Dent du Géant. Disdaining the fixed cables he reached the summit by a new route over the north ridge and north-west face. He took part with Oscar Eckenstein in the 1902 expedition to the Karakorum. He was a pioneer of ski-mountaineering and on this expedition established a ski height record on the Windy Gap (20,450 ft.).

Paul Preuss' most sensational climb was his solitary conquest of the east face of the Guglia di Brenta (Campanile Basso) on July 29th, 1911, a climb which was not repeated for seventeen years. In the Mont Blanc range he made many first ascents, including the south-east ridge of the Aiguille Blanche de Peuterey. He was killed in 1913 in the Dachstein range at the age of twenty-seven.

Guido Lammer (1862–1945) was a prominent exponent of the cult of danger for the sake of danger.

Hans Fiechtl (1883–1925), who gave his name to a piton, was considered by many to be the best rock climbing guide in the Eastern Alps. His many first ascents included the south face of the principal peak of the Vajolet towers.

Karl Blodig (1859–1956), who was elected an honorary member of the Alpine Club at the age of ninety-four, climbed every one of the seventy-nine 4000-metre peaks. Blodig was proudest of his ascent of the Brouillard Ridge of Mont Blanc with Young and Jones, but his most amazing achievements were his solitary ascents of the two remaining 4000-metre peaks which he had not till then climbed, the Grande Rocheuse and the Aiguille du Jardin. As he did not wish to venture alone on the Talèfre Glacier this veteran of seventy-three made a solitary ascent of the very steep snow couloir from the Col Armand Charlet, on the Argentière side, and redescended next day by the same route.

Germany during this same period produced some great climbers. Josef Enzensperger (1873–1903) was a Bavarian who made over thirty first ascents in the limestone ranges of the Eastern Alps, among them the first ascent of the Trettachspitze by the south face. He was one of the founders of the Akademischer Alpen-Club München.

Hans Pfann, who was born in 1873, was described by George Finch as "the best all-round German mountaineer". His greatest achievement was the complete traverse of the two peaks of Ushba on August 12–14th, 1903.

Hans Dülfer (1893–1915) was born in the Rhineland, but studied at Munich University in order to be nearer the mountains. He was killed in an artillery duel, and is buried at Bailleul. Dülfer was an artist. Like Comici he was a superb pianist and for him rock climbing was an aspect of aesthetics. A rock face was the raw material of his art, and just as Michelangelo evoked his masterpieces from marble, so Dülfer conjured out of the great limestone cliffs of the Eastern Alps the perfect line of ascent, exacting in his insistence on style for its accomplishment. "Son but suprême", write his biographers Wast Mariner and Heinrich Klier, "a toujours été l'ascension de grand style, directement vers le sommet." So far from disdaining artificial aids he welcomed them, but, like most great masters of the piton, he was also a superb free climber. Like so many German and Austrian climbers he had a great love for solitary ascents, and he was alone in 1913 when he conquered the terrible south-east face of the Fleischbank by what is now known as the Dülferriss. His father who was his companion on his early climbs did not long survive him. He vanished shortly after his son was killed, and it is believed that he sought death in some remote and unvisited recess in the Lattengebirge.

Angelo Dibona of Cortina d'Ampezzo was born an Austrian in 1879 but became Italian after the First World War. With the brothers Guido and Max Mayer of Vienna he made a series of notable first ascents in the Dolomites. Perhaps his greatest triumph was the grim 700-metre north wall of the Laliderwand in the Karwendel which he climbed with the brothers Mayer and the guide Luigi Rizzi. The same party made in 1912 the first ascent of the south face of the Meije on which Emil Zsigmondy had been killed.

Tita Piaz (1879–1948) was yet another born Austrian who became Italian after the First World War, but in his case gladly, for Piaz had always been an irredentist. His long list of first ascents includes the Guglia De Amicis, the summit of which he lassoed with a rope, the north face of the Winkler Turm, Cima Tosa, etc. Piaz was a legendary figure in the Dolomites. He was from the first an irredentist and he remained a socialist under Mussolini. He was thrown into a concentration camp by the Austrians in the First World War, escaped, crossed the Adriatic in a boat, and expected to be received by the Italians with music and applause. Instead he was thrown into another concentration camp as he was still technically an Austrian. He was later imprisoned by the Fascists and finally under Hitler. In 1932 he climbed with King Albert of the Belgians. "Don't you realise", he asked, "that you are compromising the monarchy by climbing with me?" "Why?" asked the King. "Well, when your daughter, Princess Marie-José, married the Crown Prince of Italy they put me in prison as a precautionary measure."

Piaz was an opponent of artificial climbing, and it was only on the rarest of occasions that he used pitons. To quote his biographer Giuseppe Mazzotti, he even regretted towards the end of his life having climbed the Guglia De Amicis by the famous rope lassoing. "My experience", he said, "is similiar to that of the majority of mountaineers. They begin by yielding to the magic of the mountains in its noblest form. Then they are intoxicated by the enticement of blue sky, by heights and space and then after surviving perilous conquests they end as gymnasts and climbing becomes a matter of piton and mousqueton. Without wishing to denigrate what is called acrobatic mountaineering I must admit that my long experience leads me to this melancholy conclusion." Piaz was killed riding a bicycle without brakes.

The achievements of the Duke of the Abruzzi, Vittorio Sella and Emile Rey, three great Italians who were active during this period (1882–1914) have been described in previous chapters.

The brothers Giuseppe and Giovan Battista Gugliermina, of whom the former was born in 1872 and the latter in 1874, are associated with some great climbs in the Mont Blanc range, the first traverse in August 1899 of the Col Emile Rey (13,146 ft.) and the first ascent of the Pic Luigi Amedeo (14,672 ft.). In July 1901 they made the first ascent of Mont Blanc by the Brouillard Ridge. They were elected honorary members of the Alpine Club in 1955.

Guido Rey (1861–1935) was a Sella on his mother's side, and a nephew of Quintino Sella. He began as a guideless climber but after his younger brother had been killed on the Col du Géant he never again dispensed with a guide. When Italy declared war in 1915 he volunteered for active service and a severe motoring accident near the front put an end to his mountaineering career, in the course of which he made a number of first ascents such as the Pointe Blanche on the east ridge of the Dent d'Hérens. He is mainly remembered in connection with his exploration of the Furggen Ridge of the Matterhorn. On August 24th, 1899, Rey with his guides Aimé and Ange Maquignaz was stopped by an overhang not far from the summit. He redescended, climbed the Matterhorn by the normal route, and was lowered by a rope ladder to the point at which he had been checked. He thus completed the exploration of the entire ridge. The subsequent history of this ridge is of interest. On September 9th, 1911, Mario Piacenza[1], an Italian, with Joseph Carrel and Joseph Gaspard climbed the ridge but made a big détour on to the Italian face. Finally on September 23rd, 1941, a direct ascent of the ridge, a climb of extreme exposure, was effected by an Italian party, Alfredo Perino, Louis Carrel and Giacomo Chiara.

Guido Rey described his Furggen climb in his famous book *Il Cervino*, from the admirable English translation of which by J.E.C.Eaton I have already quoted. This was the first Alpine classic by a continental mountaineer which rivalled in my affections the great English classics of Alpine literature. In his forties he made a series of difficult ascents such as the south face of the Marmolata with Tita Piaz which he described in his book *Alpinismo acrobatico*. He was elected an honorary member of the Alpine Club.

During this period (1882–1914) one of the outstanding Swiss amateurs was undoubtedly Gustav Hasler, a member of that famous club, the Akademischer Alpen Club, Berne. Many north walls and ridges had been climbed before Hasler and his guide Fritz Amatter attacked the great north-east wall of the Finsteraarhorn, but this was the first of the classic north walls and is described by a modern climber, who compiled the list of notable first ascents for that modern and admirable book *Les Alpinistes Célèbres*, as "encore une des plus belles et grandes courses des Alpes, très difficile sur 1000 m. avec deux passages de 100 à 150 m. particulièrement durs" ("Still one of the most beautiful and one of the greatest expeditions in the Alps, very difficult for 1000 m. and with exceptionally severe passages of 100 to 150 m.").

Mario Piacenza was a cousin of the Sellas. His son was killed fighting with the Partisans.

On July 8th, 1904, Hasler and Fritz Amatter[1] climbed the north-east spur leading to the Hugisattel, and on July 15th and 16th the north-east spur which leads direct to the summit. The second ascent and the first guideless ascent was made in August, 1906, by that superb climber V. A. Fynn of America with A. Brüderlin, a Swiss. A quarter of a century passed before this formidable face was again climbed, this time by the most famous of American lady climbers, Miss Miriam O'Brien (now Mrs. Underhill) with Adolf and Fritz Rubi of Grindelwald.

I remember meeting at Grindelwald Gertrude Bell who had attempted this face twelve years before Hasler and attained a point 250 m. below the summit. Miss Bell, who was famous for her Eastern journeys, spent two nights on the face of the Finsteraarhorn. During the thirty-two years under review Hasler was perhaps the only Swiss amateur who ranked as a pioneer of new routes with the best Austrians. On the other hand no country produced greater guides in the last decades before the First World War than Switzerland. Of Franz Lochmatter and Joseph Knubel I shall write in due course.

Christian Klucker of the Fextal in the Engadine was not only a great guide but a great personality. He was well educated and wrote his own excellent memoirs without employing a ghost writer. From 1889 to 1891 he made a series of brilliant first ascents with Norman Neruda, the north faces of the Piz Roseg, Scerscen, Lyskamm, and from 1891 to 1900 he explored the Bergel with A. von Rydzewski. His greatest climb was the first ascent of the Peuterey Ridge of Mont Blanc in 1893 with Paul Güssfeldt, Emile Rey and the porter, C. Ollier.

The French during this period produced no outstanding amateurs, but at least one outstanding guide, Joseph Ravanel (1869–1933) better known under his nick name "Le Rouge". His first ascents included with Emile Fontaine the Aiguilles du Fou, des Pèlerins, du Peigne, and the peaks now known as the Aiguilles Mummery and Ravanel, the Dent du Caïman, Dent du Crocodile and Les Ciseaux. He was also a pioneer of ski mountaineering. In January 1903 he was the first to open on ski the high-level route from Chamonix to Zermatt.

Conway and Slingsby (in Norway) achieved fame during this period (1882–1914) as explorers of distant ranges rather than as pioneers of new routes in the Alps. Mummery's reputation was made before the Silver Age ended and the only British climbers who made an *international* reputation in the Alps in these three decades were V. J. E. Ryan and G. W. Young. There were, of course, many first class British mountaineers who were active in this period, but their names mean little to the continental rock acrobats, whereas Young, and to a lesser degree Ryan, still command great respect.

---

[1] It was Fritz Amatter who in 1921 led the Japanese Yuko Maki on the first ascent of the Mittellegi Ridge of the Eiger, the other guides being Samuel Brawand and Fritz Steuri.

V. J. E. Ryan

V. J. E. Ryan (1883–1947) was an Irish landowner who had fought and been wounded in the First World War and who left Ireland after the Nationalist upheavals and settled in Jersey. He began to climb in 1898: 1903 was his first great season. His constant climbing companions were Franz and Joseph Lochmatter, excepting when Franz was replaced by his brother Gabriel. In 1905 this team made the first ascent of the Grépon from the Mer de Glace, but they failed to find a direct route, and struck the final ridge some distance from the summit. Ryan and the Lochmatters made various new routes of which by far the most famous are the Ryan-Lochmatter Ridge of the Plan and the south face of the Täschhorn, on which he was joined by Young and Knubel. The immense difficulties of the climb, which even by modern standards is considered, to quote a modern climber, Pierre Henry, as a "course longue, difficile et très dangereuse sur une des plus formidables parois des Alpes", were aggravated by storm and driving snow. Lochmatter's lead up the overhang—in nailed boots, without a piton and in bad weather—was an achievement which no modern rock acrobat has excelled. Georges de Rham, one of the finest of modern Swiss climbers, who made the third ascent says: "Even with all the recourses of modern technique, pitons, clasp-rings and rubber shoes, I thought the place which was so brilliantly climbed by Franz Lochmatter, in nailed boots, without pitons, exceptionally severe" (*Alpine Journal*, 1944, p. 397).

Ryan had married early in 1906 and thereafter he had two good climbing seasons, 1906 and 1914, and a very short season in 1909. From a hint which he once dropped in the course of a conversation I gathered that he gave up climbing to please his wife.

Ryan was a superb climber but nobody could possibly describe him as a great mountaineer. He seldom carried rucksack or ice-axe, and he never cut a step. He had no interest in route finding. The effective leadership he left to his guides. He never published an article on any climb, and all that we know about his routes is from information extracted verbally from Ryan, or more often from his guides. Ryan himself was often very vague about where he had been.

Franz Lochmatter was the greatest mountaineer of his time and Ryan one of the finest amateur rock climbers. Ryan's deficiencies as a mountaineer therefore in no way weakened what was perhaps the strongest mountain team climbing in the last decade before the First World War.

Ryan was defective in the technique of human relations. Any unforeseen delay or set back on a climb provoked his impatience, with the result, writes Roger Chorley, that he became incapable of treating his guides correctly and sharing in the tactics of the climb.

Guido Rey was resting on the summit of the Aiguille Verte, which he had climbed by one of the easier routes, when Ryan who had climbed the peak from the "Gouffre de la Charpoua", a difficult route, suddenly appeared. "Un froid et sûr vainqueur" was how Rey described him. Chorley, in the interesting essay on Ryan which he contributed to *Les Alpinistes Célèbres*, explains his manner "abrupt et hautain qui repoussait l'amitié" by timidity. It may be so, but I who knew him fairly well could never detect the slightest hint of timidity in his manner, or in his conversation. On the contrary, he never hesitated to express himsel, freely about the shortcomings of other mountaineers, and there were few of themf other than the Lochmatters, of whom he spoke with real respect. According to Chorley his aloofness from the mountain brotherhood was due to certain imaginary humiliations. The humiliations were not imaginary, for it is hardly a compliment to be blackballed by the Alpine Club, even if blackballed by the same type that blackballed Mummery. He never referred to this incident and I do not know whether it rankled, but his somewhat inhuman detachment from the friendly amenities of human intercourse seemed to me innate rather than induced by rebuffs real or imaginary.

I leave it to psychiatrists to explain, or rather attempt to explain his frosty detachment from his fellow men. That some people are generously endowed with that mysterious attribute charm is a fact, and that others like Ryan are wholly lacking in charm is also a fact and, not being a psychiatrist, I am content to record such facts without trying to account for them.

I saw a great deal of Ryan when I had a chalet in Grindelwald, and I ran into him more than once in later years when he was on his way to or back from the City of London Chess Club, for he lived in a hotel near my flat. He was an accomplished tournament chess player, and as I was often the only player in Grindelwald who could extend, and occasionally beat him, I was much in request during his prolonged summer visits to Grindelwald. The ritual of our chess evenings was unchanging. Somewhere about ten p.m. he would turn to me, when we played at his hotel, and ask me if I would like a drink. I would reply in the affirmative, whereupon he would order two glasses of water. In my chalet the ritual would be slightly different. I would ask him whether he would like a glass of beer, and he would reply sternly that he would prefer a glass of water. I suspect that he regarded the association of alcohol and chess as derogatory to the austere dignity of the game.

On the rare occasions when I could tempt him to talk about mountaineers and mountaineering he never failed to be interesting, and I was always glad when I ran across him in London. He was a man whom I found it equally impossible to like or to dislike.

Geoffrey Young, like Whymper and Mummery, is the symbol of a particular age of mountaineering, for he stands in much the same relationship to the last decade before the First World War as Whymper to the Golden Age and Mummery to the Silver Age of mountaineering. No mountaineer of that period, not even Ryan, had a record of new ascents comparable with Young's. These included a route up the Weisshorn from Zinal which bears his name, the first direct ascent of the east face of the Weisshorn, the first ascents of the east face of the Zinal Rothorn, the Younggrat on the Zermatt Breithorn, the south face of the Täschhorn with Ryan, and the following climbs in the great year of 1911 with H. O. Jones; the Jorasses from the Col des Grandes Jorasses and the first descent to the Col des Hirondelles, the first complete ascent of the Brouillard Ridge of Mont Blanc from the Col Emile Rey, the ridge itself having been climbed by the Gugliermina brothers, and the first direct ascent of the Mer de Glace face to the actual summit of the Grépon in which Todhunter joined the party. Ryan had made the first ascent of the Grépon from the Mer de Glace but he had struck the Grépon-Charmoz Ridge some distance below the summit.

Finally Young and Siegfried Herford made the first ascent by the grim Red Teeth Ridge of the Gspaltenhorn in 1914.

Young had often climbed without guides in his early years and made with Mallory and Donald Robertson one of the very few all British guideless first ascents, the first ascent of the south-east ridge of the Nesthorn, but once he had met the incomparable Joseph Knubel the partnership between the greatest amateur and the greatest professional of that particular decade was never again broken.

In an entertaining paper read to the Alpine Club, *Two Days With a Guide* (*Alpine Journal* 1909, page 472), Young writes:

> "I admit that I climb with a guide. The confession is painful but necessary, and I must hope that the weakness will be attributed not so much to a want of originality as to a preference for a sense of security. I find that, take him all round, the guide meets me in better training, lasts rather longer, and occasionally climbs even better than the majority of amateurs with a month's holiday. . .
>
> Yet the gentle art of managing a guide, digging him out of the depressing public opinion of the hut, humouring his local climbing superstitions, pressing him when he is only pouting, knowing where to yield when his real instinct is speaking, cheering him along when he's off under full sail, has its own fascination for the pseudo-psychologist, apart from the pleasing sensation of his stability at the further end of the rope."

The guided climber hardly exists for the modernists of the French school, but they make an exception for Young. Alain de Chatellus in *Les Alpinistes*

Célèbres remarks that he possessed that power which Talleyrand regarded as the hallmark of personalities who were superior, the power to use other people to ensure one's own success. "Thus Young, who was one of the best amateurs of the period, having found in the person of Joseph Knubel the ideal companion inspired him with that self-confidence without which so many of the professionals of the period refused to branch out from traditional climbs. For our hero is anything but a mere tourist. His association with Knubel has far more in common with that which unites members of a guideless party ...

"Young loved to conquer, even to conquer easily. Bivouacs appeared to him incompatible with self-respect. The excessive difficulty of the slab on the east face of the Grépon irritated him probably because he was conscious of a feeling, in itself very honourable, that it was not 'fair play' to conquer thanks to the exceptional courage of his guide."

During the First World War Young was in command of an ambulance unit, and severely wounded on the Italian front. His right leg had to be amputated, but he returned to the mountains after the war and climbed the Matterhorn, Grépon, Weisshorn, Monte Rosa and Zinal Rothorn. "Misfortunes only break mediocrities", writes Alain de Chatellus, "but reveal their powers to men who are worthy of this name. His victory on the south face of the Täschhorn would have evoked from the generations that follow no more than their admiration mingled with some envy, but his courage in adversity entitles him to their respect."

My friendship with Geoffrey Young began when I was an undergraduate at Oxford. His first book of poems, *Wind and Hill*, was sent for review to *The Isis*, the undergraduates' weekly of which I was then the editor, and I never open that slim grey covered book without a wave of nostalgic memories. Many poets had sung of mountains without climbing them but here for the first time a member of our own brotherhood had translated into noble poetry the aspirations and the ardours of mountaineering.

I was bed-ridden when I first opened *Wind and Hill*, recovering from a severe mountain accident, and doubtful whether I would ever climb again, and few indeed were Young's readers to whom the lines

> If but the kindly years may grant us still
>   To track the lonely valley to its end,
> And view, though from afar, the crag-bound hill
>   Lift its long greeting.

could have meant more than they meant to me.

Many poets have worshipped mountain beauty from below, but Young was the first poet to interpret the ardours and ordeals of serious mountaineering.

138

Young's influence on young mountaineers at the universities was marked. As an undergraduate he had invented the sport of roof climbing, and had written a climber's guide to the roofs of Cambridge, and but for his encouragement I doubt if I would have ever produced *Oxford Mountaineering Essays*. His role is mentioned in the preface to this little book which also records the foundation of the Oxford University Mountaineering Club in 1909. H. E. G. Tyndale accepted the presidency.

Members of the Oxford Mountaineering Club have played such an important role in the more recent story of mountaineering that I hope I may be forgiven for quoting the light-hearted story of its foundation.

"Oxford, they tell us, is the home of movements; Cambridge the home of men. Certainly the miniature movement that took shape in this little book was inspired by a Cambridge man. It was at an Oxford tea-party, where the talk had been unashamedly of mountains and their metaphysics, that Mr. G. Winthrop Young gave the first impulse to the scheme that ultimately produced this collection of essays. To Mr. Young the editor and contributors have been indebted for constant help and advice. He has heartened the despondent and has inked cold daylight into more than one 'sunset' passage.

"At Oxford there are a number of Alpine clubs. The oldest and most sedate meets once a year in New College Hall. A less dignified association meets at irregular intervals on New College Hall and other hospitable roofs. Lastly, there is a genial little society which owed its beginnings to some twenty undergraduates who agreed they could spare an occasional arduous evening to the revival of their Alpine memories. One confiding member brought a lantern, and has since endeavoured—with indifferent success—to recoup himself out of spasmodic subscriptions. We shall none of us forget the first meeting. In our innocence we had hoped that a scientist might know something of electricity, and Mr. Bourdillon[1] was in consequence entrusted with the lantern. After much hissing on the part of the machine, and of the audience, a faint glow appeared on the sheet, and enveloped in a halo of restless hues we dimly discerned the dome of Mont Blanc. A pathetic voice from behind the lantern sadly inquired whether we would 'prefer Mont Blanc green and spluttering or yellow and steady'. The chairman then proceeded to read a paper illustrated or rather misrepresented by lantern slides, and at the conclusion proposed a very hearty vote of thanks to himself for his interesting and entertaining lecture. The House then divided, and the motion was lost by an overwhelming majority. The minutes also record that a member moved to inhibit the secretary of the Church Union from issuing a printed prayer for 'faith to remove mountains'. This motion was lost, as Mr. Tyndale ably pointed out the value of a publication that might facilitate the transfer of some superfluous mountains from the Alps to the monotonous surroundings of Oxford."

None of those who were present at an informal dinner in 1912, at which we sat down thirteen, were likely to forget the support which that dinner party might give to one of the silliest of superstitions. Of those present, three were to die in

---

[1] Father of Tom Bourdillon, of Everest. When he joined the Club he was appointed lanternist to maintain the tradition.

the mountains Mallory on Everest a few years later, H. O. Jones and Hugh Pope within a few weeks of the dinner. Young Claude Elliott, now Provost of Eton, and two members of the Oxford Mountaineering Club, both of whom were killed in the war, Nigel Marden and Finlay and I went out to the Pyrenees to look for Pope who was killed on the Pic du Midi d'Ossau and the others present at the dinner were involved in the search party for H. O. Jones.

Geoffrey Young's father, Sir George, was my first landlord after my marriage, and the few months which I spent at Cookham before the outbreak of the First World War were idyllically happy. None of the many homes which we occupied in later years, not even the Chalet Berna at Grindelwald, meant more to us than Suttoncroft, Cookham. It was a great privilege for a young man to meet Sunday after Sunday at Sir George's home, Formosa, that group of gifted men and women who came down from London. Elsewhere[1] I have tried to recapture the climate of opinion which I associate with the Formosa Salon, the Indian summer of Liberal Humanism.

In his book of war memoirs, *The Grace of Forgetting*, Geoffrey Young recalls the high hopes which he himself entertained and the disillusion of the post-war years.

The pen is mightier than the ice-axe. We should have heard a great deal more of Slingsby and Collie, had their books been as effective as Mummery's in catching the imagination of the mountaineering world, and Geoffrey Young's place in Alpine history would have been less secure against the erosion of time but for his books.

Shortly before the First World War I persuaded Methuen's that the Badminton volume on mountaineering was out of date, and that Geoffrey Young should be approached to edit an up-to-date study of mountaineering technique. *Mountain Craft* was the result. To the first edition various experts on other ranges than the Alps contributed chapters, and I wrote a chapter on ski-mountaineering.

In later editions these outcrops were dropped. My own chapter became a book, *Alpine Ski-ing*, and *Mountain Craft* in its modern form is Young's unaided work. It must be one of the few text books on a sport which will continue to be read as literature, even when some of its technical chapters are out of date.

On High Hills was published in 1927, and in 1951 *Mountains with a Difference*, which describes his one-legged climbs, appeared in *The New Alpine Library*, a series which I persuaded Eyre and Spottiswoode to launch. In the literature of adventure there can be few more thrilling narratives than Young's account of the first ascent of the south face of the Täschhorn in the first of his books, and of his remarkable escape from death on his one-legged descent from the Zinal Rothorn, his last climb.

To describe scenery is even more difficult than to record adventure. The

[1] In my book *Memory to Memory*.

140

secret of the successful word painting of scenery is, as I have elsewhere suggested, the power to differentiate similar scenes – a mountain sunrise as seen, for instance, from the plains on distant snows, the theme of Tennyson's perfect quatrain describing the dawn on Monte Rosa as seen from Milan, or the nuances which distinguish different mountain sunsets seen from on high, a differentiation which is the motif of one of the subtlest passages of mountain description that I know, a passage to be found on page 186 of *On High Hills*:

"There are evenings in the Alps", writes Young, "when the sunset pours out its whole colour-box on to the sky above us, but when the snow peaks, the glaciers, and the rock walls about us will have none of it. They remain colourless, ghostly, and unreceptive; as we may see the forms and faces of sleepers in a dark room startled only into outline and a resentful pallor by the passage of a candle. And there are evenings when every corner of rock, every snow prism, and every ripple of falling glacier, catches fire and colour, and contributes its own varied light to the illumination.

"Our few moments of triumph on the summit were transfigured by this blaze of sympathetic celebration. The nearer rock spires reached up towards us their late glowing torches. The recession of snow peaks along the Oberland bore each its dying beacon, ash-red at the heart and hurrying gold at the edges. The uneven snow on the northern slopes descending from our feet caught the shallow waves of retreating colour, and threw them back lower and fainter at each instant as the sun sank. Until the interrupting rock crests of the north ridge hemmed the rays finally beyond our sight; and the snows about us took shelter from the cold inrush of darkness under a uniform monotony of steely disregard."

CHAPTER XIII

SKI AND WINTER MOUNTAINEERING

I devoted a long chapter in my book *A History of Ski-ing* (1927) to winter mountaineering on foot. An appendix of twenty-three pages records every first winter ascent and first ski-ascent known to me. In my book *The Story of Ski-ing* (1953) I brought the history of ski mountaineering up to date. I refer the reader who wants a fuller treatment of the subject than he will find in this chapter to the above mentioned books.

Winter Mountaineering on Foot

Many people, as I have already remarked, crossed passes because they had to, but nobody climbs a peak unless he enjoys getting to the top. Winter mountaineering may therefore be said to date from the ascent of Prato al Saglio (4921 ft.), by Dante, in the winter of 1311. Four centuries pass before another great poet writes the second page in the history of winter mountaineering. Towards the end of November, 1779, Goethe visited Switzerland, climbed the Dôle near Geneva, visited Chamonix, walked up to the Montenvers, crossed the Col de Balme and tramped over the Furka in deep snow.

Professor Franz Joseph Hugi, a Swiss teacher of science by profession and one of the pioneers of summer mountaineering, was the father of winter mountaineering. On January 14th, 1832, Hugi reached the summit of the Strahlegg Pass (10,994 ft.). On January 16th he reached a point on the way to the Mönchjoch just below the Bergli rocks. The Hugihorn, a fine peak in the Schreckhorn Group, perpetuates his name.

On January 6th, 1862, T. S. Kennedy, the first to climb the Dent Blanche, reached a height of about 11,000 ft. on the Matterhorn. On December 23rd, 1866, A. W. Moore and Horace Walker left Grindelwald at 3 p.m., walked through the night, crossed the Finsteraarjoch (11,024 ft.) and returned by the Strahlegg (10,994 ft.) to Grindelwald which they reached at 1 p.m. after twenty-two hours of continuous walking, in the course of which they climbed and descended an aggregate of 10,000 vertical feet. Their guides were Christian Almer, Melchior Anderegg and Peter Bohren.

Coolidge with Miss Brevoort made the first winter ascent of the Wetterhorn and Jungfrau in 1874 and of the Schreckhorn without Miss Brevoort in 1879, the leading guide in every case being Christian Almer.

Lady mountaineers were very prominent in this new development of mountaineering. Miss Brevoort, as we have seen, took part in the first winter ascent of the Wetterhorn and Jungfrau. Miss Straton, with the guides Jean Charlet, Sylvain Couttet and Michel Balmat, climbed Mont Blanc on January 31st, 1876. In the winter of 1887–88 Mrs. Jackson, accompanied by Emil Boss, with Ulrich Almer as the leading guide, made the first winter ascent of the Lauteraarhorn on January 5th, of the Klein Fiescherhorn on January 6th, of the Gross Fiescherhorn on January 11th, and on January 16th traversed the Jungfrau from the Bergli to Guggi; a desperate venture, for the traverse of the Jungfrau even in summer is an ice climb of some difficulty. The party was forced to bivouac on the Guggi Glacier, and both Mrs. Jackson and Almer lost several toes through frostbite.

Mrs. Jackson describes her adventures in a lively article, "A Winter Quartette", which appeared in *The Alpine Journal* (A. J. xiv, p. 200).

By far the most remarkable of the winter mountaineers was Mrs. Aubrey Le Blond (formerly Mrs. Main and Mrs. Burnaby, her two previous husbands having died). She was the author of the first book devoted entirely to winter mountaineering, *The High Alps in Winter; or, Mountaineering in Search of Health*.

Mrs. Le Blond was a consumptive who was sent to the Alps by her doctors. She arrived in Chamonix in the summer of 1881 in bad health. "As for mountaineering, I knew nothing of it and cared less." A few weeks later she attempted Mont Blanc, but was beaten by bad weather. Next summer she returned again to Chamonix, climbed Mont Blanc and the Grandes Jorasses—on which she was benighted—and "enjoyed herself immensely". The winter of 1882–83 found her in Chamonix again, with an insatiable appetite for new experiences. The Col du Tacul had never been crossed, not even in summer. Mrs. Le Blond decided to inaugurate her career as a winter mountaineer by traversing a virgin col. She succeeded. A few weeks later she tried Mont Blanc, but was defeated by bad weather. On this, as on all the climbs described in her book, she was guided by Edouard Cupelin. On January 15th, 1883, she crossed the Col des Grands Montets, and on the 19th walked up to the Montenvers, intending to climb the Aiguille du Midi (12,600 ft.) next day. Even in summer the ascent of the Midi from the Montenvers direct would be a stiff day's work, but this gallant lady, who had been packed off to the Alps by her doctors, was far from exhausted by her twelve hours' climb to the summit. The good folk of Chamonix witnessed her arrival and fired off a canon in her honour. They spent a night at the Montenvers. "While descending to Chamonix next morning we considered what more we could do to make the good people below open their eyes."

"What should I do next?" asked Mrs. Le Blond. "Cupelin, what do you advise?"

Cupelin suggested crossing the Col du Chardonnet and returning by the Col du Tour. Actually they crossed the Col du Chardonnet and later the Col d'Argentière.

The insatiable Mrs. Le Blond then turned her attention to Monte Rosa, and met Vittorio Sella who had previously made the first winter ascent of the Matterhorn[1], and who had just returned from an unsuccessful attempt on Monte Rosa.

The two parties joined forces and on March 3rd they succeeded in reaching a height of 4200 m. on Monte Rosa, before they were forced to retreat by violent storms. Mrs. Le Blond parted from Signor Sella on the Gorner Glacier, as he was returning to Breuil, whereas she was returning to Zermatt.

"I do not know", writes Signor Sella, "if the cold and my large woollen gloves prevented me giving due significance to the cordial handshake with which I took my leave of Mrs. Burnaby, but, in any case, I will make amends by giving expression here to my great admiration for her courage."

For Mrs. Le Blond's winter climbing did not cease with climbs recorded in her book. In the Engadine she made a whole series of first-class winter ascents, of which the most remarkable were the first winter ascents of the Piz Palü, Piz Sella and Piz Zupô in January 1898, and the first winter ascent of the Disgrazia with Martin Schocher on February 16th, 1896. This last-named climb is probably one of the longest, if not the longest, expedition ever attempted in mid-winter, involving as it did some 8000 ft. of climbing, some of it very difficult, under winter conditions. Mrs. Le Blond left the Forno Hut at 3.15 a.m. and reached the summit of Sissone at 5.40. "After a wearisome descent of 2000 ft. on the Italian side, during which much step-cutting was necessary", the party skirted the long ridge between Sissone and Disgrazia, eventually reaching the summit in the teeth of a gale and driving snow at 10.35 a.m. The Forno Hut was regained that same evening at 6.30 p.m.

Mrs. Le Blond also enjoys the distinction of being the only lady who has led a guideless party in winter and in spring.

Among the most enterprising of winter mountaineers may be mentioned the great Swiss climber Gustave Hasler who with Christian Jossi made the first winter ascent of the Aletschhorn, Gspaltenhorn and Aiguille Verte, and Lt. Colonel E. L. Strutt, later president of the Alpine Club. With that great Engadine guide, Martin Schocher, he made more than thirty winter ascents of over 12,000 ft., among others the first winter ascents of the Bella Vista and Piz Argient, the second winter ascents of the Zupô, Piz Palü and Piz Roseg, and the third, seventh and tenth winter ascents of the Bernina.

[1] For Sella's winter climbs and summer ascents see pp. 128—129.

PIZ LUNGHIN
Giovanni Giacometti (1933)
(By Courtesy Zurich Municipal Authorities)

Modern Developments of Winter Mountaineering

Winter mountaineering has followed the same evolution as summer mountaineering. The first winter ascents were made by the easiest routes but when every great peak had been climbed by the normal routes, their more difficult faces and ridges were attacked in winter.

Among many such notable winter ascents may be mentioned the Peuterey Ridge of Mont Blanc by the Swiss O. Gerecht, H. Huss and E. Meier (1948); the south ridge of the Aiguille Noire de Peuterey by the Italian guides Toni Gobbi and Henry Rey (1949); the Route Major on Mont Blanc by the guides Toni Gobbi and Arturo Ottoz (1953), and the north face of the Grosse Zinne by the Italians W. Bonatti and C. Mauri.

Many of the six-degree climbs in the Eastern Alps have been climbed in winter by Germans (Adolf Goettner and Rudolf Peters) and Austrians (Fritz Kasparek, Josef Brunhuber, Hermann Buhl, K. Rainer among others).

Ski Mountaineering

Winter mountaineering is only a minor variation of mountaineering. There is often less snow on a rock peak in January than in July, and even normal winter conditions merely aggravate the difficulties of an ascent without creating any radically new problems of mountain craft or mountain technique.

Ski mountaineering, on the other hand, is no mere variation of mountaineering. It is the result of the marriage of two great sports, mountaineering and ski-ing. Whereas the winter mountaineer has the same objectives as the summer mountaineer, the ascent and descent of his peak on foot, the ski mountaineer is concerned not merely with the ascent of a peak or crossing of a pass, but also with the ski-ing possibilities of the descent.

To the skier the mountains offer a new and enchanting way of mountain love. The problems of planning are therefore very different. The mountaineer, whether he climbs on foot or on ski, is of course confronted with the problem of security, and security in the case of ski mountaineering, mainly means the avoidance of avalanches, but planning for the skier also means picking the ideal ski-ing line for the descent, and timing the descent to secure the best snow conditions.

Timing is never more important than in the late spring when a particular slope may yield ski-ing which is both perfect and safe at one moment of the day, and ski-ing which is not only unenjoyable but dangerous an hour later. The hard frozen crust which is normal in the early hours of the day is a less attractive running surface than crust which is superficially softened. The skier will therefore normally time his descent to the moment when the crust is beginning to soften.

If the skier is returning from some lofty peak to a club hut high above the valley it is usually easy to time his descent so as to ski down slopes which have been softened by the sun but which still retain their firm under-surface of crust, but if he is ski-ing down to the valley he may have to choose between good snow on the lower slopes and an icy crust above, or good snow on the summit slopes and snow rotted by and rendered dangerous by the sun lower down.

On the other hand if the hard crust be covered by a thin soft layer of brittle ice, which I have called film crust, he may be able to enjoy ideal ski-ing at dawn on the glacier slopes and perfect spring snow lower down. In this case the skier will be well advised to overcome the reluctance of his guides, a conservative race, and insist on leaving the hut, as I have often done, before midnight. Film crust yields ideal ski-ing even before it is softened by the sun. As the ski cut round on a turn the film of soft ice falls away and splashes down the slope with a sound like the soft ripple of a mountain stream. Film crust provides an ideal surface. "Will there be film crust on the summit slopes, and if so should we leave the hut before midnight?" This is one of the innumerable problems of snowcraft which the skier has to solve.

All that the summer mountaineer need know is whether snow is likely to be hard enough to bear his weight, and whether, if soft, it is likely to avalanche. The simple categories into which he divides the snow are complicated in a thousand ways for the ski-runner, who must learn not only to recognise, and often to recognise while travelling at a high speed, but also to foretell a whole gamut of snow values each with its significance and its own particular demands on the technique of ski-ing.

It is not surprising that the snowcraft of the old pioneers seems rudimentary to the modern skier. Even the greatest guides in the past made the kind of mistake which none but the most inexperienced of ski-tourers could possibly make. Christian Almer, for instance, on a January ascent of the Jungfrau gaily led his party up the path to the Bäregg in spite of the fact that the previous day's rain had rendered the snow extremely dangerous. The whole party narrowly escaped death from a tremendous avalanche which swept down the cliffs of the Mettenberg and crossed the path just ahead of them. A skier would instinctively choose the safe route on the opposite side of the glacier under the Eiger cliffs, which is the end of the Eismeer run.

This above statement when published in my *History of Ski-ing* provoked indignant protests from Colonel Strutt and the late P.J.H. Unna, both of whom resented the suggestion that Almer could possibly have made a mistake which mere skiers, then regarded in Alpine Club circles as gate-crashing arrivistes, would have avoided; but the only attempt at an argument was Unna's suggestion that conditions then may have been very different to those today. On the contrary then as now, the Bäregg Route is often a death trap, and now as then the route which all skiers follow on the Eismeer run is normally safe.

The First Decade

The first great ski mountaineering expedition was the incomplete traverse on ski of the main massif of the Bernese Oberland (Meiringen–Oberaarjoch–Grünhornlücke–Belalp–Brig) by a German party, W. Paulcke, de Beauclair, W. Lohmüller, Ehlert, and Mönnichs on 18th–22nd January, 1897. Ehlert and Mönnichs were subsequently killed in an avalanche on the Susten Pass on 2nd January, 1899, the first fatal accident on ski.

In the following year Paulcke made an almost successful attempt to climb Monte Rosa on ski with the well-known Swiss pioneer, Robert Helbling, who in February, 1903, was the first to complete on ski an important section of the high-level route from Chamonix to Zermatt.

Dr. Henry Hoek whose father was Dutch, and whose mother was English, a descendant of one of Nelsons's captains, traversed the Oberland on ski in November, 1901, climbed the Finsteraarhorn and Mönch, and in 1903 made the first ski ascent of the Wetterhorn.

On February 25th, 1904, Hugo Mylius, a German, with the Meiringen guides A. Tännler, Kaspar Maurer and H. Zurflüh made the first ski ascent of Mont Blanc. Among the famous German ski mountaineering pioneers may be mentioned O. Tauern, Hofmeier, the author of a valuable book on ski mountaineering, Martin Hoferer and Roegner.

In Austria no man did more to develop ski mountaineering than Colonel Bilgeri. In Switzerland Professor F. F. Roget of Geneva was outstanding among the pioneers of ski mountaineering. He was nearer fifty than forty when he began to ski, and carried out his finest expeditions when he was well over fifty. In 1906 he made the first ski ascent of the Aiguille du Tour; in 1907 of the Grand Combin and the Aiguille du Chardonnet. On the latter expedition he was accompanied by Marcel Kurz, whom he introduced to ski mountaineering. In January, 1909, the professor traversed the Oberland by the high-level route. In March, 1910, he traversed the Diablerets, Wildhorn and Wildstrubel; on the second day he crossed in succession the Diablerets and Wildhorn and reached the Wildstrubel Hut, a very good day's work for a young man, and a magnificent achievement for a climber over fifty. In 1911 Professor Roget and Marcel Kurz traversed the high-level route from Bourg St. Pierre to Zermatt, making the first winter ascent of the Dent Blanche en route.

Professor Roget published the first book on ski mountaineering to appear in the English language, Ski Runs in the High Alps.

147

No skier has a finer record as a pioneer of ski mountaineering than Marcel Kurz, an honorary member of the Alpine Club, Alpine Ski Club and Ski Club of Great Britain. His first winter ascents, on all of which ski were used, include the Dent Blanche, Täschhorn, Gabelhorn, Zinal Rothorn and Grand Combin, etc. He is the author of *Alpinisme hivernal* and of ski guides to the Valaisian Alps.

Among the great Swiss pioneers of ski mountaineering may be mentioned Paul Montadon of Thun, Robert Helbling who made an early ski attempt on Monte Rosa with Paulcke, and who was the first to cross the Finsteraarjoch on ski, and the first to complete on ski an important section of the high-level route from Chamonix to Zermatt, and Carl Egger, one of the best editors that the *Swiss Ski Year Book* has ever had, and one of the first skiers to explore distant ranges on ski. With Miescher he made the first ascent on ski of Elbruz just before the outbreak of the First World War, on July 28th, 1914, to be precise.

Among the more notable pioneer ski expeditions in which the Swiss took part may be mentioned the Aletschhorn by G. Hasler and guides in 1904, the first ski traverse of Mont Blanc from Courmayeur to Chamonix on April 20th, 1924, by R. von Tscharner and M. Wieland, the traverse of the Jungfrau from south to north by W. Amstutz and P. von Schumacher on June 11th, 1924, the Nesthorn and Lötschentaler Breithorn by H. Morgenthaler and Lauterburg in 1917.

Ski Mountaineering in Italy

Count Aldo Bonacossa was the outstanding ski pioneer in Italy. He was not only president of the Italian Ski Federation and the representative of Italy on the International Ski Federation for thirty years but he was also one of Italy's greatest mountaineers. In summer he had more than two hundred new routes to his credit, among others a climb which is still regarded with unqualified respect by the modern desperados, the south-east ridge of the Aiguille Blanche de Peuterey (l'arête des Dames Anglaises), which he climbed in 1913 with P. Preuss and C. Prochownick. Most of his climbs were accomplished without guides.

He is perhaps the only skier who has skied in almost every Alpine region. He was the first thoroughly to explore on ski the Graians and the Cottians. His wife, Contessa Bonacossa, who in the Second World War earned the proud title "Mother of the Partisans", was one of the leading ski mountaineers of Europe. In 1925 she made the first ski ascent of the Breitlauihorn (12,018 ft.) in the Bietschhorn Range, and in 1925 the first winter traverse of the Gran Paradiso on February the 9th, both with her husband.

The contribution of French skiers to the exploration of the High Alps only began to be important after the First World War, and the subsequent history of ski mountaineering in France is closely connected with the G.H.M. *(Groupe de Haute Montagne du Club Alpin Français)* which was founded in 1919 and which provided the main initiative for the brilliant development of French mountaineering since that date.

Among the pioneers of ski mountaineering in France may be mentioned the following members of the G.H.M.: Albert Plossu, president at the age of eighteen years of the Students' Club at Grenoble, who with R.Michelet made the first ski ascent in 1925 of the lower summit of the Ecrins, the Dôme de Neige des Ecrins; Mlle Collet, Pierre Caillat, M. Henriot and D. Challonge who both by their example and by their writings helped to found a school.

The G.H.M. campaign reached a brilliant climax in the winter of 1925–26 when twelve of the great Dauphiny peaks were conquered, among them the Meije and Ecrins. Ski were not used on the first ascent of the Meije (March 16th, 1926) by Pierre Dalloz and D. Armand-Delille. On February 21st, 1926, Armand-Delille made the first winter ascent of the Ecrins. Armand-Delille and two ladies climbed on ski to the Bergschrund where the ladies, who did not wish to compromise his chances of success, waited for six hours of a February afternoon till Armand-Delille rejoined them after a solitary ascent of the peak.

In 1922 Captain, now Colonel, A. de Gennes, a member of the G.H.M., translated my book *Alpine Ski-ing* into French, and a little later organised an expedition, the object of which was officially described as a study of snow conditions on the glaciers in April, taking as a basis de Gennes' translation of *Alpine Ski-ing*.

Another active pioneer was Captain Schindler who had many fine first ski ascents to his credit, among others the Pic Coolidge and Le Râteau.

Samivel

I cannot conclude my brief sketch of ski mountaineering in France without a tribute of gratitude to the inimitable Samivel. If Samivel were not a brilliant cartoonist, the greatest interpreter of the humour of mountaineering and of ski-ing, he would long have won recognition as a great mountain painter, but it is difficult for the versatile to win recognition in more than one field, with the result that most people identify Samivel with his humourous cartoons and seldom pause to consider and to appreciate the lyrical beauty of some of his mountain scenes.

No mountain artist has more successfully interpreted the fantasy, mystery and occasional horror of the mountains. His mountain world has something in common with the fairy world of Hans Andersen's Ice Maiden, and I was not at all surprised to find an article by Samivel on mountain myths and legends in that splendid French Encyclopaedia of Mountaineering, Maurice Herzog's *La Montagne*.

The picture of Napoleon's army crossing the St. Bernard in Samivel's *Contes à Pic* is an enchanting blend of history and fairyland. In this, as in all his work, one is impressed by the combination of delicacy and precision. The book itself consists of essays and short stories on mountain themes, essays which reveal in prose qualities which recall those which give to his art its inimitable character.

The British Contribution to Ski Mountaineering

The Alpine Club which had played so distinguished a role not only in the development of summer but also of winter mountaineering contributed nothing to the first phase of ski-ing.

During the winter of 1897–98 a friend sent Colonel Strutt a pair of Norwegian ski without any bindings. "This being", writes Colonel Strutt, "I believe, only the second appearance of these weapons at St. Moritz,[1] the first having been worn by Sir Arthur Conan Doyle."

Unfortunately, there were at that time few good runners in the Engadine, and the Engadine guides strongly discouraged the use of ski on winter climbs for the good reason that at that distant period they felt more secure on their feet. Colonel Strutt witnessed the agonies of an incompetent party who were attempting to descend a glacier on ski and on a rope. He was not impressed, and in a friendly criticism of an article which I contributed to the *Field* on roped ski-ing he recalled the "ludicrous spectacle and unsafe proceeding" of the party in question and concluded:

> "Ski", he wrote, "are only suitable as originally used in Norway, for the ascent of gentle grass or shale summits or as aids to serious mountaineering to enable one to reach a club hut."

I can trace no record of an important ski ascent by the British before 1908.

British ski mountaineering began in 1908. Early in January that year Cecil Wybergh, a member of the Alpine Club who had only been on ski for two days, and I, without guides, crossed the Wildstrubel from Montana to Lenk, and thence in two more days skied across the passes to Villars. In March of the same year, C. Scott Lindsay and G. W. Hutchison, an Alsatian F. A. M. Noelting and a German Oscar Kuntze, reached on ski the Furggrat and Adler Passes, this being the first time when the 13,000-foot line had been crossed by British skiers.

[1] Captain J. P. Farrar had tried ski-ing at Grindelwald in the winter of 1891–92.

On March 7th, 1908, the Alpine Ski Club was founded in London under the presidency of Sir Martin Conway. This, the first ski club with a ski mountaineering qualification, was conceived in the course of a conversation with Owen O'Malley, later Sir Owen O'Malley, Ambassador to Poland and Portugal, in his room in Magdalen, Oxford. The club published the first ski-guide to a Swiss region, the present writer's *Alpine Ski Guide to the Bernese Oberland*, the first volume of which appeared in 1912, the second in 1920.

In January 1909 Professor F. F. Roget and I, with the guides Gyger and Schmidt and Adolf of Kandersteg, carried out the first end-to-end traverse of the central Bernese Oberland on ski, Kandersteg to Meiringen (Petersgrat, Lötschenlücke, Grünhornlücke, Finsteraarhorn, Oberaarjoch).

In the same winter W. A. Moore and J. R. Dixon with the guide Louis Theytaz made the first ski crossing from Zinal to the Val d'Hérens.

In 1909 I shattered my right leg in a rock-climbing accident and an open wound in the shin did not heal until some years after the War. I was rejected more than once from the Army and resigned myself to looking after British prisoners of war in Mürren. During the four winters which I spent in the Alps I made daily notes of snow conditions which formed the basis of my book *Alpine Ski-ing at all Heights and Seasons*[1]. A few years later Gerald Seligman, a member of the Alpine Club, equipped with the training of a scientist, published *Snow Structure and Ski Fields* recognised throughout the world as the leading work on this subject.

The first outstanding ski expedition by a British lady was the first winter ascent of the Gabelhorn from the Mountet Hut in February, 1928, by Miss Maud Cairney with the guides Théophile and Hilaire Theytaz. Among other enterprising ski mountaineers may be mentioned Miss Marjorie Pugh who crossed the Valaisian Alps from Saas Fee to Martigny in 1928, and the Central Alps from Saas Fee to Disentis in 1929, her companion on the former expedition being Miss Rosamund Lyster, and on both expeditions Miss Mary Powell. Miss Angela Stormonth-Darling's traverse of the Eigerjoch on ski from the Jungfraujoch to the Scheidegg has already been mentioned.

The following were the more important British ski expeditions in other ranges. In 1930 Frank Smythe took ski almost to the summit of the Ramthang Peak (21,982 ft.). In 1931 R. L. Holdsworth reached Meade's Col (23,420 ft.) a height record for ski. In 1934 Sir Norman Watson, Bart., E. B. Beauman, Clifford White and Camille Couttet made the first ski crossing of the Coast Range (British Columbia).

---

[1] Of this book Marcel Kurz wrote in the preface to his *Alpinisme hivernal*: "It is a curious fact that the English who were the first to explore our Alps, and the last to explore them on ski, possess since 1921 the best work on the subject." Of the French translation of this book and of *The Complete Ski-Runner*, Robert Michelet wrote in a chapter contributed to Paul Gignoux' *Ski sur les Alpes* (p. 139): "*Le ski en hiver et au printemps et sur les glaciers* et *Le Ski Alpin* torment une nouvelle génération de skieurs."

Glacier skiers may be divided into those who are primarily skiers, and those who are primarily mountaineers. The former are quite content to repeat the classic routes, such as the high-level traverses of the Bernese Oberland or the glaciers between Zermatt and Chamonix. But those who are primarily mountaineers are happiest when pioneering. Certainly there are few mountain days which I recall with greater pleasure than those spent making first ski ascents, the Dom for instance which is the highest mountain wholly in Switzerland, on which Knubel and I took ski to the actual summit (June 18th, 1917), or the Eiger via the Eiger Glacier with Walter Amstutz, W. Richardet and Fritz Amacher, without guides, or the traverse from the Weisshorn Hut (after climbing the Weisshorn) to the Biesjoch, and the ski descent thence to the Turtmanntal (May 27th–29th, 1920). It is a little surprising how few of the ski passes I pioneered in the Oberland (Gredetschjoch, Bieligerlücke, Hühnerthäli Pass, etc.) have been repeated. Indeed the only ski pass which I discovered, incidentally from an aeroplane photograph, and which has become really popular is the Galmilücke which I had explored with Fritz Amacher in 1922, and combined with the crossing of the Bächilücke to the Rhone Valley in 1923, my companions being Peter Schlunegger and Adolf Amacher. On the Bieligerlücke, my companions were Prince Chichibu of Japan and Max Amstutz (Walter's brother) and the guides Fritz Steuri and Adolf Rubi.

Prince Chichibu of Japan

Prince Chichibu of Japan, the brother and at that time heir apparent of the Emperor, arrived in Mürren in January 1926. The Emperor had asked me to accompany him on his first expeditions in the High Alps, and I made the necessary arrangements for our glacier tours in the Oberland in May.

The Prince was a competent rock climber and a competent skier. He was not outstanding as a skier or as a climber, but few men have loved the mountains more passionately. There is a touch of near-mysticism in an article which he contributed to a magazine which circulated among the Imperial Princes, an article which ends: "The mountains themselves stand as the symbols of Eternal life, and serve as the expression of a mighty Spiritual being." The Prince, be it noted, would not have incurred Michael Roberts' criticism, cited in a later chapter, of those who worship the symbols rather than the reality.

The Prince and his great friend and A.D.C., Viscount Matsudaira, were both strongly opposed to the war and showed great courage when the war had broken out, in expressing their sympathies with the British, so I was informed by Sir Robert Craigie, Ambassador in Japan till Pearl Harbour, who added that when the British were interned in the Embassy the Prince sent in a great deal of food which was most welcome as they were on very short rations.

Prince Chichibu, I am glad to say, died an honorary member both of the Alpine Club and also of the Ski Club of Great Britain. Shortly before he died I sent him my *Mountains of Memory* in which our expeditions are described.

"I must tell you", he wrote, "how much delighted and consoled I was by reading it myself at a most depressing time. Having lost all books on mountains and ski, including the British Ski Year Book, when my Tokyo house was burnt down by one of the air raids, I was particularly pleased to find the record of my un-forgettable ski tour with you in the Alps in Spring 1926."

CHAPTER XIV

THE IRON AGE

The east face of the Grand Capucin, which Tom Bourdillon described in a lecture at the Alpine Club, is one of those climbs where the climber progresses from one iron piton to the next, and where every now and then, to quote a classic phrase, "the angle eases to the vertical". It is only about 2000 ft. in height, but difficult enough to involve a bivouac. Bourdillon's was a fascinating talk, all of which I enjoyed, and one remark in particular was unforgettable. "For the next hour we were hardly in contact with the rocks." I looked round hopefully wondering whether by any happy chance R. L. G. Irving, that great traditionalist, could be in the audience. I could imagine his reactions: "And what in heavens name do we go to the mountains for? To be in contact with rocks or in contact with ironmongery?"

Bourdillon's companion, H. G. Nicol, has described their climb in *The Climbers' Club Journal* for 1956. "The next roof", he writes, "was the biggest on the climb, and Tom had no difficulty in surmounting it in textbook fashion, *body held well away from the rock*" (Italics mine). Avoiding contact with the rocks would seem to me the "text book fashion" of the new rock-climbing. Equally characteristic of the neo-cragsman is a revealing sentence: "No pitons and no cracks! In this unusual situation it became necessary to *climb* for a short distance, which on the Capucin is something of a surprise."

Nicol and I were joint guests at the Oxford Mountaineering Club dinner in 1956. We discussed the objections to artificial climbing. "I know", said Nicol, "but what our critics never allow for is that we *enjoy* this kind of climbing. It's fun." And a legitimate form of fun for those who enjoy that kind of thing. And not only fun but an exacting test of physical fitness, acrobatic talent and courage. Nicol's defence reminded me of Leslie Stephen's reply to critics who suggested that mountaineers did not really enjoy climbing but merely risked their lives from fashion or the desire for notoriety. "No more argument is possible than if I were to say that I liked eating olives, and someone asserted that I really eat them only out of affectation. My reply would be simply to go on eating olives."

The equipment of a modern rock-climber consists of *pitons* (iron pegs) most of which are provided with a *mousqueton* (an iron snap-ring) which is clipped to the

154

piton head and through which the rope is threaded, a piton hammer to hammer the pitons into cracks, *étriers* that is miniature rope ladders which are suspended from the mousquetons, and, for more extreme climbs, rock drills to bore holes where there are no suitable cracks for the pitons, expansion and contraction bolts to fit into the holes thus bored and rock anchors to hold the cragsman in position. A modern climber will start up a smooth rock face with a generous supply of hardware clanking from his waist. Such is the characteristic climber in this Iron Age of mountaineering.

The purists condemn *all* artificial aids, and many who would make free use of pitons condemn boring holes in rocks and fitting into these holes expansion bolts. They contend that so long as one confines oneself to driving pitons into cracks which exist there is still a place for the genuine route finding which consists of discovering a route with adequate cracks for pitons.

Every phase of modern climbing from completely free to the most extreme forms of artificial climbing is represented on the various routes up the Eiger, and its minor summit (Eigerhörnli).

(1) The *Lauper* route up the north-east face is a masterpiece of traditional climbing in the free style, mainly on ice.

(2) *The Mittellegi Ridge*. The first ascent of this ridge was made on September 10th, 1921, by the Japanese Yuko Maki with the guides Fritz Amatter, Fritz Steuri and Samuel Brawand.

The worst pitch was climbed by means of an 18 ft. long pole, to which a rope was attached and which was provided with devices for holding it in position.

This device was analogous to the ladders so often carried by the early guides. There is a radical distinction between an aid, like a ladder, which leaves the structure of the mountain unaltered and pitons driven into the rock.

(3) *The south-east face*. First climbed by O. Eidenschink and E. Moeller of Munich on August 10th–12th, 1937. None but a purist could cavil at the three pitons used, only for security, on this magnificent climb.

It is important to note the radical distinction between pitons *used for security purposes* (belays, running belays) and the manufacture of artificial footholds, and the various devices to pull a climber up rocks otherwise unclimbable.

(4) *The Eigerwand*, the ascent of which in 1938 is described below, and which is still considered one of the most desperate of Alpine climbs. It was condemned by the traditionalists because of the unavoidable objective dangers such as falling stones and ice, avalanches and the difficulty of retreat in bad weather.

Pitons have been used by all parties, but mainly for security purposes. The Eigerwand is not an artificial climb, as that term is generally understood. It is, on the contrary, one of the most exacting tests of free climbing.

(5) *The east face.* Under the heading "Freak Expeditions" Colonel Strutt wrote: "The most remarkable and ridiculous performance was the nailing of the east (Bäregg) face of the Eigerhörnli after four months drilling, divided equally between the midsummers of 1936 and 1937." (*A.J.*, 49. 277.)

This, of course, was artificial climbing, a reduction *ad absurdum* which would be condemned today not only by the few surviving traditionalists but also by most masters of the modern technique.

Until the young climbers returned to the Alps after the Second World War the traditional attitude of the Alpine Club was that crystallized by Mummery in his account of the descent from the Grépon. "Here Burgener", he writes, "tried to fix one of the wooden wedges.... Someone then mooted the point whether wedges were not a sort of bending the knee to Baal, and might not be the first step on those paths to ruin where the art of mountaineering becomes lost in that of the steeplejack."

As early as 1924 J.H.Doughty, who was unfettered by tradition in his original and brilliant approach to mountaineering, read a paper before the Rucksack Club on "The Conventions of Mountaineering":

"I remember", he wrote, "listening to a well-known climber who objected to the ascent of the Eagle's Nest direct in rubbers on a dry day. 'It does not', he complained, 'give the rocks a chance.' This is a hard saying, and suggests a grim doctrine; but I think we may find in it the clue to what really lies at the bottom of mountaineering conventions, or at any rate those which are worth discussing. *They are the unwritten rules of the game.* Our Spartan friend was adopting precisely the attitude of those others, who, in their several spheres, object to batsmen defending the wicket with their legs, or golfers using ribbed clubs, or sportsmen shooting at sitting birds; all things which tend to make the job in hand too easy, which fail to give the pitch, the course, the bird, or whatever animate or inanimate opponent it may be, a chance.

Of course it may be urged that mountaineering is not a game. 'A sport, I grant you', one may say, 'but with the competitive element entirely eliminated.' Do not believe it. The grosser forms of competition may not be tolerated in the best mountaineering circles but the thing is there....

Moreover, if he is successful in the struggle he may well desire, without being chargeable with vanity, to estimate the measure of his triumph; and how can he do this so readily or with such comfort as by comparing his own with the performances of other men....

We want a rough idea of what bogey really is. Else what is to prevent some unscrupulous fellow from securing our plaudits by leading Walker's Gully, when all the time he has had a rope privily fixed, up which to swarm over the final chockstone? Emotions are not to be trifled with like that....

And what is to distinguish your own achievement, when reported, from the performance of the shameless trickster, if once such things become common? To particularise about the purity of your methods would be offensive: you want to be able to say with all due modesty that you have climbed Walker's Gully—and leave it at that."

Doughty had, without knowing it, predicted what the great exponents of artificial climbing now admit to be a drawback to pitons. Prior to the Iron Age the standard of a climb tended slightly to change. Psychologically a second ascent is easier than the first even apart from the information which those who follow acquire from their predecessors, but at least the physical details remain substantially the same. Climbs on the other hand on which pitons are used tend to become progressively easier, for successive parties increase their speed up the climb by adding a few extra pitons here and there to those already in place. The Eigerwand for instance is definitely easier than it was.

This degeneration of a climb can be checked. There is an informal society known as "The Squirrels" which from time to time remove all pitons they regard as superfluous, and they do this the more readily because good pitons are expensive and it is cheaper to replenish one's stock by cleansing a cliff than by emptying one's pockets. Nicol told me that Bourdillon and he used up four pounds worth of pitons which they had to leave in place on the Capucin. Removing a piton is often a lengthy and always a tiresome process and many pitons are left in place because climbers have no time to remove them.

The Alpine Club and Artificial Climbing

The attitude of the Alpine Club to the developments of technique between the wars was influenced by the fact that most of the outstanding climbs of the period were achieved by Germans and by Italians, and exploited on behalf of the Nazi and Fascist dictatorships. A great traditionalist quoted with disgust the following passage:

> A climber has fallen. Let a hundred others arise for the morrow ... All our wars will always take place in the mountains, and the cult of mountaineering passionately pursued, and spreading more and more among our young men, will contribute to the military preparedness of the young generation.

But what deductions may be drawn from this rhetoric? That the writer correctly interpreted the ideals of young Italian mountaineers? Or that some ardent Fascist was exploiting the achievements of these mountaineers for political ends?

Italian climbers who thought as we did, were powerless to protest against this kind of rubbish, but it was difficult for Englishmen, born and bred in a climate of freedom, fully to appreciate life under a dictatorship, or to realise that what was written by or about German and Italian mountaineers was no guide to what they thought. Only those who knew them, and knew them intimately, could form a just impression of their mountaineering outlook. Captain A. F. Marples, M.P., for instance had climbed with Bavarians for many years. He knew them well, and rejected as absurd the theory, popular among our mountaineers, that the motive which inspired their most desperate climbs was the desire "to bring prestige to the Nazi party". "In my opinion", he wrote, "they climbed desperately as a form of excapism from Nazism.[1] Most of them joined the party because they could not obtain employment otherwise." Before we judge them too harshly let us remember that we entertained as honoured guests in the England of 1956 Khruschev and Bulganin, representatives of a régime as odious as the Nazi. We were prepared to overlook the crimes of Soviet Russia in the interests of international peace, and should not therefore condemn young Germans and Italians who conformed for the sake of individual peace. There is something unattractive about the selective indignation which condemns in others what it condones in oneself.

My knowledge of the German and Italian skiers of this period leads to conclusions similar to Marples'. They joined their respective parties because they had to. Of all those whom I met, year by year, at international race meetings I cannot recall more than three or four who seemed to me to be genuine and fanatic supporters of their respective régimes. Most of them acquiesced without enthusiasm, as the German and Italian mountaineers of that period acquiesced, in régimes which they were powerless to change. As Jean Franco so rightly remarks: "Dans les poitrines décorées par les médailles offertes aux vainqueurs par le Führer ou le Duce battaient des cœurs d'alpinistes."

The unchanging motive

In *The Times* of June 23rd, 1956, I wrote a long article on artificial climbing in the course of which I remarked that mountaineers of the old school dispensed with pitons "not because they were more idealistic but because they were luckier than their successors. The contrast is a contrast of opportunity rather than of ideals. No pitons were used on the first ascent of the west ridge of the Jorasses, and no pitons would have been used on the first ascent of the north face had this face, whose tremendous challenge was irresistible, been climbable by the traditional technique. But surely it would have been unreasonable to expect the young to acquiesce in the perpetual virginity of the last unscaled precipices of the Alps, merely because these could not be conquered by the orthodox methods so brilliantly described in Mr. G. W. Young's *Mountain Craft*."

[1] Marples' views are quoted at some length in *Switzerland and the English*, pp. 247–249.

To this Geoffrey Young replies that he refrained from using pitons not because he was "luckier" than the moderns but on principle. "Call it prejudice if you prefer. But, while we knew about pitons and their uses, *we did not use them because we did not wish to spoil climbing*, or lessen the fine judgements and skills which climbing on our own powers alone produced. It was a deliberate refusal to use aids; *not* a lucky happening of new climbs still left which could (just) be done without them."

The masters of piton technique would not accept the implied alternatives, "fine judgments and skills" *or* artificial climbing. It is the exceptional climb which is mainly artificial, and on most of the more famous modern climbs pitons are only used where "fine judgments and skill in climbing" would avail nothing without their help, used in fact for exactly the same reason that Geoffrey Young's party hammered in a piton on the first descent of the east ridge of the Grandes Jorasses. Only one piton was used on that climb, but *magis et minus non mutant speciem*.

The sentence in my article, on which Geoffrey Young commented, was not intended to deny that a real principle was at stake in the use of pitons, but rather to question the theory that those who objected to piton were more "idealistic" than those who use them. Between the wars this problem of technique was so bedevilled with politics that reactions to the new technique were confused by our hatred of Nazism and Fascism, but the time has now come frankly to admit that it was a mistake to attribute unworthy motives to mountaineers whose views on these disputed points differed from ours. The theory that the crack German and Italian climbers of this period were mainly inspired by the ambition to bring prestige to their countries and to the political systems of those countries is untenable for two reasons. The dictators were only interested in *first* ascents, and the more extreme climbs of the period were repeated not only by Germans and Italians but as in the case of the north face of the Matterhorn by one of the best of modern guides, the Swiss Hermann Steuri. In the second place these climbs continue to attract the younger mountaineers in this post-Nazi age.

The motives which inspired Whymper and Mummery and Geoffrey Young are indistinguishable from those of a Buhl or a Comici or a Magnone.

I attended in June 1956 a meeting of the Alpine Club at which Gaston Rébuffat showed a superb film, in which every form of climbing, free and artificial, was displayed. His audience included some who disliked artificial climbing but none who could have failed to recognise in the lecturer not only one of the greatest climbers of all time but also a man whose love of the mountains was as disinterested and as single minded as that of the most conservative of traditionalists.

Artificial climbing has come to stay and all that remains is to assess its influence on the sport. Traditional mountaineering is virtually unaffected by the use of an

159

occasional piton (as on the south face of the Eiger) to overcome an exceptionally difficult pitch, and much controversial ink need never have been spilled had the more extreme forms of artificial climbing been classified not as mountaineering but as rock gymnastics. The relationship between rock gymnastics and mountaineering may be illustrated from an analogous relationship in ski-ing.

The pioneers of Alpine ski-ing were as concerned to master mountain craft as the technique of ski-ing, for they skied on natural snow as shaped by frost, sun and wind, and in those days a man was deemed to be a good skier if he could pick a good line when travelling at fair speed over ground on which he had never skied before. Today the majority of Alpine skiers are *piste* skiers. They ski not on natural snow but on snow which has been transformed by Kurverein employees into a hard smooth unvarying surface which makes no demands on snow craft. The ability to choose a good line is at a discount, for most piste skiers spend their time trying to beat the clock down a piste with every curve of which they are familiar.

Now piste ski-ing, especially in its ultimate form ski-racing, is an exacting test of balance, technique and courage, and as such deserves our respect. And the same is true of rock-gymnastics, even though both developments of their respective sports represent a development of mechanisation, the ski-lift corresponding to the pitons, expansion bolts, etc.

"It is not inapt to recall", writes Geoffrey Young, "that a silver cup shaped by the hands has life transmitted to it, and is alive to our eye, but that no machine-made cup is anything but dead and unbeautiful. If we assume that any principle of beauty and life inspires the forms and surface life of hills, the more we interpose mechanisms between our natural senses and their rhythmic lines and planes the less chance is there of a real interplay being established or of our uncovering its pleasures."

The Spenglerian distinct contrast between culture (in close touch with nature) and civilisation (largely the product of science and mechanism) applies both to ski-ing and to mountaineering. In the hierarchy of sport culture takes precedence of civilisation, mountaineering of rock gymnastics, but precedence does not imply condemnation.

I am not in the least ashamed of all that I have done to promote ski-racing. High speed down a piste is a legitimate pleasure and is none the less enjoyable because natural snow ski-ing is incomparably more enjoyable. Similarly it is legitimate for a mountaineer, who admits that rock gymnastics rank far lower in the hierarchy of sport than mountaineering proper, to desire none the less to extend his climbing experience by mastering this new technique. It is unreasonable to condemn piste ski-ing but not unreasonable to persuade piste skiers to master the technique of natural snow ski-ing. It is unreasonable to condemn

rock gymnastics but not unreasonable to seek to entice the piton specialists to develop into all round mountaineers. I am told that there are an increasing number of young climbers who specialise in rock gymnastics, and devote their entire holidays to rock gymnastics on Chamonix Aiguilles without ever attempting the classic climbs of the Mont Blanc Range, for instance the Peuterey, Brouillard or Sentinel routes on Mont Blanc. If this be so, it is, I feel, a pity.

E. A. Wrangham, the Honorary Secretary of the Alpine Climbing Group, remarked in a letter to *The Times* that few climbers would quarrel with what he was kind enough to describe as my "statesmanlike remarks" about artificial climbing, and he then proceeded to point out that comparatively few Alpine climbs are "in any great part artificial", and that the "piton specialist" is a "rare bird". It may be so, but a contemporary of Wrangham's, with a fine record in the Himalaya and in the Alps, J. B. Tyson, who would of course have agreed with Wrangham that there is no piton-specialist who would not jump at a chance of Himalayan exploration, none the less added sadly that it is becoming increasingly difficult to entice some of these modern experts from Chamonix and its Aiguilles to a classic centre of traditional mountaineering such as Zermatt, and this statement of his could be supported by quotations from an article which Wrangham contributed to *La Montagne* (June 1956), in which he claims that Chamonix is still the favourite climbing centre of the British. "Zermatt", he writes, "n'attire plus que les débutants et les alpinistes âgés ou fatigués." One meets few "aged and tired" climbers on the north face of the Matterhorn and few "débutants" on the Young Ridge of the Breithorn.

It would indeed be a sad development if our best climbers were to become pure specialists in difficult rock climbing, but I do not regard such a development as probable, if only because so many of our own and of the continental cracks are all-round mountaineers, as for instance that great French climber Lucien Devies who is not only a master of all aspects of mountain craft but also a brilliant interpreter of mountain moods. Here, for instance, is a convincing analysis from his pen of the prelude to a great climb, in this particular case the north-west face of the Olan:

> «L'immensité de la muraille, les difficultés et les dangers qu'elle réserve s'impose peu à peu puissamment à l'esprit et la menace du lendemain pénètre en vous. L'inquiétude sert d'excitant à la sensibilité. On prend intérêt à l'atmosphère sereine et mélancolique, à la poésie des choses, au bêlement triste des brebis, au rythme du torrent, aux ombres qui creusent le relief sous le ciel noir... On s'accroche à la moindre palpitation du monde, comme si elle était unique, irrenouvelable.»

The indirect influence of artificial climbing on the technique of free climbing has been partly mischievous and partly beneficial. Mischievous in so far as the art of climbing down, on which Geoffrey Young wrote a masterly chapter in *Mountain Craft* is neglected. The modern piton expert seldom climbs down for the fun of climbing down and prefers wherever possible to rope down. On the other hand it is only on exceptional climbs, such as the east face of the Capucin, that there is more artificial than free climbing. On most classic artificial climbs a cragsman can only carry a limited number of pitons and therefore he has every inducement to be economical of pitons and to climb what can be climbed without their aid. Many free pitches on artificial climbs are at least as difficult as the greatest rock climbs of the pre-piton age.

The greatest masters of artificial climbing have led without pitons on rocks of a standard of difficulty never attained before the opening of the Iron Age. This is certainly true of Joe Brown whose friends believe him to be the finest cragsman in the world; as there is fortunately no world-championship in rock climbing, this is a claim which can neither be proved nor disproved.

Many a splendid climb in the classic traditions, such as those described in Graham Brown's *Brenva*, were accomplished during the Iron Age, an age which coincided with the Golden Age in Himalayan exploration, but the justification for describing this period as the Iron Age is that it was during this epoch that the great development of artificial climbing took place with its corollary, an increasing tendency to substitute artificial for natural footholds. The rock gymnasts often claim that there is no radical distinction between making holes in a rock or cutting steps in ice, but there is surely a real difference between the kind of climbing in which ones foot rests on rock or ice and the kind of climbing in which it rests in an étrier suspended from an iron ring, and it is to emphasise this distinction that I have suggested for the modern era the name "Iron Age".

The Iron Age in the Alps coincided with the Golden Age of Himalayan exploration which ended with the ascent of Everest. Though artificial climbing reached its full development between the two World Wars the classic tradition was dominant during the early years of this period.

Many of the greatest mountaineers between the two World Wars, such as Willi Welzenbach, were supreme masters of free climbing.

Willi Welzenbach (1900–1934)

Welzenbach, a Bavarian born in Munich, was the greatest mountaineer between the wars. He died young, at the age of thirty-four, and his mountaineering career was interrupted for three years by an illness which permanently damaged his right arm, and yet in his fourteen seasons he achieved a list of expeditions which no other mountaineer has ever surpassed, nine hundred and forty in all, of which seventy-two were over 4000 m. and fifty were first ascents.

162

His first striking success was the first ascent of the north-west face of the Gross-Wiesbachhorn, the most difficult ice climb till then achieved in the Eastern Alps. It was on this face that Tony Schmid, of Matterhorn fame, was killed. Many of his first ascents were rock climbs of exceptional difficulty in the Wetterstein Range. He never climbed with a guide.

In 1925, with Eugen Allwein, he made the first direct ascent to the actual summit of the north face of the Dent d'Hérens, and climbed in all one hundred and forty-nine peaks. After another brilliant season in 1926 he was incapacitated by illness and did not return to the Alps until 1930 when he startled the mountaineering world by his direct ascent of the north face of the Gross-Fiescherhorn with Heinz Tillman. In 1931 with W. Merkl he climbed the north face of the Aiguille des Grands Charmoz in continuous storm and in the course of which they spent four nights on the face of the peak. Bad weather seems to have stimulated him, for in the eight days of mixed weather, some of which was very bad, he made three brilliant first ascents in the Bernese Oberland, a variant and the most direct route up the north face by the Lauterbrunnen Breithorn, the north face of the Gletscherhorn and the north-east face of the Gspaltenhorn. His companions were Eric Schulze, Alfred Drexel and Hermann Rudy. In the following year he rounded off his remarkable and still unrivalled list of Oberland first ascents by the first ascent of the north wall of the Nesthorn. Welzenbach was killed in an attempt on Nanga Parbat in 1934.

No other mountaineer of the period equalled Welzenbach's record of achievement, but the fame of Munich as the cradle of great climbers was reinforced by many other expert performers of whom I have only space to mention the most notable.

On August 4th, 1925, Emil Solleder and Gustav Lettenbauer, both of Munich, conquered the highest and most impressive of Dolomite cliffs, the north-west face of the Civetta. On the 4000-feet ascent only fifteen pitons were used, and these exclusively as security belays. On August 26th–27th, 1930, two young Munich climbers, Carl Brendel and Hermann Schaller achieved a long coveted and extremely difficult first ascent, the south ridge of the Aiguille Noire de Peuterey, and finally two Munich brothers, Franz and Toni Schmid conquered on August 1st, 1931, the Swiss National holiday, the north face of the Matterhorn.

The North Face of the Matterhorn

When the outbreak of war in 1914 sent the mountaineers hurrying back to their countries to take part in a sterner game, the greatest of Alpine problems were still unsolved. Many north faces had been climbed and many remained to be climbed, but there were three outstanding problems which some of the pre-war mountaineers had vaguely considered, but which none of them had seriously attempted. The "Big Three" were the north faces of the Matterhorn, Grandes Jorasses, and the Eiger.

The first to fall was the north face of the Matterhorn. The brothers Franz and Toni Schmid, like so many of the young German climbers, were impecunious. They had bicycled from Munich and camped out. The key to this north face is the couloir, but unfortunately this couloir is also the natural channel for falling stones, and of course the drier and more snow-free the face the greater the risk of stone fall. The Schmid brothers, with the insight of mountain genius, fully realised that the heavy snowfalls of that particular July, though they would aggravate the difficulty of ascent, would also diminish its dangers. They started just after midnight on July 31st, 1931, and climbed the couloir. No stone fell and after bivouacking at a height of 4150 m. they reached the summit in a violent storm at 2 p.m. on August 1st, having celebrated the Swiss National holiday by conquering the most savage face of the greatest of Swiss peaks.

A year later Toni Schmid was killed on the north-west face of the Gross-Wiesbachhorn. An ice piton on which he relied broke away and Schmid and his companion slid down an ice slope some 1600 ft. in height. Schmid was killed and his companion, Ernst Krebs, grievously injured.

The Grandes Jorasses

The second of the "Big Three", the north face of the Grandes Jorasses, was the dream of many a fine climber from 1920 onwards, and the tomb of a German climber, R. Haringer, killed in a 1934 attempt.

On June 28th–29th, 1935, two Munich climbers, Martin Meier and Rudolf Peters, made the first ascent of the north face. On July 1st–2nd an Italian party, G. Gervasutti and R. Chabod, and a Genevese party, Raymond Lambert and Loulou Boulaz, repeated the ascent without realising that the Germans had reached the summit. Lambert was to play a prominent role in the Swiss attempt on Everest. Mlle Boulaz was not only a brilliant mountaineer but a fine skier, who raced for Switzerland in the 1936 World Championship. These three parties had climbed the north face up to the Pointe Croz which is not the highest point. The first direct ascent of the north face to the Pointe Walker, which is the highest peak was accomplished on August 4th–6th, 1938, by an Italian party, R. Cassin, G. Esposito and U. Tizzoni. The height of this face is 4000 ft., and the climb is still considered to be one of the most formidable in the Alps.

What may justly be described not as the last Alpine problem but the last of the great problems in which every mountaineer had been interested, was solved when the Eigerwand was climbed on July 20th–24th, 1938.

The first attempt on the Eigerwand was made by two young Munich climbers in 1935. They spent three nights on the mountain before the weather broke and died of exposure. In 1936 two Germans and two Austrians spent three nights on the mountain. They descended in a storm and reached a point just above the Eigerwand Station of the Jungfrau Railway. The rocky traverse leading to easy ground was iced, and the only hope was to *abseil* (rope down) to the easy ground just below the station. An employee of the Jungfrau Railway heard the shouts of the party on Tuesday night and telephoned for a rescue party. They reached the station by special train and emerged from the tunnel about a hundred metres below where Toni Kurz was hanging on the rope. The *abseil* had failed. Kurz was the only survivor. Rainer was frozen to death, Hinterstoisser had fallen to his death, and Angerer had strangled himself in the attempt to rope down. It was already dark and the rescue party could do nothing but shout encouragement.

Early next morning the guides reached a point about forty metres below Kurz. He had hung in a rope sling on the face of a cliff bombarded by falling stones and swept by rain-fed torrents. And now Kurz began his last fight for life. He needed more rope, and his first task was to climb back to one of his dead companions, to cut the rope which bound him to the corpse and to attach this rope to the rope previously used for the *abseil*. His hands were frozen, and the cliff was so smooth that he could find no secure stance while he carried through these intricate manoeuvres. For *six hours* he forced mind and body to the limit of mental and physical endurance and then—at last—he was ready for the final effort. He lowered the two ropes, tied together, and the guides (Adolf Rubi, Hans Schlunegger and Arnold Glatthard) attached a 40-metre rope, and to this rope they tied pitons and a piton-hammer. Kurz used his last reserves of ebbing strength to drive the piton into the rock, and to complete the difficult preparations with the ropes. And then very slowly he began to lower himself. The guides below saw his feet appear over the overhang. Very slowly the feet crept nearer until they could all but touch the soles of his boots with their axes. And then suddenly all movement ceased. Kurz was dead. He had endured four nights on the mountain. He had watched his companions die. His valiant heart had resisted the terrors of storm and solitude and misery such as mountaineers have seldom been called on to endure. He had hung in his rope-sling buffeted by the storm, but determined not to surrender. And he did not surrender. He died. In the annals of mountaineering there is no record of a more heroic endurance.

In 1937 two Italians were killed on the north face, bringing the death roll up to eight.

On July 20th, 1938, two Austrians (Kasparek and Harrer) started for the north face. On July 21st they were joined by two Germans (Heckmaier and Vörg), who had profited by the steps which the Austrians had cut on the previous day and overtaken them. The two parties joined forces. One climber was struck by a falling stone which ripped all the skin off his hand. The combined parties were all but wrenched from their holds by snow slides which poured over them incessantly. Enfeebled by exposure and prolonged exertion, they battled their way to the summit through a blizzard. During the final phase of the climb, before victory was assured, they heard the shouts of searchers who had climbed the Eiger by the ordinary route. They refused to entertain the option of rescue. "'*Nicht* antworten', ging es bei uns von Mund zu Mund" ("'Don't answer', we said to each other"). The Austrians had been on the mountain for four days, the Germans for three. The issue between life and death was still in grave doubt. Only those who have been very close to death can measure the stubborn courage of the men whose ambition forbade them to accept help in the last desperate phase of their climb.

Harrer's career did not end with this Eiger climb, he was caught in India by the war, interned and escaped from an internment camp to Tibet, where he spent the war.

Groupe de Haute Montagne

It was in the course of the second ascent of the Aiguille du Peigne that Jacques de Lépiney and his friend Paul Chevalier, who had been severely wounded in the war, resolved to found a section of the French Alpine Club to be restricted to expert climbers, and to be called the *Groupe de Haute Montagne*. Their proposal was enthusiastically supported by Henry de Ségogne.

On August 10th–11th, 1924, Jacques Lagarde, Jacques de Lépiney and Henry de Ségogne were the first French guideless party to accomplish a really outstanding virgin climb, the first ascent of the north face of the Aiguille du Plan, the climb which Mummery's party had attempted and which is described in a famous contribution to the *Alpine Journal*, "Two Days on an Ice Slope".

De Lépiney and Ségogne gathered round them a remarkable group of young Frenchmen all of whom had first ascents of outstanding difficulty to their credit, a group which included Tom de Lépiney, Jean-Antoine Morin who was killed in the war, Georges Vernet who died in Dachau, Andéol Madier de Champvermeil and Edmond Stofer both of whom were killed in the mountains.

It was the influence of the Groupe de Haute Montagne which accelerated the development of a new type of guide, the amateur-guide. The word "amateur" is derived from *aimer* and once it meant a man who practised a sport for the love of it. By "amateur guide" I mean the guide who when he is not engaged as a professional still continues to climb for the joy of climbing. Prominent among the guide-amateurs of this period were men like Armand Charlet, Gaston Rébuffat and the Italians Emilio Comici, Cesare Maestri and Walter Bonatti.

Alain de Chatellus points out that Joseph Knubel's limitation in the mountains was only those of his companions. "In the company of climbers of his own class he would certainly have had the capacity to resolve the 'last problems' which were the glory of our contemporaries." If, for instance, Knubel had joined forces with Franz Lochmatter, there was no problem soluble by free climbing which they could not have solved, and none by artificial climbing had they been able to overcome their repugnance to pitons. It was the partnership of guides without amateurs which was responsible for some of the outstanding climbs of the inter-war period. Armand Charlet, for instance, pioneered a new and sensational climb on the Nant Blanc face of the Aiguille Verte.

Some Great Italians

Emilio Comici (1901–1940) was born at Trieste and his first job was as an official at the port, but the call of the mountains proved too strong and he became a professional mountaineer as the only means of gratifying his genuinely amateur passion for the mountains. With Giuliano Perrugini, who organised the ski school at the Lago del Mucrona above Biella, he founded the first mountaineering school in Italy near Trieste, and was later appointed to the control of the military school of mountaineering in Aosta.

Comici was a born leader and he made innumerable disciples among the young Italians to whom the doctrines of the Iron Age had a very special appeal. Comici had the realism of the Italians and he did not think it necessary to ignore the existence of national rivalries in mountaineering. "For the sake of our prestige", he remarked to his biographer, Severino Casara, "we must not allow the trans-alpine climbers to surpass our standards, for if we do, our most difficult climbs will be conquered by Germans and Austrians." He had studied with great care the methods of the moderns, Dülfer and Solleder, and felt convinced that given intuition and an improved style this technique could produce the ideal method of overcoming obstacles with the minimum of physical effort and the maximum of security. And it was this conviction which was the basis of what came to be known as *l'école comicienne*.

There is no basis for a belief, more often implied than stated, that the exponents of artificial climbing are necessarily devoid of any artistic appreciation of the rocks which are the raw material for their particular art. Comici summed up his own artistic credo in a memorable sentence.

> "The power to conceive the most elegant line to the summit, rejecting with contempt all easier approaches, and the skill to follow one's chosen line with muscle and nerve taut, to resist vertigo and the lure of empty spaces below one's feet, are qualities which can create an authentic work of art, a masterpiece outlined in those rock walls which will endure eternally."

Of the many first ascents in the Dolomites which conform to this definition of his aims, the most famous was the first ascent of the north face of the Cima Grande di Lavaredo (Drei Zinnen). This wall is 1800 ft. in height and the first 600 ft. overhang. A climber who fell from the wall on this first section would hit the scree without rebounding from the cliff.

On August 12th–14th, 1933, Comici with the Cortina guides Angelo and Guiseppe Dimai conquered this grim cliff with the help of eighty pitons. They spent two days on the wall. On his second (and solitary) ascent Comici climbed the wall in the fabulous time of three hours and a half. Julius Kugy's mot has become famous; when he heard of this piton ascent he exclaimed: "Now at last I am convinced that the north wall of the Grosse Zinne can never be climbed." But whether we agree or disagree with Kugy we can hardly deny to Comici the attributes of an artist. He not only interpreted rock climbing in relation to aesthetics but he was also a most accomplished musician, with a special love of Bach, Mozart and Beethoven. He died young. The defects of iron were responsible for the tragic end of this great master of the Iron Age, for an iron ring which he was using for a rappel snapped and the great modernist fell to his death.

The Italians were well represented among the masters of the Iron Age. Giusto Gervasutti who was born in 1901 and graduated from Turin, a great centre of active mountaineers, established his reputation by his first ascent of the north-west face of Olan (1934) which was then regarded as the most important problem in the Dauphiny. With the same companion, Lucien Devies, he made the first ascent of the north-west face of the Ailefroide, another desperate climb. He was killed in 1946 in an attempt on a new route on Mont Blanc du Tacul.

On July 14th–16th, 1937, R. Cassin, G. Eposito and V. Ratti conquered the north-east face of Piz Badile. M. Molteni and G. Valsecchi had joined their party, but the struggle with storm and precipice proved too much for them and they both died from exhaustion on the descent.

168

Cassin's climb on the Grandes Jorasses will be described below. Another great climb during this period was the first ascent of the north face of the Dru, made by Pierre Allain and R. Leininger on July 31st–August 1st, 1935. Pierre Allain who, like so many of the best French climbers of this period, had trained systematically in the forest of Fontainebleau, was a master of free climbing. He made many first ascents in the Chamonix Aiguilles, of which only one included a short passage of artificial climbing. The north face of the Dru was perhaps the most difficult climb as yet accomplished with only an occasional piton.

The Swiss Mountaineers

The guideless climbers of Switzerland had no outstanding successes to their credit before the First World War. Hasler, as we have seen, was guided on his great Finsteraarhorn climbs.

After the War the first great successes were achieved by Bernese members of the Akademischer Alpen-Club, Zürich. In 1921 Hans Lauper and Max Liniger climbed the north face of the Mönch. In 1924 Daniel Chervet and Willy Richardet (killed later on the Aiguille Blanche de Peuterey) climbed the north face of the Lauterbrunnen Breithorn. In 1926 Lauper and Pierre von Schumacher made a direct ascent of the north face of the Jungfrau.

Hans Lauper of the Akademischer Alpen-Club, Berne, was one of the outstanding mountaineers of the period. The Eiger, Mönch and Jungfrau is the most famous mountain trinity in the world, and it was a magnificent achievement of Lauper's to make the first direct ascent of the north faces of these peaks. His pioneer climbs on the Jungfrau and Mönch mentioned above were accomplished without professional assistance, but on the Eiger, Lauper and his friend, A. Zürcher, secured the services of two supreme masters of the craft, Joseph Knubel and Alexander Graven.

The north face of the Eiger is the greatest precipice in height: 6000 ft. It is divided by a ridge which separates the north-east face, which Lauper climbed, from the north-west face, the notorious Eigerwand. Stonefall, avalanches and the perils of a retreat if the weather changes are among the terrible objective risks of the Eigerwand. The climb is impossible without the occasional use of pitons. Lauper's route is free from objective dangers and was climbed without using a single piton. His climb was a masterpiece in the classic tradition.

Lauper's success gave particular pleasure to the editor of *The Alpine Journal*, Colonel E. L. Strutt, a resolute opponent of artificial climbing.

> "We must congratulate our members", wrote Colonel Strutt, "on a superb expedition, by far the most important problem of the 1932 season. We might add that it is a source of gratification to us that the north face of the Eiger, the last

important problem of the Bernese Oberland, should have been solved by this unsurpassed all-Swiss party."

Colonel Strutt's views of the Eigerwand were expressed with his customary vigour in his valedictory address:

"The Eigerwand still unscaled, continues to be an obsession for the mentally deranged of almost every nation. He who first succeeds may rest assured that he has accomplished the most imbecile variante since mountaineering first began."

Lauper and Zürcher were members of the Alpine Club and in general sympathy with its conservative traditions. Lauper in particular might have been a reincarnation of a Victorian conservative. He never used pitons and he was particularly scathing in a letter to his friend Walter Amstutz about that alleged competition for the Blue Ribbon of the Alps which figures so conspicuously in Wilhelm Lehner's excellent history of mountaineering. Lauper watched with increasing misgivings the approach of the Iron Age. He was only forty when he died and did not live long enough to read in *The Alpine Journal* itself an article by E. A. Wrangham on artificial climbing.

The Bernese lead was soon followed by the Genevese. On September 20th, 1931, André Roch, one of the greatest mountaineers of the inter-war period and the author of an excellent book, *Climbs of my Youth*, and Robert Gréloz, solved one of the last of the remaining great problems of the Alps, the first ascent of the north face of the Aiguille de Triolet, an exceptionally difficult climb. Mlle Loulou Boulaz with Raymond Lambert, both Genevese, made the second ascent of the north wall of the Jorasses without being aware of the fact that the Germans, who had just beaten them, had completed the climb while they were actually on the face.

In England the attitude of the Alpine Club to ski-racing at first was faintly censorious but many of the finest Swiss climbers of this period were ski-racers or associated with ski-racing. The first ascent of the south face of the Jungfrau was made by Ernst Gertsch and Fritz Fuchs in 1927, the first descent of that north face which Hans Lauper and Pierre von Schumacher were the first to climb, by Ernst Gertsch and Hans Schlunegger. Ernst Gertsch was not only a great ski-racer in his youth but the creator of the famous Lauberhorn race. Schumacher, André Roch and Richardet, all raced in the early Anglo-Swiss University Races. Walter Amstutz, who with Schumacher made the first ascent of the Gross Fiescherhorn by the Fiescherwand (the direct route to the actual summit was one of Welzenbach's climbs), was my first continental ally in the campaign to obtain recognition for downhill and slalom racing. Dr. Oscar Hug, who in 1935 made the first ascent of the west face of the Schreckhorn, was an early president of the

Swiss University Ski Club, the primary object of which was to race against the British.

Finally the best all-round competitive skier of the period was undoubtedly Ernst Feuz who won the championship title awarded in 1924 on the combined result of Nordic and Alpine competitions. Feuz was also among the best climbers of the day.

Every skier knows that Mürren, Ernst Feuz's birthplace, is the cradle of modern ski-racing, and headquarters of the Kandahar Ski Club, but it is curious how few mountaineers realise that a group of Mürrenites carried out some brilliant climbs between the two World Wars. Feuz's achievement in discovering new routes up Oberland north faces rivals that of Welzenbach.

Within three days Feuz and Walter von Allmen, now head of the Mürren ski school, made two splendid first ascents from the Lötschental, the first direct ascent to the summit (north-east of the Flach-Kalbermatten-Rubin line made in 1897) of the Lötschentaler Breithorn, 12,412 ft., on June 18th, 1936, and the first ascent of the north face of the Breitlauihorn, 12,019 ft., on June 21st.

On July 8th–9th, 1934, Ernst Feuz and Walter von Allmen climbed the north face of the Grosshorn by a variation of the Welzenbach route. Feuz's route was more direct and an exceptionally difficult ice climb.

On August 1st, 1940, Feuz and Emil von Allmen (of the Blumental pension) made a new route up the north face of the Lauterbrunnen Breithorn (via the west ridge). Feuz finally rounded off his superb series of new routes in the Oberland by the first ascent of the north face of the Tschingelgrat and Tschingelspitz (outliers of the Gspaltenhorn). This climb on which his companions were Walter von Allmen and Hermann Salvisberg (the only non-Mürrenite to take part in these new ascents) was accomplished with one bivouac on July 6th–7th, 1935.

On June 29th, 1941, Feuz and Walter von Allmen made the first descent of the north face of the Mönch following the Lauper-Liniger route of the ascent. Ernst Feuz tells me that he took a few pitons with him on these climbs but only used them as an occasional security belay.

In July 1947 Emil von Allmen of Mürren with Willi Roth of Berne made the first ascent of the difficult south wall of the Gspaltenhorn, a splendid climax to the achievements of the Mürren mountaineers.

Some Post-War Climbs

As the technique of artificial climbing improved, no cliff, however, repellant was deemed impossible. Walter Bonatti of Monza and L. Ghigo of Turin conquered the east face of the Grand Capucin in 1951 by a climb which was almost entirely artificial, overhanging for the last 1000 ft. The west face of the

Dru was conquered in two stages by a French party consisting of Guido Magnone, who has written a book on this climb, Lucien Bérardini, Adrien Dagory, reinforced on the second stage by M. Lainé. They spent five days from July 1st to July 5th, 1952, hammering and nailing their way up the west face and then returned to their base. On July 16th they climbed the easier north face and after a bivouac traversed across the west face, a traverse which involved among other modern methods drilling holes in the rock and inserting expansion bolts. They thus reached the west face at the highest point attained on their previous attempt and continued to the summit which they reached on July 18th. Seven days in all were spent on the climb.

In 1955 J. Brown (later a member of the successful Kangchenjunga party) and Don Whillans bivouaked twice on the west face and climbed it from base to summit in about forty-eight hours. The difference between the seven days spent by the first party on this face and the two days spent by the third party was, of course, largely due to many of the pitons which had been left in place, but even so the Chamonix guides were astonished that the west face could be climbed—so quickly.

The reaction of the Alpine Club to the Iron Age and the achievements of British mountaineers from the ending of the First World War to the present day will be discussed in the next chapter. Meanwhile we can conclude our survey of continental achievements by a brief reference to the most fantastic exploit which commands the reluctant respect we must concede to reckless courage and super-human endurance.

From August 17th until the 22nd, 1955, the Italian Walter Bonatti made a solitary and first ascent of the south-west buttress of the Dru. He spent five nights alone on the face. There were points on his climb where he roped down before resuming the ascent. Had he failed to reach the summit there were pitches which he had *descended* on a double rope which he could never have reascended. No climb in Alpine history has equalled this for improvidence and courage, folly and endurance. No climber has shown a more complete mastery of his medium under more appallingly difficult circumstances.

Bonatti's career illustrates some points that have been made in another connection. He took part in the expedition which climbed K2 and was offered a very good position in a factory to be in charge of the Dopolavoro Department which is concerned with providing entertainment for workers after office hours. He was to organise their mountaineering and ski-ing. He replied that he would far prefer to be a guide. Even the greatest of guides would find it difficult to earn the equivalent of 400 pounds a year and that was far less than the salary offered to him by the factory. He became a professional guide because of his amateur passion for the sport.

Again, Bonatti is one of many masters of artificial climbing who has a great love for classical mountaineering. In the winter and spring of 1956 he traversed the Alps on ski from the Adriatic to the Mediterranean.

The Lady Mountaineers

The Iron Age witnessed a remarkable advance in feminine mountaineering. Nini Pietrasanta after a bivouac in a storm made the first ascent with G. Boccalatte of the west face of the Aiguille Noire de Peuterey. "Ici", writes Mme Micheline Morin, "ce n'est plus le bal, mais le bivouac qui décidera de l'avenir d'une jeune fille", for the lady subsequently married her climbing companion.

Claude Kogan actually *led* a party up the grim south ridge of the Aiguille Noire de Peuterey. Madame Kogan was a member of the expedition to Peru in 1951. On August 13th, 1951, her husband Georges Kogan of Nice, Jacques Jongren of Brussels and Raymond Leininger and Maurice Lenoir made the first ascent of the lovely ice pyramid of Alpamayo (20,079 ft.), and five days later Mesdames Claude Kogan and Nicole Leininger made the second ascent of Quitaraju (20,276 ft.), a height record for a manless expedition. Nicole Leininger is joint author with Georges Kogan of *The Ascent of Alpamayo*, one of the recent books on mountain exploration. Even more than Nicole Leininger's admirable account of Quitaraju I enjoyed the story of the return to civilisation, the lorry drive with the little Indian who "looks like a peasant by Brueghel the elder...." ...As he gets off the lorry the little Brueghel peasant takes out his knife and calmly cuts a pair of soles for himself out of the spare tyre against which he has been leaning. No one is the slightest bit worried. True the owner of the lorry isn't there.

"At that moment his hatchet face appears under his enormous sombrero. He solemnly delivers the following speech in Spanish. 'Senors and senoras, my professional conscience forces me to tell you that I cannot take you any farther. For such a long journey I cannot accept less than 200 soles.' We are looking forward too much to a bed and a bath to argue. When we get to Monterey, after unloading all our baggage into our store, we obviously pay only what our own professional conscience tells us."

The "manless" expeditions began in 1932. Micheline Morin and Miriam O'Brien climbed the Mönch from the Jungfraujoch. Miriam O'Brien, now Mrs. Underhill, was already a famous mountaineer, undoubtedly the greatest lady climber that America has produced. The "voie Miriam" on the Cinque Torri was so named in her honour. Having satisfied herself on the Mönch that she could dispense not only with men but with guides, Miriam O'Brien and Alice Damesme traversed the Grépon. Then Micheline Morin, Nea Morin and Alice

Damesme traversed the Meije, the three points of the Blaitière, the Aiguilles Mummery-Ravanel, etc. Loulou Boulaz and Lucie Durand traversed the Droites, Charmoz, etc., and finally Mme Nea Morin and her daughter Denise with no other companions achieved a succession of brilliant climbs of which the most sensational was the Grépon from the Mer de Glace (1955). It is difficult to resist quoting Leslie Stephen's remark about the three stages of an Alpine climb, a remark which Mummery popularised, but this famous climb will never reach the final stage "an easy day for a lady" or indeed for a man. It is also important to note that the first party made the ascent in nailed boots, and of course without using a single piton. Be that as it may the conquest of this famous climb by a mother and her daughter must rank among the greatest achievements of modern mountaineering.

Mrs. Bullock Workman's height record for women, 22,737 ft., on Pinnacle Peak was established in 1906 and successively beaten by Frau Dyhrenfurth on Sia Kangri, 23,622 ft., in 1934, by Madame Claude Kogan in an attempt on Cho Oyu pushed as far as 24,935 ft. The record for a purely feminine party is held by two members of a strictly feminine expedition to the Himalaya, two Scots, Monica Jackson and Elizabeth Stark. They climbed a peak 21,982 ft. in height.

"In recent years", writes Mr. Ullman, "man-and-wife teams have reached the summits of Alaska's highest mountains; Bradford and Barbara Washburn on Mount McKinley, Andrew and Betty Kauffman on Mount St. Elias."

Among many other distinguished American mountaineers may be mentioned Elizabeth Cowles and Elizabeth Knowlton who have climbed not only in their own country and in the Alps but also in the Andes and Himalaya.

CHAPTER XV

BETWEEN THE WORLD WARS

M. Lucien Devies in *Les Alpinistes Célèbres* expressed the view, widely held by continental climbers, that British mountaineering suffered if not a total at least a partial eclipse between the two World Wars.[1] "Les grimpeurs anglais demeurent étonnement à l'écart du mouvement de conquête. Les détenteurs d'une grande tradition n'ont pas su transmettre l'esprit de découverte aux jeunes générations." The same verdict is recorded in *La Montagne*, an encyclopaedic work produced under the general editorship of M. Maurice Herzog. In a joint contribution by Professor Jean Escarra and Bertrand Kempf the surprising statement occurs that British climbers had hardly begun to experiment with artificial climbing, and that their literature was scarcely touched by these modern influences. And this in a book published in 1956. For some years before this date it would have been difficult to open any of the numerous climbing journals published in Great Britain without chancing on a narrative of the kind of climb in which the progress is from piton to piton rather than from rock to rock.

The 1956 *Climbers' Club Journal*, for instance, contains H. Nicol's account of the climbing of the east face of the Capucin, and the previous issue the story of the third ascent of the west face of the Dru by Joe Brown and Don Whillans. The revolution in the British attitude is the theme of a moving lyric by David Yeoman in the *Climbers' Club Journal* for 1955.

> Anything goes!
>> Perhaps its iron pegs you use
> Wooden legs you use
>> Abseil rings you use
> Etriers you use
>> A psychic belay you use
> Nobody will oppose . . .

An article by E. A. Wrangham on the technique of artificial climbing even found its way into *The Alpine Journal*. The case for the traditionalists was admirably

---

The best *Alpine* climbs by continental mountaineers in this period are described in Chapter XIV.

stated by T. A. H. Peacocke in a letter of protest against the publication of the article in question. He wrote:

> "Mountaineering is a sport and not a form of war. A sport is governed by a set of rules which allows each side a fair chance. Why must we use 'all out' methods in mountaineering? Why not let the mountain win sometimes, . . . Let the Alpine Club lead the world back to sane methods and fair tactics and give the mountains a sporting chance."

To this the editor, F. H. Keenlyside, replied:

> ". . . the use or otherwise of artificial aids appears to us to be purely a matter of individual taste. . . . Traditions develop or die, and ours have not died."

But I am anticipating for I am quoting from the May 1956 issue of *The Alpine Journal*, my excuse being that I am anxious to rebut the statement quoted above that the British are still completely out of touch with these modern developments. What is certainly true is that the prejudice against artificial climbing was still strong between the wars, and is at least a partial explanation of the fact that our record in the Alps was less distinguished than that of mountaineers with no such prejudice.

The British in the Alps (1919–1939)

The British record in the Alps during these twenty years was not particularly distinguished, but none the less some fine new routes were carried out, notably the following.

The first great climb after the War was the first ascent of the Innominata Ridge of Mont Blanc by S. L. Courtauld and E. G. Oliver on August 20th, 1919, with the guides Henri and Adolphe Rey and Adolf Aufdenblatten.

On August 2nd, 1923, George Finch, T. G. B. Forster and R. H. K. Peto, without guides, made the first ascent of the north face of the Dent d'Hérens, the last section of the climb being up the east ridge. The climb is described in Finch's *The Making of a Mountaineer*.

On July 16th, 1924, Captain J. P. Farrar (who was then sixty-six!) with Miss F. R. Wills, grand-daughter of Alfred Wills of Wetterhorn fame, and the guides Peter Almer (father and son) and Fritz Boss, made the first ascent of the north ridge of the Ebnefluh, and on August 11th, the first passage of the Grossjoch (without Boss).

On September 10th, 1929, N. S. Finzi with the guides Josef Knubel and Franz-Joseph Biener climbed the north-west face and east ridge of the Scheidegg-Wetterhorn.

The best British climbs between the Wars were the four superb routes on the Brenva Face of Mont Blanc which T. Graham Brown has described in his famous book *Brenva*, on September 1st–2nd, 1927 (guideless), with Frank Smythe; Route Major on August 6th–7th, 1928, also with Smythe (guideless); and finally the Via della Pera on August 5th, 1933, with the guides Alexander Graven and Alfred Aufdenblatten, and the Col Major on July 26th, 1933. These climbs rank among the outstanding achievements of this period.

Perhaps the most difficult British expedition of this period was the first ascent of the north ridge of the Dent Blanche by Ivor Richards and Dorothy Pilley, now Mrs. Richards, with the guides Joseph Georges, and his brother Antoine. There is a most evocative description of this climb which was accomplished in 1928 by Dorothy Pilley in *Climbing Days*.

On August 14th, 1919, R. W. Lloyd crossed the Col de Bionnassay for the first time, and on July 18th, 1926, Lloyd, who was then in his fifty-ninth year, made the first direct ascent of the north face of the Aiguille de Bionnassay, a splendid climb. The guides on both expeditions were Joseph and Adolf Pollinger.

The Himalaya (1919–1939)

The theory of the partial eclipse of British mountaineering between the Wars only applies to the Alps. Clearly the exploration of distant ranges, notably the Himalaya, must be taken into consideration.[1]

The foundation of the Himalayan Club on October 4th, 1927, proved of outstanding value to future expeditions, British and Continental. The *Himalayan Journal* which began publication in 1929 is an invaluable source for the historian of Himalayan mountaineering.

Between the Wars unsuccessful attempts were made by German parties on Kangchenjunga and Nanga Parbat. In 1930 an international party, which included Marcel Kurz and Frank Smythe, made an attempt on Kangchenjunga. They climbed the Jongsong Peak (24,344 ft.), the highest summit attained before Kamet and reached 23,442 ft. on Nepal Peak.

In 1936 Paul Bauer led a small party consisting of Adolf Göttner, G. Hepp and Darjeeling porters which made the first ascent of the loveliest of all ice peaks, Siniolchu (22,620 ft.).

On October 5th, 1936, five Japanese, Takebushji, Hotta, Yamagata, Yuasa, Hamano and the porter, Ang Tsering, made the first ascent of Nanda Kot (22,510 ft.).

In 1939 the great Swiss climber André Roch with the Swiss guides Fritz Steuri and David Zogg, both famous skiers, climbed Dunagiri (23,184 ft.). These

---

[1] One of the English members of the Alpine Club, H.E.L. Porter, was very active in New Zealand during this period.

were, perhaps, the most outstanding successes achieved by non-British mountaineers during this period. Between the Wars the British were extremely active and successful in the Himalaya.

During the same period there were seven British expeditions to Everest, led respectively by Colonel C. K. Howard Bury in 1921, by Brigadier C. G. Bruce in 1922 and by Colonel E. F. Norton in 1924; in 1933 and in 1936 by Hugh Ruttledge, in 1935 by Eric Shipton, and in 1938 by H. W. Tilman. Though none of these expeditions was successful, Norton, Wyn Harris, L. R. Wager and Smythe reached, without oxygen, a height of 28,126 ft., far greater than any height attained until the Swiss reached 28,200 ft. in their 1952 attempt on Everest.

In 1931 Frank Smythe (leader), Eric Shipton and R. L. Holdsworth with the Sherpa Lewa, made the first ascent of Kamet (25,443 ft.). Wing Commander E. B. Beauman was in support. Two days later Dr. Raymond Greene and Captain E. St. J. Birnie with the porter Kesar Singh repeated the ascent. It was on this expedition that Holdsworth established a height record for ski, taking ski to Meade's Col (23,420 ft.).

In 1935 C. R. Cooke, who believed that weather and snow conditions in late autumn were more suitable than those just before the monsoon, made the first ascent of Kabru (24,002 ft.), with G. Schoberth and six Darjeeling porters[1]. It took them from October 28th to November 18th to find their way and lay out their camps. "Surely", writes Kenneth Mason, "no-one, after reading Cooke's account can still believe that this was the mountain climbed by W. W. Graham in three days in 1883."

In 1936 T. Graham Brown and the American Charles Houston organised a party which climbed Nanda Devi. It was composed of four British, Graham Brown, N. E. Odell, H. W. Tilman and Peter Lloyd, and four Americans, W. F. Loomis, Charles Houston, Arthur Emmons and Adams Carter. On August 29th Odell and Tilman reached the summit (25,645 ft.), the highest peak that had then been climbed.

In 1937 F. Spencer Chapman and Pasang Dawa Lama made the first ascent of Chomolhari (23,997 ft.). "As a feat of endurance", writes Geoffrey Young, "it stands quite unsurpassed. The descent was made in a five-days blizzard from the peak, bringing with him a Sherpa, out of his mind, safely down."

Chapman described this climb in *Memoirs of a Mountaineer*, but his best known book, so far as the general public is concerned, is *The Jungle is Neutral*, one of the classics of the Second World War, in which Lt. Col. Spencer Chapman was awarded the D.S.O. and Bar.

The most persistent Himalayan explorers of this period were Harold William Tilman and Eric Shipton. Tilman, whose partnership with Shipton on Mount

---

[1] Cooke alone reached the top.

178

Kenya is referred to later in this chapter, was the leader of the Mount Everest expedition of 1938, and with Odell made the first ascent of Nanda Devi.

He served as a Regular Officer in the First World War and was awarded an M.C. and Bar. He rejoined the Army in the Second World war, at the age of 41, and had just the kind of war that an explorer might be expected to enjoy, serving in France, Syria, Irak, Western Desert, Tunisia, and with the Albanian and Italian Partisans. He and Shipton revolutionised the whole conception of Himalayan exploration by their successful demonstration of what small parties could accomplish. His books are vivid in their descriptions of mountain adventure and distant exploration, and are enlived by attractive wit. I particularly enjoyed *When Men and Mountains Meet* and *China to Chitral*.

It is of interest to note that it was on the Everest expedition of 1951, which was the first to explore the route to the Western Cwm on the Nepal flank of Everest, that Sir Edmund Hillary, K.B.E., made his debut as an Everest climber. Shipton told me the story of how he came to include him in the party. "I happened just by chance to call in at the Royal Geographical Society before starting for the Himalaya, and there I found a telegram from the President of the New Zealand Alpine Club asking me if I would allow two New Zealanders to join my party. Their names were not stated and my first inclination was to refuse, and then—I don't know why—I took a chance and telegraphed my acceptance. I nearly didn't, and if my prejudice against inviting climbers, whose names I didn't know, had not been overcome, Hillary would in all probability never have climbed Everest."

The British achievement in the Himalaya between the two World Wars may be briefly summed up as follows. During this period the British established on Everest height records more than 2000 ft. higher than any point attained on other peaks, and climbed two peaks which at the time they were climbed were the highest summits till then attained. In the Himalaya we made four splendid first ascents, Kamet, Kabru, Nanda Devi and Chomolhari.

It is undoubtedly true that the more brilliant Alpine climbs of this period were achieved by Continental climbers, and that the technique of mountaineering which the Alpine Club did so much to develop in the Golden Age, and indeed up to the First World War, was developed by Continental mountaineers between the Wars. Meanwhile in the Himalaya we were laying the foundation for the strategy and technique of mountaineering at high altitudes. The lessons learned on Everest have proved of benefit to all subsequent explorers.

Before attempting a brief summary of what was accomplished in other ranges, a few pages must be devoted to a great Himalayan explorer of this period.

Eric Shipton C.B.E.

"Eric Shipton", writes Geoffrey Young in his forward to Shipton's *Upon That Mountain*, "stands in the forefront of our present day explorers. Since boyhood he has been an adventurer, and since boyhood a rebellious intelligence has held him back from all conventional openings, and steered him inevitably into the single positive alternative, the life of a pioneer. He has refused to accept conventional methods even in exploration, and he has gone far to perfecting a new technique of toughening by travel. He is an illuminating writer."

He is indeed. In the first chapter of his book *Upon That Mountain*, a classic of mountaineering literature, there are a few paragraphs which illuminate the contrast, ignored by Shipton, between the majority of those who frequent winter sports centres and the occasional eccentric who is more interested in mountaineering than in ski-ing. As a boy Shipton spent a winter in Adelboden. "Fortunately", he writes, "that year there was no snow in the lower valleys for ski-ing." "*Fortunately!*" In apparent innocence of the horror which this statement would provoke and perhaps was intended to provoke, in a skier, he proceeds to explain how he persuaded some other guests to share the expenses of guides for the Gross Lohner, on which he was introduced to the ritual of the rope and the ice-axe.

> "I felt when I got back to the hotel that all my senses had been sharpened and my whole outlook changed by the crowded experiences of the last twenty-four hours. In the Gross Lohner I now had a priceless possession. I bought a big picture of the mountain, looking in its mantle of winter snow as fine as any Himalayan giant and hung it in my room at home."

There is a curious resemblance between Shipton's memories of Adelboden and mine. The Lohner is no ski-ing peak, nor is the Albristhorn which I climbed on foot from Adelboden, having persuaded the Milligans, father and son, to accompany me. And like Shipton I hung a photo of that beautiful mountain in my room at Harrow. I doubt if these winter ascents of the Lohner and the Albristhorn have been repeated since then even by those "fortunate" enough to find inadequate snow for ski-ing in Adelboden.

Shipton's explorations have not been confined to the Alps and the Himalaya. There is an excellent chapter in his book on Mount Kenya, the highest summit of which, Batian (17,058 ft.), was first climbed by Sir Harold Mackinder with César Ollier and Joseph Brocherel of Courmayeur on September 13th, 1899. Shipton with P. Wyn Harris repeated the ascent in 1929 and also climbed the slightly lower Nelion (17,022 ft.). In 1930 Shipton and H.W. Tilman made the first ascent of the Midget Peak, by far the most difficult aiguille in the range.

They narrowly escaped death on the descent. The first ascent of Batian by a woman was made in 1938 by Miss Una Cameron.

Shipton is the great advocate of small Himalayan expeditions, even where ample funds are available. His own belief in the virtue of small expeditions is based on personal experience.

On his first Everest expedition the thought occured to him:

> "Why not spend the rest of my life doing this sort of thing? ... I had always rather deplored the notion that one must sacrifice the active years of one's life to the dignity and comfort of old age. Also the less conservative of my monitors assured me that things had a way of panning out so long as one knew what one wanted."

How things panned out is described in the chapter on his exploration of Nanda Devi with another great explorer (and also be it noted another gifted writer), H. W. Tilman. Try as he could Shipton could not bring the estimate to below £ 150. Luckily Tilman managed to fix up return passages by cargo steamer for thirty pounds each to Calcutta, including baggage.

Geoffrey Young's remark that Shipton was an "illuminating" writer would not be disputed by anybody who had read the psychological reasons which he advances in defence of small expeditions.

> "It is vitally important that no members of a party should at any time feel that he is superfluous, or that he is simply there in case someone else breaks down.... It is merely tactless to remind a man that he is lucky to be there at all, and that there are hundreds of equally good climbers at home who would be only too glad to take his place.... The strongest mountaineering party is one in which each member has implicit confidence in all his companions, recognises their vital importance to the common effort, and feels himself to have an indispensable part to play. This ideal ... can only be achieved by a relatively small, closely knit party. Only then can you talk (if you must) about team spirit. How is it possible, when at least 50% of the members are destined to remain in reserve to avoid all feeling of competition? Only a saint could expunge from deep down in his soul all hope of another man falling sick, that he might take his place. How different from the joyous partnerships we have known on other climbs."

The book is refreshing in its realism. There is, as Shipton rightly remarks, a tendency to ignore in written accounts of the expeditions, "the difficulty of preserving harmony", but Shipton's analysis of the things which make for disharmony is as realistic as it is entertaining.

He was accompanied on one expedition by two scientists, Spender and Auden, both of whom he liked, but "it was generally prudent to keep them separated as much as possible. This was odd because each was untiring in his co-operation in the work of the other. Perhaps it was because they both had unusually hearty appetites or, perhaps, because both had brothers who were celebrated poets. I find that scientists are often intolerant of one another."

I hope these necessarily bleak quotations will tempt such of my many readers as have not yet read *Upon That Mountain* to remedy that deplorable omission.

So far my examples of Alpine Club activity in this period has been mainly drawn from the Alps and Himalaya. Actually British mountaineers were not very active on the American Continent.

The American Continent

The outstanding success by a subject of the King between the Wars was undoubtedly the ascent of Mount Logan (19,850 ft.) by a party led by a distinguished Canadian member of the Alpine Club, Captain A. H. MacCarthy. The climbers were partly Canadian and partly American (H. F. Lambert, Lt. Col. W. W. Foster, British Lennox Lindsay, Norman Read and Allen Carpè). Mount Logan, the second highest summit on the North American Continent, was climbed on June 23rd, 1925.

The great achievements of this period were mainly American, as for instance the first ascent of Mount Lucania (17,150 ft.), the second highest peak in Canada, by that distinguished American mountaineer, Bradford Washburn of Harvard, and Robert Bates on July 9th, 1937, and the first ascent of a peak, long reputed utterly inaccessible, Mount Waddington, on July 21st, 1936, by Fritz Wiessner, a German born American, and William House of the American Alpine Club.

Our Native Mountains (1919–1939)

On our own mountains the standard of rock-climbing approximated to the highest standards of free climbing attained on the Continent. Pitons were still suspect.

The standard of rock-climbing on our native cliffs began to rise after the War under the influence of men like H. M. Kelly and C. F. Holland. Kelly's ascent of Moss Ghyll Grooves on Scafell in 1927, and A. S. Pigott's lead up the East Buttress of Snowdon's till then unclimbed cliff, Clogwyn du'r Arddu, in 1927, and J. L. Longland's lead of the West Buttress acted, as W. H. Murray remarks, "like the firing of a fuse to explode the latent energies of England's rock-climbing youth".

An important influence in changing the emphasis from muscular strength to balance and rhythm, the feet being used as much, the hands as little as possible, was Young's book, *Mountain Craft*, but the individuals who did most to raise standards at this period were Menlove Edwards and Colin F. Kirkus, who was killed in the Second World War. "Kirkus' example", writes Murray[1], "was a personal one of audacity and tenacity. He accepted very long run-outs of rope without much, if any, use of slings and pitons." Kirkus was perhaps *primus inter pares;* he worked out the new technique with A.B. and A.T.Hargreaves, A.W.Bridge, M.Linnell, Dr. G.Graham Macphee, and J.M.Edwards.

After the Second War standards of rock climbing were again raised by men like A.J.J.Moulam, A.R.Dolphin and Joe Brown. Brown was to prove on the west face of the Dru that he was as good as the very best Continental cracks.

Pitons once barred are now accepted. "There has come a reaction", writes Murray, "from Kirkus' example of personal courage in accepting exposure without protection of any kind in favour of a kind of Dutch courage drawn from much use of slings and pitons, so that technical standards remain high but routes tend to become nasty, brutish and short."

Moreover, as in the Alps, pitons are used by the less competent on routes which experts climbed without pitons. The ideal would obviously be for pitons only to be employed where free climbing is impossible, but if they are to be hammered by second class climbers into routes which were climbed without them they should at least be removed. R.R.E.Chorley cited to me as an example of the consequent degradation of a great climb, the south ridge of the Aiguille Noire de Peuterey on which three pitons is the maximum which is justifiable, but on which he found thirty pitons left in place when he climbed it. On our cliffs it should be possible to create a tradition that pitons should only be used on climbs which are wholly impossible without their use.

As I have quoted so freely from the chapter which W.H.Murray contributed to James Ullman's book, I should like to conclude with a tribute to a book of which Murray is sole author, *Mountaineering in Scotland*, the best book, perhaps, in the literature inspired by our native mountains, and welcome evidence of the fact that among the most finished exponents of modern cragsmanship there are men whose vision has not been clouded by preoccupation with technique, men who write as well as they climb, and whose work is not only precise and scientific in its description of exciting climbs, but convincing in its interpretation of mountain beauty.

"We had set out in search of adventure, and we had found beauty. Thus we had found them both in their fuller sense, for in the architecture of hill and sky, as in great art and music, there is an everlasting harmony with which our own had this night been made one. What more may we fairly ask of the mountains?"

The book, from which I have just quoted, was published after the War, and something should be said about the British contribution to mountaineering

[1] I am quoting from Murray's excellent chapter contributed to *The Age of Mountaineering* by James Ramsey Ullman.

literature between the Wars. Many of the best books published during this period have already been mentioned, but there are others, beside those from which I have quoted, which helped to maintain a great tradition, notably Geoffrey Young's *On High Hills* and R.L.G.Irving's *The Romance of Mountaineering*.

Few men have written with more passionate sincerity of all that mountains have meant to those that love them, and Irving's books, as I know, appeal not only to mountaineers but also to all in whom mountains evoke that near-mystical adoration which finds expression in the best passages of Ruskin.

Of the outstanding books of this period which have not already been mentioned in previous chapters and whose authors were British perhaps the most widely read were Conway's *Mountain Memories*, Frank Smythe's *Climbs and Ski Runs*, *After Everest*, by T. H. Somervell, and Claud Schuster's *Men, Women and Mountains*.

Michael Roberts, whose untimely death was a great loss to English letters, published during this period *Poems*, some of the finest of which, notably *Elegy for Fallen Climbers*, were inspired by the mountains.

John Pascoe's *Unclimbed New Zealand* is a classic in the literature of the New Zealand Alps, and *The Mountains of Snowdonia* by Herbert R.C.Carr and George Lister is a standard work on the subject. And among the many other books to which I owe a tribute of gratitude may be mentioned *Hills and Highways* by Katharine Chorley.

Let me bring this study of the Alpine Club between the Wars to an end by tributes to the memory of two great presidents who held office during this period, Captain J. P. Farrar and Lt. Col. E. L. Strutt, and to Frank Smythe, perhaps the best known British mountaineer during this period, who died shortly after the conclusion of the Second World War.

Captain John Percy Farrar D.S.O. (1857–1929)

Farrar was educated in Lausanne, spent some years on the shores of Lake Geneva, fought with distinction in the South African War, and achieved a great business success in South Africa. It was, perhaps, this cosmopolitan background which gave him his unique position in the mountaineering world. Certainly no man did more than Farrar to re-unite the mountain brotherhood after the First World War.

Farrar knew the Alps from end to end. This list of his expeditions occupies more than seven pages in Mumm's Alpine Register. The climb which he recalled with greatest pride was perhaps the second ascent of the Peuterey Ridge of Mont Blanc. For many years he climbed without guides and at the age of sixty-seven he climbed the Piz Badile and the Grépon.

184

He was president of the Alpine Club during the First World War and though only Assistant Editor and Joint Editor of *The Alpine Journal* from 1909 to 1926 he was in effect the guiding spirit. He never wrote a book but his contributions to *The Alpine Journal* were, as Geoffrey Young rightly says, "always in character, virile, brusque, eloquent, strict in censure but all of a sudden aflame with admiration and generous praise". His tribute to his guide Daniel Maquignaz has been quoted on page 81 of this book.

I was introduced to him by Geoffrey Young, and shortly afterwards he asked me down to his house for a week-end. At the time I was still fighting for the recognition of ski-mountaineering as a legitimate branch of our sport, and Farrar gave me an occasional encouraging pat on the back in the columns of *The Alpine Journal*. I remember how delighted I was when he described me as "the liaison officer between mountaineering and ski-ing". He was candid in his criticisms and sparing of praise, but his rare compliments meant a lot. "You're a hard worker", he said to me one day in reference to my researches into the history of winter mountaineering. I was only one of the very many young men who turned to Farrar for counsel and who felt when he died that the mountain brotherhood would never be quite the same again. Nothing could be at once more felicitous and accurate than Geoffrey Young's tribute in *The Alpine Journal* (LIV, p. 117):

"I know nothing comparable with the affection and respect in which Farrar was held by the climbers, young and old, of nearly every land. During the troubled interlude following the last war, his tireless work in promoting international understanding through a common mountaineering interest, seemed to me — when engaged upon parallel lines — the most successful undertaking of the kind in Europe. Among ourselves, protesting fierce prejudices, he encouraged or shared in every new form of adventure with vigorous indulgence. His catholic sympathies embraced every age and variety of climber, and his finger was upon the mountaineering pulse of every country. With ageing or afflicted mountaineers, wherever he could trace them, he would start a mountaineering correspondence about the past with a charming deference that in itself consoled; and with the young and enterprising — if any man or boy had the mountaineer's faith in him and the courage to practise it, for Farrar he could do no wrong. It was a heroic effort, and an all prevading presence, which for some years held together the loosening strings. . . . With Farrar we may say with some certainty that even the revised version of the later prophets was finally closed."

A charming tribute to Farrar's memory was paid by thirty-two members of the American Alpine Club who presented the British Army in 1940 with an ambulance and a sum for one years maintenance, "in memory of Captain John Percy Farrar".

Colonel Edward Lisle Strutt C.B.E., D.S.O. (1874–1948)

Strutt who was president of the Alpine Club from 1935–1937 was a fine all-round mountaineer and perhaps the most experienced winter mountaineer of his period (page 142), and was a member of the 1922 attempt on Everest.

He was editor of *The Alpine Journal* for ten critical years, 1927–1937, and probably did more than any other man to convince the advance guard of Continental mountaineers that the Alpine Club was hopelessly out of touch with modern developments. Strutt fought a stubborn rearguard action against ski-mountaineering (as I know from my own relations with him), crampons, oxygen on Everest, and artificial climbing. I have already quoted (page 170) his contemptuous references to the Eigerwand adventurers.

He had a vigorous style and was a master of controversial dialectics. He never bothered to translate his dislike of individuals who sinned against his conception of the mountain code into the language of diplomacy. From time to time cries of distress from his victims would reach the Alpine Olympians. "It's all very well", Farrar would reply, in soothing tones, "but it's not too easy to get anybody to edit *The Alpine Journal*." Certainly *The Alpine Journal* has never been livelier than during the ten years of his editorship. One opened it in a mood of pleasurable and yet anxious anticipation. Whose turn would it be for the Strutt guillotine?

There was no malice about Strutt. Few men who have been so outspoken in their condemnation of individuals and methods of which they disapproved were so wholly free from vindictiveness, nor so ready to revise an unfavourable verdict on an individual whom they felt they had misjudged. As I have good reason to know. There exists a letter which he wrote to Coolidge in reply to a demand for information about "Young Lunn", a letter which would have given more pleasure to my enemies than my friends, but some years later we became great friends, and the episode described on page 101 proves the lengths to which he was prepared to go in defence of a friend.

He was a gallant soldier. In the front line of battle, courage is taken for granted, and men only remember the extremes, cowardice or exceptional gallantry, and it was for exceptional gallantry that Strutt was remembered by those who served with him in Flanders. He was not only physically brave, for he signalised his appointment as editor of *The Alpine Journal* by an act of great moral courage; the publication of an article which was nothing less than a scathing exposure of *himself*. He had taken three young companions for a short winter climb above Sils Maria and they had been caught in a sudden blizzard. Two of the party slipped on a traverse of hard snow and fell over a cliff. "I, alone", writes Strutt, "was really responsible for the fall. I had committed a series of unpardonable mistakes. . . . Providence had averted disaster in a place where the odds were a thousand to one in favour of death. . . . The humiliation to myself is everlasting; my admiration of my companions eternal." Some years later I told him that I thought that he had judged his own conduct far too harshly, and he replied that his self-exposure was useful because it gave him the right to criticise others as severely as he had criticised himself.

In his resistance to innovations Strutt was often mistaken, but he was basically right. Mountaineering is a sport, not a substitute for warfare or a criterion of national greatness, and extreme risks which are legitimate in war are not legitimate in mountaineering.

The eminent seldom advertise their own errors, and few such examples of unqualified self-condemnation are to be found in the literature of sport, and none, so far as I know, in the literature of mountaineering. Even Strutt's sternest critic could not deny that he had given irrefutable proof of his integrity. A man who criticised himself so unsparingly could hardly be accused of criticising others for the sake of being disagreeable, or attacked for condemning in others what he had condemned in himself. Strutt was a brilliant ice-man. Josef Pollinger, no mean judge, described Strutt as the finest amateur ice-man and Farrar as the finest all-round mountaineer with whom he had ever climbed.

Frank Smythe (1900–1949)

There was no British mountaineer between the Wars who was better known to the general public than Frank Smythe. His fame, solidly based on a foundation of achievement, was reinforced by the fact that he was also a popular lecturer and a skilful journalist.

Smythe was born on July 6th, 1900, and resolutely resisted Berkhamstead's attempt to educate him. He was said to have a weak heart and was not allowed to play football. Raymond Greene writes: "Physically on his mountains, intellectually in his books, he strove always to attain heights which were just a little beyond his powers, great though these were."

At the age of fourteen he cycled all the way to Wales to climb, and from then onwards insisted that all his holidays should be spent among the mountains.

In 1926 Smythe joined the R.A.F. and went to Egypt. He was not suited to that type of life and after several months he became very ill, and in the letters to his mother the doctors write: "He has all the signs and symptoms of typhoid and we fear his heart may be considerably affected." He was invalided out in 1927.

For a year he accepted an appointment with Kodaks, and for the rest of his life he supported himself by books, articles and lectures on mountaineering. From 1930 onwards he was *The Times* correspondent for mountaineering.

Nobody assumes that a great scientist is only or mainly interested in his salary, or that judges have only a minor interest in justice, but there are people who make an analogous assumption in the case of a man who derives most of his income directly or indirectly from a particular sport. It was for the benefit of such critics that Raymond Greene thought it as well to refute in *The Alpine Journal* the view that Smythe "climbed mountains not for the love of mountains but for the love of gain." Smythe, as a professional writer and lecturer on mountains, was the precursor of guides like Rébuffat who have become professionals because they were impelled into this way of life by the flame of a devouring mountain passion.

Smythe was a competent but not a brilliant rock climber. The Mummery crack, according to a climber who led him up the Grépon, was just above the limit of what he could lead, but he was a safe and seasoned cragsman capable of leading on most classes of rock found in the Alps.

It was in the 1933 attempt on Everest that Smythe "showed to the full", according to Raymond Greene, "his superb icemanship. His approach to the North Col seems to me the finest piece of ice-climbing I have ever seen."

Smythe never climbed with a guide until he joined a guide on a search party. He learned to mountaineer by mountaineering. Dr. Graham Macphee writes:

> "Although physically of light build, he had amazing powers of endurance, and could carry a heavy rucksack all day without apparent fatigue. A careful perusal of the accounts of the great climbs he did on the South Face of Mont Blanc reveals the hours of step-cutting he carried out. He was extremely good on snow and ice, with a wonderful knowledge of varying conditions, and had an uncanny sense of direction in difficult route-finding.
>
> It was my good fortune in my first Alpine season to accompany him on the Pétéret Ridge. Surprised by sudden bad weather soon after leaving our bivouac high on the Aiguille Blanche, he never faltered, and led the first successful descent on the Rochers Gruber from the Col Pétéret in a storm I have never since seen equalled. Descending and crossing the complicated and difficult Fresnay Glacier, he was never once at fault and unerringly attained the foot of the couloir leading to the Col Innominata in dreadful weather conditions, so that we safely returned to the Gamba Hut thirty-six hours after setting out from Courmayeur."[1]

As a skier he was steady but by no means accomplished, somewhere between the standards of the British Third and Second Class tests. His ski-mountaineering record is relevant to the question of his position in Alpine history. His record of exploration in distant mountain ranges was exceptionally good. His pioneer ascents in the Alps, notably the new routes on Mont Blanc, are among the very few great climbs which have been first accomplished by an all-British *guideless*

---

[1] Geoffrey Young has paid a tribute to the characteristic that *made* Smythe a great mountaineer, "the slow inner flame that burnt the fiercer as things went wrong and contrary winds blew up".

party. If his claims were based solely on his record as a summer mountaineer it would not be easy to prove that any other British mountaineer had a finer record between the Wars, but what establishes Smythe's position as perhaps the best all-round British mountaineer of this period is the fact that he knew the mountains not only in summer but also in winter and in spring, and had mastered the techniques of *modern* mountaineering, ice-craft, rock-climbing and also ski-ing which is more and more being recognised as an integral element in the education of the all-round mountaineer.

I must not omit a tribute to his skill as a mountain photographer. Some day, we shall, I hope, be given a book containing the best of Frank Smythe's writings and the best of his photographs. Such a book should be a very good book indeed.

Of his leadership on the Kamet expedition, Raymond Greene writes:

"He was the best kind of leader for such an enterprise, the leader who makes all the plans with meticulous care and having, as it were, created the world leaves it to run itself, giving it only a gentle push if it slows down or begins to wobble on its axis, but remaining personally inconspicuous.

At great altitudes a new force seemed to enter into him. His body, still apparently frail as it had been in boyhood, was capable of astonishing feats of sudden strength and prolonged endurance and his mind, too, took on a different colour. At sea-level the mistaken sense of inferiority so unfairly implanted by his early experiences rendered him sometimes irritable, tactless and easily offended. The self-confidence which flowed into his mind and body, the emanation as it were of the mountains whose strength he so greatly loved, changed him almost beyond recognition. It seemed impossible above 20 000 ft. to disturb his composure or his essential quietism. I remember the Kamet expedition as a period of calm, unbroken by more than a rare small ripple of disagreement, and the calm was the result of Frank's confident but always modest and unassuming leadership.

In the Himalaya he was equally good as a follower. Under Ruttledge on Everest he was as imperturbable, reliable and good-tempered in circumstances far harder and consequently more troubled."

Smythe was not indifferent to his fame, but I, who knew him well, am convinced that he was at heart a genuinely modest man, who found it difficult to believe in his own achievement.

Eric Shipton told me that he had been particularly impressed by a kind of Yogi-like power which Smythe seemed to possess to detach himself from his surroundings. "There is something inevitably squalid", said Shipton, "about a high camp in the Himalaya. Things and food get spilled and climbers are often too weary to keep things ship-shape. On Everest one might have to remain some days on the North Col, but Smythe never got impatient or irritable, he preserved a complete detachment."

No British mountaineer of the period was read more widely than Smythe. It was his particular merit to convey to those who had never climbed something of his own passion for mountains. He was admirable as an interpreter of mountain adventure, less admirable in his attempts to construct a religion out of his mountaineering experiences.

"Mr. Smythe's observations on life, death and judgment", wrote Lord Schuster in a review of one of his books, "are neither as original nor as profound as he seems to think",

but it would be a mistake to assume that Smythe wrote for effect or invented emotions which he did not feel. Like the poets who

> Mar their mortal melodies
> With broken stammer of the skies

Smythe often failed to find the right words to describe a genuine spiritual experience. And the kind of remark which provoked Schuster's dry comment was largely due to his resolute refusal to read anything which other explorers of the borderland between the natural and the supernatural had troubled to report. "I avoid reading that kind of book", he once remarked to me, "because I want to be sure that my interpretation of the mountains is my own and is not confused or influenced by anything I might have read about religion or mysticism." In those days he was not prepared to consider the possibility that a study of the subject might have clarified rather than confused his beliefs, and might, for instance, have helped him to distinguish between the worship of mountains, which is silly, and the worship inspired by mountains which is anything but silly. In the late twenties he sent me a succession of indignant epistles in which I was upbraided, much as an apostate might be upbraided by an apostle, for perverting the true mountain faith. I had been infected, so he believed, by the heresy of "Downhill-Only", and instead of insisting that young men should climb up mountains was actually encouraging them to race down them. "Don't you realise", he pleaded, "that mountains are meant to be worshipped, not treated as slides?"

But the worship of limestone and granite is—in the exact sense of the word—idolatry.

It is odd that Smythe, and those mountaineers who agreed with him, did not realise that they had adapted Ruskin's taunt for use against skiers. Ruskin accused mountaineers of treating mountains as if they were greased poles; Smythe attacked skiers for treating mountains as greased planes.

Smythe was a man who matured late. One of his earlier mountaineering companions once remarked to me that "he thought in clichés". When I first met him he was something of a monomaniac for whom history seemed to begin with the beginnings of Alpine exploration, but his strong prejudice against reading gradually disappeared. Towards the end of his life he was a voracious reader of history, biography and even of religious literature. His work as a photographer had educated his eye for colour and line, and he had begun to make a collection of reproductions of Alpine paintings from the Middle Ages onwards. I was impressed by his erudition and flattered that he should have asked me to collaborate in a book on mountains in art.

I have mentioned his modesty. Of his other personal traits I must not forget his good humour. He was often in the centre of controversy, but he was incapable of malice. Our own friendship was founded on the two poles of firm agreement and no less firm disagreement. I recall no hour spent in his company which I did not enjoy.

CHAPTER XVI

THE ALPINE CLUB DURING AND AFTER
THE SECOND WORLD WAR

The Alpine Club during the War

Shortly after Dunkirk I spent a few minutes with Lord Lloyd, who was a member of the Government, in his office. He assured me that we should be invaded. "And what then?" I asked. Lord Lloyd shrugged his shoulders, and for the first time I faced the fact that we might conceivably be defeated.

As a boy I had always re-read *The Playground of Europe* when I felt depressed and it was the same instinctive lifting up of one's eyes to the hills which sent me into the Alpine Club which had not yet evacuated its library and pictures. I paused before the gallery of ex-presidents. Never had those splendid heads, John Ball, Kennedy, Leslie Stephen and Grove seem more characteristically Victorian, the epitome of a serene Augustan age.... *They* had never faced the possibility of a conqueror gloating over stricken London from the balcony of Buckingham Palace.

O fortunati ninium sua sit bona norint.

And if we fell, what then? Of one thing I felt certain. If the mountaineers of Europe were to be regimented under Sport-Führers, German and Austrian climbers, themselves the heirs of a great tradition, would remember, if only with unspoken gratitude and concealed regret, the Mother Club of mountaineering, which had from the first regarded itself the trustee for something infinitely more important than national prestige, the tradition of a mountain brotherhood transcending all frontiers, and united in their devotion to the noblest of sports.

England did not fall and the Alpine Club did not die. Not even its structure was damaged by the Blitz.

The Club was fortunate in its war-time presidents, Lord Schuster, president at the outbreak of the war; Geoffrey Young, president for three years of war, from January 1941 to December 31st, 1944; and Leo Amery, president during the last year and a half of the war.

It would not have been surprising if the Club had tended, during these war years, to live nostalgically in the past, but this was very far from being the case, as I can testify for I served three years on the Committee from January 1st, 1944, onwards.

MONTE ROSA
Emil Aufdenblatten (1946)
(Swiss Foundation)

Schuster's valedictory address emphasised the need to revivify our traditions. Geoffrey Young, ably assisted by his lieutenants Geoffrey Bartrum and Bryan Donkin, the Hon. Secretary, and J. E. Q. Barford, representatives of three different age-groups, reasserted for the Alpine Club its interest in our native mountains, and prepared for the post-war extension of its activities beyond the Alps. Young revived the Alpine Club meets in the Lakes, and with the help of John Barford created the British Mountaineering Council, on which the Alpine Club and all mountaineering clubs with their headquarters in this country are now represented. He got into touch with the Military Education authorities and the Club naturally co-operated with the War Office in the development of schools for mountain warfare.

Geoffrey Young was also actively associated with starting the camps, short-term schools on Hahn's lines, joint experiments of the Army, Navy and Civil Institutions. Young was living in Holland Street at the time, and his house was the focal point of many of these new developments. He was indefatigably assisted by Donkin and Barford. One sub-committee was engaged on Alpine Club internal reforms, and another on external relations.

The Club was a very live affair during the war, and the seeds of a great renaissance of British mountaineering were laid before we returned to the Alps.

Schuster and Amery, who were also, as we have seen, presidents during these difficult times, have since died.

Lord Schuster G.C.B., C.V.O. (1869–1956)

More than forty years have passed since Claud Schuster published *Peaks and Pleasant Pastures*, but it is not difficult to recall the delight with which I read this book as a young man. Claud Schuster described no desperate climbs, but few mountaineers have recaptured with greater skill or translated into words of greater felicity all that mountains mean to those who love them not only as an avenue of adventure but also for their beauty. It is difficult to repeat a success, but *Postscript to Adventure* (in *The New Alpine Library*) published in 1950 did not disappoint the admirers of the earlier work, and nothing in his books moved me more than the noblest Valedictory address ever delivered by a president of the Alpine Club. He was speaking on December 10th, 1940, when the world believed England to be lost, when our Club meetings had to be held in the afternoon before the bombs began to fall, and when Greece was heroically resisting invasion.

"Countries and clubs are not impersonal abstractions, but collections of those who compose them or inherit their history. To them those who came before have transmitted, as in our case, imperishable memories and indestructible traditions. While they hold fast by those memories and traditions, and yet allow them to be permeated and revivified by the continual struggle for the best, they need not grow old and decayed, but stronger, tougher and more vigorous. 'Past ruin'd Ilion Helen lives.' The bust survives the city. The spirit of man survives physical trials and misfortunes. It lives on, using its own achievement to inspire the young who fill the ranks, as the old fall by the wayside, and march on to victory; so that in the rough and desperate gorges of the Pindus, the Greek peasant still goes forward fired by the memory of Leonidas and of Miltiades."

Schuster was president not only of the Alpine Club but also of the Ski Club of Great Britain, and he helped to build a bridge between the clubs. Many of the old guard were not at their best in their references to ski-ing. "Fashionable winter sports", wrote one of them, "are like jazz music, an instance of the return to the primitive delights practised by savages", and the writer proceeded to compare ski-ing, the most aesthetic of all forms of swift motion, "to the tobogganing of savages down steep slopes."

In a paper read before the Alpine Club in 1943, Schuster poked fun at mountaineers who accused skiers of pot-hunting. There was, as he rightly said, a touch of the Pecksniff in this attitude, "Competition has in the past entered into mountaineering.... There are those who collect summits like postage stamps. But apart from this, competition in athletic sports is not in itself an evil. We do not deprecate the successful track-runner, and there is nothing particularly immoral in either running or ski-ing faster than your neighbour...."

Leopold Amery P.C., C.H. (1873–1955)

No president of the Club had had a more distinguished career than Amery. When he was offered the presidency he remarked with hardly a smile that of his two ambitions he had set the presidency of the Alpine Club above the premiership. It is conceivable that had there been no Winston Churchill, Amery would have been offered the premiership after his dramatic speech on May 7th, 1940, which brought down the Chamberlain Government, a speech which he ended by quoting the words with which Cromwell had dismissed the Long Parliament.

"You have sat too long here for any good you have been doing. Depart I say, and let us have done with you. In the name of God, go!"

Amery was a brilliant writer, and his political autobiography, *My Political Life*, will be an indispensable source book for historians of this troubled period. He had held many high offices under the Crown, among them First Lord of the Admiralty, 1922–1924, and Secretary of State for India and Burma, 1940–1945. Mountains, however, meant even more to him than politics.

"Mountaineering", writes Geoffrey Young, "was the practical outlet for the adventurous and artistic side of Leo Amery's gifted and many-sided personality. To no man of great powers and great position have mountains meant more. Statesman, scholar, linguist, athlete and of the first rank in all, it was in the rhythm and romance of his climbing that he realised himself most happily."

Many of his mountain adventures and his ski-ing memories were described in his delightful books, *Days of Fresh Air* and *In the Rain and the Sun*, titles which he took from the most famous of Bowen's Harrow songs.

In the Alps he had no sensational first ascents to his credit, but he must be the only mountaineer who has made the first ascent of a peak which was named after its conqueror *before* it was climbed. It was in 1929 that he made the first ascent of Mount Amery in Canada, called after him by the Geographical Board of Canada while it was still a virgin peak.

Amery was twice elected president of the Ski Club of Great Britain, from 1936 to 1938 and from 1946 to 1948.

He married a Canadian, Miss Florence Greenwood, with whom, he tells us, he "lived happily ever afterwards". Indeed, few marriages can have been happier.

Amery and my father had been friends, and I had in consequence first met him when I was a young man. I had served under him as president on the committees of the Alpine Club and Ski Club of Great Britain. We often met in England and in the winter Alps, and as the years passed he would talk to me with increasing freedom of his political experiences. There is nobody from whom I have learned more of the inside political history of the past fifty years.

If we define a statesman as a man who is primarily concerned for the welfare of the State, and a politician as a man who is primarily concerned for the welfare of a political party, then most certainly Amery would be classified as a statesman. Of course this is an over-simplification, for the statesman has to take consideration of the fact that his own plans for the welfare of the State will come to nothing if his party loses its majority, and therefore every statesman must master the technique of politics. None the less, the distinction between those whose first concern is for the good of the State, and those whose first concern is for the good of the Party is important, and certainly Leo Amery was a classic example of the high-minded statesman. Had he been readier to sacrifice his principles for office he might have risen even higher than he did.

There are two qualities above all others which we associate with Leo Amery: integrity and courage. His courage, which had often been put to the proof in the mountains, was severely tested in a family tragedy which might well have broken a man of less outstanding fortitude.

In July 1955 he spent a very happy week at Zermatt during the Centenary celebrations of the first ascent of Monte Rosa, and of the first opening of the

Monte Rosa Hotel. He was elected honorary president of the organising committee. At the Centenary dinner he spoke, mainly in German, and I have seldom known a speaker more successful in capturing and holding his audience. He spoke simply but effectively of all that the mountains had meant to him, and I was not the only mountaineer in this gathering who felt that we were listening to Amery's farewell to the mountains.

That week in Zermatt was a perfect ending to his long and happy associations with his beloved mountains. A few weeks after leaving Zermatt he died quietly in his sleep in the early hours of September 16th, 1955.

The Post War Return to the Alps

When the Second World War ended, many of our younger mountaineers had never seen the Alps. For their immediate seniors the war had meant an exile of at least seven, and in some cases eight years from the Alps. It was among our own native crags that the younger climbers were initiated into mountaineering. Many of them spent their leaves in Cumberland, Wales or Scotland, and some were trained for mountain warfare under Frank Smythe.

Currency difficulties, under which term I include shortage of pounds sterling, delayed the return of the younger climbers to the Alps, and the Alpine tragedies of 1947, which robbed the younger generation of the example of two brilliant mountaineers, Barford and Kretschmer, still further postponed the renaissance.

After both World Wars the revival of outstanding mountaineering began in the Universities. After the First World War it was the guideless ascent of the Brouillard Ridge of Mont Blanc by Wyn Harris and Van Noorden, both of Cambridge, which set a standard soon to be followed by the leading mountaineers of the University Clubs. After the Second World War Tom Bourdillon of Oxford and Cym Smith of Cambridge, killed in a motor accident in 1952, fired their contemporaries with the ambition to prove that Grade VI climbs were not the monopoly of continental climbers.

Some of our younger mountaineers had begun to experiment with artificial climbing shortly before the War, and it was even then apparent that they were not to be deterred from mastering the new techniques by appeals to the traditions of the Alpine Club.

The University mountaineers, and a group of Northern climbers who had founded the Rock and Ice Club, provided the nucleus for the Alpine Climbing Group which was founded in the Old Dungeon Ghyll Hotel on January 31st, 1953, and modelled on the Groupe de Haute Montagne.

Even before the war ended the dialectic between the pitonists (if one may coin a word for the experts in piton technique) and the traditionalists was not

196

wholly dormant, and in a book written during the war I criticised the association in the minds of many traditionalists between artificial climbing and the Nazi-Fascist dictators. My arguments were in substance the same as those which I have advanced in this book.

In the post-war period our younger mountaineers were in the main converted to what they described as "progress in technique", thereby placidly begging the question as to whether artificial climbing represents progress or decadence. The traditionalists retorts that legitimate progress in mountaineering may be compared to telescopic sights; hammering pitons up an otherwise inaccessible cliff to the use of atomic weapons in Big Game shooting.

My own view is that the conflict between the traditionalists and the pitonists is best described by borrowing Hegel's definition of tragedy: "The conflict not between Right and Wrong but between Right and Right." The traditionalists and the pitonists both have an arguable case, and perhaps we should seek for a Hegelian synthesis in this development of Dialectical Alpinism.

"We climb to please ourselves", writes the editor of *The Alpine Journal*, "and ideally each peg is removed by the party placing it." *Ideally*, perhaps, but in practice many pegs are left in place, even on climbs where they need never have been used. Let the thesis of the traditionalists and the antithesis of the pitonists be resolved by the synthesis of a concordat restricting the use of pitons to those ridges and faces which are beyond the powers of the free climbers, and if a piton be inserted for the use of a mediocre performer, let it be a point of honour to remove it.

Meanwhile, even those who believe that sin came into our mountain world when the first piton was planted in the Rock Garden of Eden will be consoled by the thought that our young climbers have proved that they can tackle the Grade VI climbs, and put up quite as good a performance as the continental cracks. The reputation of our younger climbers today is exceptionally high, thanks to the achievements of Tom Bourdillon, Hamish Nicol, R.R.E. Chorley, G. Sutton, George Band, Vince Ridgeway, Ted Wrangham and a remarkable Scots group, D. D. Stewart, T. Patey, J. R. Marshall and H. MacInnes. Joe Brown signalised his first appearance in the Alps by selecting for his first two climbs, the north-west face of the Olan and the east ridge of the Crocodile. His ascent of the west face of the Dru with Don Whillans has already been referred to.

Little of importance remained in the way of Alpine novelties but in the Himalaya the Alpine Club prepared for their centenary celebrations by two major achievements, Everest and Kangchenjunga.

The literary output of our countrymen has shown no sign of flagging since the war. Many of the best books produced during and after the war have already been mentioned. Among those which have not been referred to I recall with particular pleasure *Approach to the Hills* by C. F. Meade, *Mountain Paths* by H. E. G. Tyndale, *Mountain Holidays* by Janet Adam Smith, *The Delectable Mountains* by Douglas Busk and not only with pleasure but with gratitude Gavin de Beer's *Travellers in Switzerland*, an indispensable source book for anybody who is interested, either as a reader or as a writer, in the historical associations of the Swiss Alps.

CHAPTER XVII

EVEREST

The story is told that one day in 1852 an Anglo-Indian computer rushed into the office of the Surveyor-General, Sir Andrew Waugh, at Dehra Dun, and exclaimed: "Sir, I have discovered the highest peak in the world." Peak XV which he had estimated on the basis of many calculations as 29,002 ft. above the sea, was later given the name of Everest in honour of the previous Surveyor-General, Sir George Everest.

Nobody took a more active interest in the early Everest expeditions than Sir Francis Younghusband. Younghusband was born, on May 31st, 1863, into an Indian military family. His father, a Major-General, served with Sir Charles Napier in Sind. He joined the 1st Dragoon Guards and went to India in 1882, where he soon made his name as an explorer, being the first Englishman to reach India overland from China. In 1904, he commanded a small punitive expedition and imposed on Lhasa terms which the then Secretary of State for India refused to ratify for fear of antagonising Russia, a curious anticipation of far baser experiments in appeasement. Though Younghusband was warmly supported by both Curzon and King Edward VII, he was left to end his official career as Resident in Kashmir. In his later years his two all-absorbing interests were the World Congress of Faiths, which he founded, and the Everest expeditions, of which he is recognised to be the father.

The admirable chapters in Dr. Seaver's biography describing Younghusband's military expeditions near the frontier awaken a nostalgia for Victorian England. On one occasion, accompanied by only three Gurkhas—the rest of his escort had been left behind to cover the retreat if this became necessary—Younghusband penetrated into the very fortress of a chieftain who had been raiding British territory. Had his confidence faltered for one moment he would almost certainly have been shot. "He said that the Queen of England was naturally displeased that her subjects were raided, and had sent him to see their chief and arrange that this practice should cease:"

> To those people I was the embodiment, the incarnation of the spirit which animates England. And I could feel England expecting me to bear myself in a manner worthy of her. I knew that these men, who had never seen an Englishman

before, were eyeing me minutely, and through a thousand little ways were forming their opinion of England. . . .

The first expedition which was expected to make a general reconnaissance of the approaches to Everest left England in 1921 under the leadership of Colonel C. K. Howard-Bury. A full-scale attempt to climb Everest was made in 1922 under the leadership of General C. G. Bruce. Bruce, who had commanded the Gurkhas in Gallipoli and on the north-west frontier, was beloved by them. In 1951 W. H. Murray was stopped by a Gurkha outside Katmandu.

> "He told me (writes W. H. Murray) some of the tales from the Bruce saga. He so obviously worshipped the man that I had not the heart to say that Bruce was dead. And thus it is everywhere. Bruce and his exploits—feats of strength and of all manner of immoderation from Bacchanalian jest to swift decisive courage in action—have become legendary in Nepal. His memory stays alive in the Hills."

George Finch, who with Geoffrey Bruce established a height record in the course of this expedition, was the protagonist of using oxygen on Everest, and at first he was in a small minority. There was a general feeling that it would be far more in accordance with the traditions of mountaineering to climb Everest without oxygen. On May 25th Finch and Bruce reached a height of 27,300 ft.

The climbers reassembled towards the end of May at the Base Camp for recuperation. On June 7th George Mallory, Dr. Howard Somervell, C. G. Crawford and one Sherpa, climbing on the same rope, followed by thirteen other Sherpas on three ropes, had nearly reached the North Col on the ascent when the entire party was swept away in an avalanche, the lower part of which carried nine Sherpas over a cliff into a crevasse. Two were dug out alive and the rest were killed. This disaster brought the second expedition to an end.

The third expedition left Darjeeling on March 25th, 1924. On June 4th Colonel Norton and Dr. Howard Somervell made a determined attempt on the summit. At 27,500 ft. there was a sudden change, for whereas up till then they could walk comfortably taking three or four breaths a step, now seven to ten complete respirations were necessary. At the height of just over 28,000 ft. Somervell could go no further. Norton struggled on for an hour but only gained 100 ft. in height. The point at which he turned back was later established by theodolite to be 28,126 ft. above the sea.

On June 6th George Mallory and Andrew Irvine started on what proved to be their last climb.

Andrew Irvine was born on April 8th, 1902, and educated at Shrewsbury and Merton College, Oxford. He rowed in the Oxford boat in 1922 and in 1923 when Oxford were victorious. He spent some weeks at Mürren in the winter of 1923–24, and won the Strang-Watkins Slalom against some strong competitors. Irvine was an original member of the Kandahar Ski Club, the senior slalom race of which still bears his name. No man enjoyed ski-ing more. "When I am an old man", he wrote, "I will look back on Christmas, 1923, as the day when to all intents and purposes I was born. I don't think anyone has *lived* until they have been on ski."

Irvine was twelve years younger than the average age of the Everest Expedition, but, as Colonel Norton pointed out, he took his place on terms of equality with his seniors. His lack of self-assertion, combined with a certain seriousness of purpose, made him seem older than his years. He was always natural, always himself. He never tried to appear old when talking to his seniors, or young when talking to small boys. I remember the grave courtesy with which he listened to the eager questions of my own small son, who was interested in the Everest Expedition and in the scientific aspect of oxygen, etc. He hurled a succession of questions at Irvine with all the ruthlessness of a small boy who has at last discovered a patient victim. Irvine replied with as much care as if he had been giving evidence before a committee of oxygen experts. Nor did his kindness stop there. From the Himalaya he wrote three long letters to Peter. Few young men would have had enough imagination to realise the joy which such letters would cause, or enough unselfishness to make the real effort to write them among all the excitements of that great adventure.

His last letter to Peter ended with an expression of hope that they would "reach the summit on Ascension Day".

Irvine was the oxygen expert on the Everest Expedition, but his sympathies were with those who longed to conquer Everest without oxygen. "I really hate the thought of oxygen", he wrote, "I'd give anything to make a non-oxygen attempt. I think I'd sooner get to the foot of the final pyramid without oxygen than to the top with it. . . . Still, as I'm the oxygen mechanic, I've got to go with the beastly stuff."

"The English", said an old chronicler, "love rather to live well than to live long." Irvine did not live long, but he lived well. Into his short life he crowded an overflowing measure of activity which found its climax in his last wonderful year, a year during which he rowed in the winning Oxford boat, explored Spitsbergen, fell in love with ski-ing, and was chosen as Mallory's companion for the final attempt on Everest. Somewhere below the summit his body lies—*Caelo tegitur qui non urnam habet*—thousands of feet above the loftiest of all the unnumbered graves of unnumbered generations.

> Here let us leave him; for his shroud the snow
> For funeral lamps he has the planets seven.
> For a great sign the icy stair shall go
> Between the stars to heaven.

Mallory and Irvine started from Camp VI on June 8th.

"At 12.50 (writes Odell), just after I had emerged in a state of jubilation at finding the first definite fossils on Everest, there was a sudden clearing of the atmosphere, and the entire summit ridge and final peak of Everest were unveiled. My eyes became fixed on one tiny black spot silhouetted on a small snow crest beneath a rock-step in the ridge, and the black spot moved. Another black spot became apparent and moved up the snow to join the other on the crest. The first then approached the great rock-step and shortly emerged on the top; the second did likewise. Then the whole fascinating vision vanished, enveloped in cloud once more."

Odell returned from Camp V, where he had seen Mallory and Irvine within a thousand feet of the summit, to Camp IV. It was a moonlight night, and Odell and Hazard waited outside their tent watching the upper slopes with anxiety for the magnesium flares with which Mallory had promised to signal. The next day Odell returned for the second time to Camp VI. Odell's sustained efforts for day after day at altitudes varying between 23,000 and 27,000 ft. is one of the finest feats of endurance ever recorded in the history of mountaineering. Within four days he had climbed to 27,000 ft. without oxygen, and slept eleven nights at 23,000 ft. or higher. There was no sign of Mallory or Irvine. 4000 ft. below Hazard was watching him through field glasses while Odell arranged sleeping bags left in Camp VI on a patch of snow in the form of a letter T which by arrangement meant "No trace". Hazard sent the tragic news to Camp III where Norton, Bruce, Noel and Hingston were still waiting. "And the memory of these days", wrote Norton, "is such that Camp III must remain to all of us the most hateful place in the world."

Before leaving the Base Camp the expedition raised a cairn to the memory of twelve men who had fallen on the three Everest expeditions. Three more were to die before Everest was climbed.

The disappearance of Mallory and Irvine had a strange sequel. I pointed out to Sir Oliver Lodge that if spiritualists solved the problem of their last ascent, and if a subsequent expedition corroborated the spirit messages received, their success could not be explained away by telepathy between the living. In the course of the next year Sir Oliver Lodge sent me a series of scripts purporting to come from Mallory. Many such messages were received by mediums in different parts of the world, and all, so far as I know, agreed on one point. Mallory and Irvine reached the summit.

On the 1933 expedition Wyn Harris found an ice-axe at the height of about 27,500 ft. which must have belonged to Mallory or Irvine. The tilted slabs offer no definite foothold, and if one had slipped the other must inevitably have been dragged down with him. In the event of a slip on such rock the man who has not slipped will at once discard his axe to hold the rope with both hands. W.H. Murray summarises the evidence which strongly suggests that the fall must have occurred on the ascent, as it is almost certain that another line would have been taken on the descent.

Even before he died the Mallory legend was in the process of being created. His pioneer ascent of one of the more direct routes on Lliwedd was popularly attributed to the fact that he was descending one of the easier buttresses and found that he had left his pipe on the summit and returned by the shortest route to the top. It was not only his mountaineering prowess which created this legend but his exceptional charm. "He was", wrote Mr. Arthur Benson, "the most modest and least self-conscious of men. He spoke willingly of his own experiences but he never introduced the subject himself, nor showed the smallest desire for recognition. This was, I think, the essence of his wonderful charm, that he was so unconscious of his great personal beauty, his gifts, and his achievements, while his sympathy with those with whom he came in contact, their tastes, their preferences, their opinions, was deep and genuine."

As the Mallory legend took shape, it was perhaps inevitable that he should not only be credited with his own outstanding qualities, but that a non-existent profundity should be attributed to some of his sayings, as for instance the patient reply which he gave to an importunate stranger. After a lecture at Philadelphia he was intercepted by a lady who asked him: "Why do you want to climb Everest?" And his reply: "Because it is there", is a good example of the technique which lecturers develop to evade the last bore who stands between them and a much needed drink.

As a writer, Mallory was most effective in his unstudied letters, and certainly a Greek would have appreciated the dramatic irony of the sentences which bring to an end his last despatch.

"Action is only suspended before the more intense action of the climax. The issue will shortly be decided. The third time we walk up East Rongbuk Glacier will be the last, for better or for worse. We expect no mercy from Everest."

In 1933 Frank Smythe, P. Wyn Harris and L.R. Wager reached on two different attempts approximately the same height as Norton. In 1935 Eric Shipton led a monsoon reconnaissance. The 1936 and 1938 expeditions were defeated by bad weather conditions.

Tibet was closed to mountaineers after the war even before it was occupied by Communists. The first post-war attempt on Everest was made by a party which included E.P. Hillary, Tom Bourdillon and W.H. Murray, the historian of Everest. This expedition, led by Eric Shipton, forced their way up the Khumbu Icefall only to be halted by a gigantic crevasse.

The British hoped to follow up this attempt with a full-scale expedition in 1952 and were dismayed to learn that the Nepal Government would only permit one expedition a year and had granted permission for 1952 to the Swiss.

In recent years a convention has found fairly wide acceptance among Himalayan explorers that certain mountains were ear-marked for certain countries. Thus Nanga Parbat came to be regarded as a German mountain. Similarly, the British have felt that Everest is in some sense their mountain. Between the Wars the British organised two reconnaissances and five full-scale expeditions, all of which failed to reach the highest point. Clearly there was a time-limit beyond which the moral claim to exclusive right of access to an unconquered Himalayan peak could not be maintained.

I remember a conversation in America before the war with a distinguished American mountaineer, who alleged that the British acquiesced rather too easily in the fact that the Tibetans were not disposed to give permission to any parties other than British who passed through their territory on the way to Everest. It is, however, difficult to see what else the British could have done but "acquiesce" in the Tibetan disinclination to permit others than ourselves to go to Everest. The Tibetans were suspicious of *all* foreigners—less of us than of others, though they were far from enthusiastic about our expeditions. We could hardly be expected to say that we would not go unless mountaineers from other countries were allowed access to Everest.

The Swiss generously offered the British the opportunity of joining forces, and a proposal to this effect was discussed at a dinner party at Mürren at which I had the honour of entertaining Ernst Feuz, one of the greatest of Swiss mountaineers, and Basil Goodfellow, the Honorary Secretary of the Alpine Club. This offer was the more generous because the Swiss had been disappointed in 1951, as they had entertained some hopes that one or two members of the Swiss party might be allowed to join in Shipton's assault. After the Swiss had been told that it was too late to make additions, two New Zealand mountaineers were admitted.[1] The Swiss proposal was that the Swiss and British should organise Anglo-Swiss expeditions in 1952 and 1953, the Swiss to provide the leader in 1952 and the British in 1953. I was greatly impressed by the attitude of the Swiss as far as the 1952 expedition was concerned, and a remark by Herr Feuz deserves to be recorded: "It would be very nice in this Olympic year of bitter rivalry between different nations if the triumph of Everest could be shared by the Swiss and the British."

Though I was disappointed at the time when the Swiss offer was turned down, even the least chauvinistic of Englishmen must rejoice that Everest was finally climbed by a party of which every amateur was British. There were other and

[1] See page 179.

better reasons than nationalistic for Sir John Hunt's decision to restrict the amateur members of the party to British subjects. Altitude and extreme cold are an exacting strain of team-spirit even in a homogeneous party, and furthermore the difficulties of climbing Everest would be greatly aggravated if the leader had to consider national susceptibilities and rivalries in selecting his assault parties. The distasteful fashion in which Communists and Indian Nationalists exploited Tenzing's share in the victory has its own moral in this connection.

In 1952 a Swiss expedition made two attempts on the mountain, the first in the spring, the second in the autumn.

The crevasse which stopped Shipton's party was crossed in 1952 by a brilliant feat of icemanship. Asper was lowered 60 ft. to a point where the crevasse was partially choked by fallen blocks of ice. He then cut steps up the opposite side after which it was easy to construct a rope bridge. Lambert and Tenzing reached a record height of 28,250 ft. before being turned back. The Swiss made a second attempt in the autumn and *as late as* November 19th reached a height of 26,575 ft. after braving a wind of gale force and a temperature of minus 30 degrees Centigrade.

Avant-Premières à l'Everest, the story of the expedition, by Gabriel Chevalley, René Dittert and Raymond Lambert, is always readable and sometimes dramatic. Its approach varies from romanticism to uncompromising realism. "Aucun de nous, je crois", writes René Dittert, "n'est venu ici par vanité, pour la gloire."

All that is necessary by way of comment on this claim is to quote one sentence from the memorandum of the Swiss Foundation which financed the expedition: "It is worth while to climb the highest peak in the world; the deed would always be mentioned in the history books." This, as Janet Adam Smith rightly remarks, "is a refreshing acknowledgement of that wish for fame of which, unlike the first Elizabethans, we have become so scared".

And now by way of contrast let me quote René Dittert in a mood of almost disconcerting realism. He is writing of the demoralising effect of cold and exhaustion on team spirit. After describing an outburst of temper he writes: "Extreme exhaustion brings everything out of a man, his injustice and his violence. This proves nothing excepting that he is a man. Those who, when they have recovered their equilibrium wish to pass for angels are in bad faith. All those who have climbed to 8000 m. in bad conditions must admit that they have often felt bitter and hostile towards their companions on the rope. Whether we wish it or not, everybody's first thought is for his own skin, his own interests and his own life rather than the lives of others. I write of the things about which it is usual to keep silent. *Tant pis*, for I dislike phoney ideals and lies. The manifestations of the instinct of self-preservation are often brutal, and I console myself with the reflection that those who remain polite and amiable and gracious in all circumstances have not perhaps climbed to 8000 m. and endured three days of fierce tempest at that height."

A Swiss who had climbed in the Himalaya remarked to me that one of the signs of demoralisation in high altitudes is the neglect of normal precautions. He mentioned specifically the neglect to rope on snow-covered glaciers. There is a good example of this in *The Mountain World* in which Léon Flory describes an incident in the course of the Swiss expedition to Everest. He was "plodding through the melting snow above Camp III", and lost his balance as a snowbridge collapsed below him. He fell with his hands against the opposite wall of the crevasse, and by a superhuman effort saved himself. But why was he unroped? He leaves this question unanswered but adds: "This kind of incident was repeated, alas, and with less luck, might have resulted in a casualty among the Sherpas."

The initial obstacle on the Nepal face is the Khumbu Icefall which consists of two sections, each of which is about a thousand feet in height, separated by a more gradual shelf. The icefall had to be attacked, for on each side of the icefall are the receptacles for the constant ice avalanches which fall from the slopes of Everest and of Nuptse.

The first problem is the Khumbu Icefall, the second the great crevasse which separates the head of the icefall from the Western Cwm, a crevasse which was crossed by means of ladders brought specially for this purpose. The third problem is that of the Lhotse face, which rises 4000 ft. from the head of the Cwm to the South Col. The Lhotse face consists of steep slopes of hard snow, revealing occasional streaks of shining ice, and intersected by a rocky ridge, named the Eperon des Genevois by the Swiss. This ridge is extremely steep, and nowhere provides a ledge for a camp. The Swiss spent eight days exploring this face. The first party to reach the col spent a miserable night *en route* in an impromptu bivouac on a small ledge of ice hacked out by the ice-axes. They were too tightly packed into their emergency tent to get into their sleeping bags.

The British, profiting by the Swiss experience, worked out a line on the Lhotse face which enabled them to establish two proper camps between the base of the Lhotse Wall and the South Col. The establishment of these camps, and of the camp on the South Col, called for careful planning and great endurance on the part of those Sherpas who carried heavy loads without oxygen to the South Col. Of the British, both Noyce and Wylie reached the South Col without oxygen, carrying heavier loads than some of the Sherpas.

On May 26th Tom Bourdillon and Charles Evans reached the south shoulder of Everest at a height of 28,700 ft.; the highest point till then climbed by man. Finally, on May 29th, which was incidentally the five hundredth anniversary of the fall of Constantinople, Edmund Hillary and Tenzing reached the summit of Everest.

The summit is approximately the same height above the Base Camp as Mont Blanc above Chamonix. If the Base Camp could be lowered 14,000 ft. and the summit of Everest correspondingly lowered; if climbers could be certain of enjoying the climatic conditions and the same temperatures as are enjoyed by mountaineers ascending Mont Blanc in a spell of good weather; and if there were a club hut at the foot of the Lhotse face a strong party of guideless climbers could climb Everest in two days from the Base Camp.[1]

Even if the Base Camp and summit of Everest could be lowered some 14,000 ft., and alpine climatic conditions guaranteed, Everest would not be an easy mountain, for the Khumbu Icefall would rank as difficult in the Alps. Above this icefall there is nothing on the Lhotse face which would worry experienced mountaineers, and the greatest difficulty on the final ridge, the steep pitch brilliantly led by Sir Edmund Hillary, could almost certainly be avoided by a party which had time and energy to explore alternative routes on the rock face to the west.

It is therefore a measure of the difficulties due to climate and altitude that whereas an Alpine replica of Everest could be climbed in two days, the successful expedition spent forty-seven days from the Base Camp to the summit.

In *High Adventure* Sir Edmund Hillary describes the climax of the expedition. He ignores the controversy fanned by hysterical nationalism which flared up on the return of the expedition to Katmandu. His references to Tenzing are, as might be expected, consistently friendly, and there is nothing unfriendly in the factual comment that Tenzing was "an inexpert but enthusiastic step-cutter". Tenzing, in the story of his life as related to James Ramsey Ullman *(Man of Everest)* insisted that the steep pitch which was the crux of the climb, and which Hillary led, was only 15 ft. in height, but on this point Hillary's account would be conclusive even if his estimate had not subsequently been confirmed by the Swiss who made the second and third ascents of Everest.

"The next moment I was reaching over the top of the rock and pulling myself into safety. The rope came tight—its 40 ft. had been barely enough."

And here is the reaction on the summit:

"My first sensation was one of relief . . . but mixed with the relief was a vague sense of astonishment that I should have been the lucky one to attain the ambition of so many brave and determined climbers. But as it seemed difficult at first to grasp that we'd got there, I was too tired and too conscious of the long way down to safety really to feel any great elation. But as the fact of our success thrust itself more clearly into my mind, I felt a quiet glow of satisfaction spread through my body—a satisfaction less vociferous but more powerful than I had ever felt on a mountain top before.

[1] I submitted this paragraph to Wilfrid Noyce who writes: "If you removed the problem of altitude Everest could certainly be done in two days. The rock step would be nothing at 15,000 ft. even without the chimney."

An interesting paper for the Alpine Club could be written by comparing the best descriptive passages of which the theme is the first moments on the summit of a long coveted first ascent. Whymper's "Crowded hour of glorious life" on the crest of the Matterhorn is the most famous of such passages; Geoffrey Young's reflection after completing the first ascent of the east face of the Weisshorn is perhaps the most interesting. Dent on the Dru is also memorable. The few paragraphs which have the note of Greek simplicity in which Hillary recalls what he felt when he reached the crest of the world are less eloquent than Whymper and less analytical than Young.

Meanwhile Wilfrid Noyce was fighting his way up to the South Col. It was his second ascent. He had no oxygen but he contrived to coax his heavily laden Sherpas to the pass, a splendid effort. Noyce was to make the third attempt if Hillary failed. He reached the Col just in time to see Hillary and Tenzing descending the last slopes after their victory. Noyce in his book *South Col* describes what follows. George Lowe went out to meet them.

> "George had met them by now . . . then there were three figures coming down the slope towards me . . . Now they were waving his axe. 'They've done it.' He pointed his ice-axe towards the top. . . . That meant Everest climbed. Job done. Good—*wonderful*. Now we can go down. No more problems . . . At the back of my heart I knew that, had they failed, I would have been of the third party. But that mattered nothing now. I can certainly remember no disappointment for myself at all.
> 'Do you know what Ed said when I met him first?', George asked. 'He said: 'Well, we knocked the bastard off.' "

When Hillary received a letter some days later, a letter addressed to "Sir Edmund Hillary, K.B.E." he thought it was a joke, and when convinced that it was not, remarked:

> "You go and have a good time on a mountain and then this happens to you. How on earth am I going into the grocer back home now in my old trousers to ask him for pots of honey?"

Meanwhile John Hunt was waiting at the lower camp. Sir John Hunt's style in his fascinating book *The Ascent of Everest* is restrained, perhaps a little too restrained, but there are some passages in which the reader is conscious of undertones of emotion in spite of the author's reticence, notably the very moving passage describing Sir John's feeling as he waited for Hillary and Tenzing to return. The Indian wireless news bulletins had just informed the world that the expedition had failed when five men could be seen above the camp slowly approaching.

208

"The approaching climbers made no sign, just plodded on dejectedly towards us; they did not even wave a greeting. My heart sank. In my weak state this plod up the track was already an effort. This must be failure. . . . Suddenly, the leading man in the party—it was George Lowe—raised his axe, pointing unmistakably towards the distant top of Everest; he made several vigorous thrusts. The others behind him were now making equally unequivocal thrusts. Far from failure, this was IT! they had made it!!"

On the return to Katmandu, Tenzing declined to attend the official reception at the Embassy because he had asked to be put up in the Embassy when he accompanied the Swiss and had been "turned away", but a special quarter in the Embassy Compound had been provided for him on the British Expedition in 1953 and he had stayed at the Embassy with Tilman in 1949, and it was for the Swiss not for the British Embassy to provide him with accommodation when he was travelling with the Swiss. Tenzing is reported by James Ramsey Ullman as saying:

"With the Swiss and the French I had been treated as a comrade, an equal, in a way that is not possible for the British. They are kind men: they are brave; they are always fair and just, always. But always, too, there is a line between them and the outsider, between Sahib and employee, and to such Easterns as we Sherpas, who have experienced the world of 'no line', this can be a difficulty and a problem."

John Hunt, in answer to some questions which I put to him, writes:

"As in the case of previous expeditions on which he has taken part, Tenzing was engaged as Sirdar of the high altitude Sherpas; as such he was naturally on a different footing from the other members of the climbing party, in that he was a professional paid for a specific purpose. With this proviso, however, we treated him from the start as one of the members of the climbing party. He was constantly consulted, shared our tents and was free to join us socially in camp when he so desired. There is still, however—and will be for some years—a certain mutual reluctance to achieve a status of literal equality between Sahibs and Sherpas. This is a matter of background, interests, language, diet, etc., etc. In Tenzing's case we reduced this to a minimum, but in the case of the other Sherpas, many of whom we knew well already, both preferred to maintain the same happy relationship that we have always had."

When the South Col was first reached the Sherpa Anullu quietly annexed a fine Swiss rucksack containing felt boots, and when Noyce protested "Hey, other people will need that", Anullu returned the laconic reply that Tenzing had promised him that if he reached the Col first he was to have the first spoil. The initial difficulties with the Sherpas were mainly due to the fact that the Swiss had established a precedent which the British were loth to follow, handing over all surplus stores and equipment including tents to the Sherpas at the end of the expedition.

When I asked Sir John if he would review Mr. Ullman's book on Tenzing he at first hesitated and finally agreed, though very overworked at the time. He agreed because, at least I believe because, he felt that he could thereby make an important contribution to maintain the perfect team work on Everest. A lesser man might have been irritated by the invidious comparisons between the British and the Swiss, but there is nothing forced in the magnanimity of his reaction and the review is worth quoting not only as a discerning comment on the relations between the British and the Sherpas, but still more because it helps to explain the affection which John Hunt evoked in the Everest team and the secret of the leadership which ensured success.

"As we returned (writes Hunt) to Katmandu I could discern in the attitude of sections in the crowd emotions of adoration, for to many simple peoples of Nepal and India, Tenzing was visited with God-like powers. This fact, and the inevitable opportunism of others, not so simple, who saw in Tenzing's unique position a potent political axe or a magnet to entice the shekels from the pockets of the ingenuous, must be remembered when we open Tenzing's biography.

"It was because of the harm which had apparently been done in our happy relationship in the eyes of the world by those who wished us ill, that I opened my copy with some misgivings. Privately, of course, my conscience was quiet and I was not in doubt, for the Everest adventure had forged unbreakable bonds between us all, and Tenzing and I have maintained the most cordial contacts ever since. But might not the written record be designed to appeal to the sensational appetite of a larger public, which had earlier goggled at the story of squabbles in our party as to who had first set foot on the top of Everest? And could the writer be expected to interpret aright the exact meaning of words translated for him by a third party — for Tenzing is illiterate? Such were my doubts.

"I need not have worried. Here, in my view, is a most remarkable book. Remarkable because of the man it reveals. For a Sherpa, Tenzing is surprisingly widely travelled and his experiences are diverse. Throughout, his wisdom shines forth, the clear vision and understanding of life possessed by one whose mind is unfettered by the preconceived notions of formal education. Above all, we can discern his simple modesty. Tenzing has retained, despite the adulation of the millions, a sense of proportion about himself. He might well have been persuaded that he possessed supernatural powers, yet he recognises that he is an ordinary human being. By his modesty in this and his honesty in relating the vexed question of the arrival of Hillary and himself on the summit, we can appreciate the greatness of the man.

"The book is remarkable too, for the fact that Ullman has interpreted the real Tenzing whom I knew. He has revealed his frank, engaging manner, his quaint mode of expressing his thoughts, almost even his wide smile and the dancing humour in his eyes. Ullman, too, has shown himself to be a remarkable man.

"I do not propose to spoil the reading of others by summarising the contents of this delightful story. Only about two points do I desire to comment. Firstly, there is Tenzing's general opinion about Swiss and British climbers he has met, as companions. I believe there is substance in what he has said, namely, that we tend to be aloof and lack the warm camaraderie of some Continental peoples. This reserve of ours is proverbial. It has nothing to do with the background of our rule in India, but it is certainly a handicap. It naturally contrasts with the convivial temperament of the Sherpas, who find themselves in this respect more akin to certain others, in particular the Latin peoples. It should not be inferred, however, that we kept a barrier between the Sherpas and ourselves; there is no closer proximity than the inside of a small tent, and many times each of us shared a tent with them. Nor let it be supposed that the Swiss maintained relations of complete equality with the Sherpas. They did not; nor is it yet possible to have such intimate relations between people whose background, language and food preferences differ so widely. Tenzing alone was treated as a full member of the climbing party by the Swiss, as he was by us.

"The reader should also know that the Swiss, like ou selves, had to face difficulties with their Sherpas over conditions of employment. They were more fortunate in being financially more free to solve them. Every big expedition has faced similar problems and we were less troubled than most. Indeed, we would never have climbed Everest had we not been a happy, well-knit team, Sherpas and Sahibs alike." (British Ski Year Book 1955.)

The 1953 expedition succeeded for many reasons which may be enumerated as follows: In the first place it enjoyed weather conditions without which success would have been impossible. Everest can only be climbed in the brief lull between the winter gales and the monsoon, but there is no certainty of any lull between the winter gales and the monsoon. The Swiss experience of attempting Everest between the monsoon and the gales of the following winter seems to rule out this period as offering any serious hope of reaching the summit of Everest.

Secondly, the 1953 expedition would not have succeeded but for the fact that their oxygen apparatus was far in advance of the oxygen apparatus used by the Swiss. The experimental "closed circuit" oxygen equipment was developed by Dr. Bourdillon, the father of Tom Bourdillon who made the first ascent of the South Peak of Everest. Peter Lloyd was the oxygen adviser responsible to the joint Himalayan Comm ttee and perhaps the main burden of the work fell on the shoulders of A. W. Bridge, the oxygen executive. The Swiss arrived at the South Col in a far more exhausted condition because they had chosen a direct route and attempted to dispense with intermediate camps on the Lhotse face. The support parties were therefore not in a position to give the same assistance to Lambert and Tenzing in their final push for the summit as the supporting parties in the 1953 expedition. It is interesting in this connection to contrast the conditions enjoyed in the nights passed in the highest camps on Everest by Lambert and Tenzing in 1952 and by Edmund Hillary and Tenzing in 1953. The latter passed a comparatively comfortable night. Lambert and Tenzing, on the other hand, camping at 27,200 ft., had no sleeping bags, no mattresses, no stove and nothing to drink excepting snow melted by candle flames. The night was a terrible one. The fact that they climbed 700 ft. from this camp on the following day is astonishing. Well might W. H. Murray write: "No more heroic effort has ever been made to reach the summit of Everest."

The third reason for success was summed up by John Hunt in a letter to me which he allows me to quote.

> "The Swiss pioneering of the route by the south-west side had an incalculable effect on ourselves who followed them; this has been true of every great ascent in the history of mountaineering. It was not a question of oxygen bottles or food left behind, although these were useful bonuses. We gained immensely in confidence by the knowledge of what they had done, and by the evidence on the mountain that they had done it."

John Hunt is generous in his acknowledgment of all those who had helped to make success possible, with one exception. This exception is understandable, for he could not, without immodesty, have given Claude Elliott the credit which he deserves for his share in the final success. Mr. Elliott, Sir Edwin Herbert's predecessor, was chairman of the Himalayan Committee who were faced with an awkward choice between two candidates for leadership each of whom had quite exceptional qualifications. The decision for which Claude Elliott took the responsibility was inevitably criticised in certain quarters. It is no disparagement to the other candidate to state that it would be difficult to conceive of a finer leader than John Hunt.

And this brings me to the fourth, and by no means the least important factor in the success of the expedition—superb leadership. A Swiss who had climbed in the Himalaya remarked to me: "The British succeeded because no expedition has been better planned or better organised or enjoyed better leadership and better team-work."

> "The secret (writes Mr. Wilfrid Noyce) lay in his way of treating everybody as a friend, as a potential helper in a worthy cause. He believed immensely in the inspiration of Everest to the world; and officials, manufacturers, diplomats and ourselves had no choice but to agree. Behind this was a deep religious sense. John once said, round a camp-fire at Thyanboche: 'I don't mind admitting that mountains make me pray.' And the sense of so earnest a conviction added to the charm of the convinced. On the mountain he could have persuaded the most ambitious that he was doing the one vital job of the expedition, peeling potatoes at Base Camp."

John Hunt's *Ascent of Everest* is a book in which every material factor contributing to the success is recorded with scientific accuracy and it is interesting to find that due importance is attached to non-material imponderables. Sir John had been sent a crucifix by an Ampleforth monk with a request that this should be taken to the summit of Everest, and in acknowledging the gift Sir John asked for the prayers of the community. The crucifix was handed over to Hillary and buried in the snow on the summit of Everest next to the thank-offering placed on the summit in honour of Buddha by Tenzing. After enumerating all the factors which contributed to this great triumph Sir John concludes: "And I would add one more asset, intangible, less easy to assess: the thoughts and prayers of all those many who watched and waited and hoped for our success. We were aware of this hidden force and we were fortified by it."

The Members of the 1953 Everest Expedition

John Hunt, Edmund Hillary, Tenzing, Charles Evans, George Lowe, Wilfrid Noyce, George Band, Alfred Gregory, Tom Bourdillon, Charles Wylie, Michael Westmacott, Michael Ward (expedition doctor), Griffith Pugh (physiologist), Tom Stobart (photography), James Morris (*The Times* correspondent).

The leading Sherpas were Anullu, Dawa Thondup, Da Tenzing, Thondup, Da Namgyal and Ang Nyiama.

Tom Bourdillon, who was the first to reach the South Summit of Everest, was killed with R. M. Viney on the Jägihorn in the Baltschiedertal on July 29th, 1956.

Bourdillon and Viney were members not only of the Alpine Club but also of the Oxford Mountaineering Club and of the Climbers' Club, of which Viney was Honorary Secretary.

In Chapter XVI, which was written before Bourdillon was killed, a tribute is paid to Bourdillon's immense influence on the post-war climbers in Great Britain. Viney had many gifts which would have been of great value to the mountaineering fraternity. Their untimely deaths have robbed the Alpine Club of men who will be difficult to replace.

CHAPTER XVIII

A GREAT DECADE (1946—1956)

Everest was, of course, the supreme achievement of the post-war years, years which however were notable for a series of splendid successes. It is clearly impossible to do more than mention briefly the outstanding climbs, of this period, in those great ranges which still offer the climber virgin peaks in abundance.

In the Andes the most notable ascents were those of Alpamayo in 1951 which has already been mentioned (page 173), and FitzRoy (11,286 ft.) in Argentina. The peak is named after the commander of the "Beagle" in which Charles Darwin, who was the first to record the peak's existence, made his celebrated voyage. It is a peak of outstanding difficulty and only surrendered after a month of siege. It was climbed by Guido Magnone and Lionel Terray, one hundred and ten pitons were used and the climb is recorded in a book which is a notable literary achievement.

One of the most difficult climbs ever accomplished on the American continent was the ascent of the south face of Aconcagua, a face some 10,000 ft. in height, on February 25th, 1954 (four bivouacs), by a French party: Lucien Bérardini, Edmond Denis, Adrien Dagory, Pierre Leseur, Robert Paragot and Guy Poulet.

The Swiss Foundation for Alpine Research

The first recorded statement leading to the formation of the Swiss Foundation for Alpine Research appeared in *Die Alpen*, 1938, being an appeal for Swiss expeditions abroad.

> "Englishmen, Italians, Germans and Frenchmen have sent their best men to explore unclimbed mountains. Switzerland alone, a country of native mountaineers, stands inactively aloof. Matters cannot rest thus. Now more than ever we may not remain mere spectators of the solution of the final and greatest problems; we must contribute our best in noble emulation, to the fame of our mountaineers and the honour of our country.
>
> "From time to time advocates have been heard urging Swiss expeditions abroad; if such appeals have hithertoo fallen on deaf ears, the idea has remained active. Some time ago a group of climbers, members of the Swiss Alpine Club, took up

the idea again and resolved to put all their energy into its realisation. A Swiss Foundation for Extra-Alpine Research was brought into being."[1]

The Foundation was formally constituted on February 10th, 1940, under the presidency of Dr. Robert Schöpfer, ex-President of the Swiss Alpine Club.

The driving spirit behind the Foundation has been from the first Karl Weber. At the beginning of 1951 the Foundation Committee consisted of only five members, Karl Weber, President, Dr. Werner E. Iten, G. Hasler, Dr. Walter Amstutz and Ernst Feuz.

No Continental mountaineering group has done more than the Swiss Foundation to defend the conception of mountaineering to which the Alpine Club attaches supreme importance, the supra-national ideal of a mountain brotherhood. Their titular emblem is a cross enwreathed with a climber's rope and of this emblem Othmar Gurtner writes in the first issue of *The Mountain World*:

"It (the Foundation) trusts that this device may not be identified with the emblem of any nation. As the Red Cross exactly reversing the colours of the Swiss national flag while maintaining its form, raised it to an expression of world wide validity, so we regard the acceptance of our simple rope-encircled cross upon a supra-national level as a symbol of a common endeavour, an *e pluribus unum*, dedicated to Alpine achievement in exploration and mountaineering."

Even before the Foundation was officially instituted an expedition was organised to the Garhwal Himalaya in May 1939, led by André Roch. His two guides were Fritz Steuri of Grindelwald and David Zogg of Arosa. Ernst Huber, the topographer, produced an admirable map of the Kosa and Rataban glaciers.

On July 5th Roch, Zogg and Steuri made the first ascent of Dunagiri (23,184 ft.). On August 8th Huber and two Sherpas made the first ascent of Rataban (20,230 ft.) and on August 18th Roch, Zogg and Steuri made the first ascent of Ghori Parbat (22,010 ft.).

On September 10th the party was overtaken in camp by an avalanche from which the Swiss escaped unhurt but the two Sherpas were killed.

In 1947 the Swiss Foundation organised an expedition to the Garhwal Himalaya, consisting of Mme Annelies Lohner, André Roch, Alexander Graven, Alfred Sutter and René Dittert, and a Rakaposhi reconnaissance.

Three attempts were made on Kedarnath (22,853 ft.). On the second attempt Sutter and the Sherpa Wangdi Norbu fell. Norbu survived two nights in the open with a broken leg. On July 11th Sutter, Dittert, Roch, Graven and Tenzing reached the summit. On August 1st, Sutter, Dittert, Graven and Roch made the first ascent of Satopanth (23,213 ft.). On August 14th Sutter, Dittert and Roch made the first ascent of Kalindi Peak (20,020 ft.) and on August

[1] *The First Ten Years*. Swiss Foundation for Alpine Research, 1951.

25th all the members of the expedition including Mme Lohner climbed the Balbala (21,050 ft.).

In 1948 the Foundation organised an expedition to the Tibesti, a mountain region in the heart of the Sahara. The expedition, which consisted of four members, Chappot, Hildebrand, Dr. Tschudi and Dr. Wyss-Dunant, made the first ascents of Eli Mushgu (9515 ft.) and Ehi Timmi (9914 ft.).

In 1949 the Swiss Foundation organised an expedition consisting of Alfred Sutter, Mme Lohner, Dr. Ed. Wyss-Dunant, medical officer, René Dittert, Jakob Pargätzi-Almer, guide, Adolf Rubi and R. N. Rahul, Indian liaison officer. Sutter, Dittert and Pargätzi made the first ascent of the lower summit of the Pyramid Peak (23,294 ft.).

In 1950 a small expedition was organised by the Foundation to the Garhwal Himalaya. The only English member of the party fell ill at a high camp, but Dittert, Tissières and Dr. Chevalley made the first ascent of Abi Gamin (24,130 ft.).

In 1950 the Swiss Foundation co-operated in an expedition to Baffin Island.

The attempt on Everest in 1952 has been, and the second and third ascents of Everest in 1956 will be described in due course.

Annapurna

In 1949 Lucien Devies obtained permission for a French expedition under the leadership of Maurice Herzog to enter Nepal. At that time, though the 8500-metre mark had been passed on Everest no 8000-metre[1] peak had been climbed, and it was the intention of the French expedition to concentrate on one or other of two 8000-metre peaks, Dhaulagiri (26,811 ft.) and Annapurna (26,492 ft.), the tenth highest mountain in the world. After reconnoitring Dhaulagiri, Herzog decided to attempt Annapurna.

On June 3rd, 1950, Herzog and Louis Lachenal, a famous guide, left the highest camp. They had no oxygen cylinders, and long before they reached the summit they were suffering from the height. Their hard-won triumph was tempered by anxiety, for grey mists swept across the sun as they began their descent, and fought their way down against the rising wind. They were sluggish from lack of oxygen, and suddenly Lachenal noticed that Herzog's hands were bare. He had lost his gloves, the first of many catastrophies.

Lionel Terray and Gaston Rébuffat were awaiting them in the Top Camp. As they approached Lachenal slipped down 300 ft. and, though he broke no bones, he was suffering from shock, when Terray picked him up. Next day they fought their way down to forward Camp IV but failed in the blinding snowstorm

---

[1] 8000 metres = 26,247 feet.

to find it. As night fell they began to dig a hole in the snow. Suddenly Lachenal disappeared into a concealed crevasse, fortunately only a few yards deep—he was less lucky with his next crevasse five years later. In this crevasse they spent a miserable night. They removed their boots, put their feet into their rucksacks and lay close together to generate heat. Before dawn a mass of snow worked loose, fell into the crevasse and buried not only the mountaineers but also their equipment and their precious boots. For over an hour in stockinged feet they dug and groped desperately for the boots. As the sun rose Lachenal and Rébuffat struggled to the rim of the crevasse and shouted for help, and fortunately for them Marcel Schatz had already begun to climb up to Camp IV and heard their shouts.

Schatz led them down in one day to Camp II; shortly before leaving, Annapurna struck again, and overwhelmed Herzog, Rébuffat and two porters in an avalanche. Somehow they contrived to extricate themselves, and to reach Camp II where Doctor Oudot was awaiting them. In the dimly lit tent Oudot worked throughout the night, injecting novaine acetychlorodine to stimulate the blood circulation. The transport down to the Base Camp was an agony for Lachenal and Herzog, and their troubles were by no means over. Amputation was essential, Lachenal lost all his toes, and Herzog all his toes and his fingers. But they would not admit that the price was too high for the glory of the moment when the Tricolour of France flew from the highest peak till then conquered by man. Herzog's book of the expedition deservedly became an international best-seller.

Five years later Lachenal was ski-ing down in November from the Aiguille du Midi. He was unroped, even though he must have realised that the glaciers are never so perilous as in November, when the crevasses are masked but not securely bridged by powdery snow, which has not consolidated. Suddenly he broke through into a concealed crevasse, and, less lucky than on Annapurna, fell to his death. So perished one of the greatest of modern guides.

Tirich Mir

On July 21st, 1950, the monarch of the Hindu Kush Range, Tirich Mir (25,263 ft.) was climbed by Per Kvernberg. Professor Arne Næss, Henry Berg, both Norwegians, and Captain Tony Streather, made the ascent on July 22nd.

Streather, an officer of the Gloucesters who fought in the Korean engagement in which his regiment was acclaimed as "The Glorious Gloucesters", was to take part a little later in the second American attempt on K2 and in the successful assault on Kangchenjunga.

Shortly after Everest had been climbed the long siege of Nanga Parbat (26,660 ft.) ended in a sensational, because solitary, victory of the Austrian mountaineer, Hermann Buhl.

No mountain has made man pay more dearly for victory than Nanga Parbat. The first victim of Nanga Parbat was Mummery whose body has never been found.

In July 1934 Willy Merkl, a Bavarian, whose first attempt on Nanga Parbat had been defeated by storm, was the leader of a brilliant group which included Welzenbach, perhaps the greatest mountaineer of the period. One member of the party died at the base of pneumonia. His friends reached the Silver Saddle at a height of 25,000 ft. before a terrible storm broke. In the desperate retreat through the blizzard Welzenbach, U. Wieland, Merkl and six Sherpas perished, a tragedy redeemed by great heroism. Gaylay the Sherpa, who could probably have saved himself, remained behind with Merkl who was at the end of his strength, and died with him. Another Sherpa, Ang Tsering, was awarded the medal of the German Red Cross in recognition of his gallantry.

In 1937 a new assault on Nanga Parbat was launched by a party which included Müllritter, who had survived the 1934 disaster, and which was led by Karl Wien. Every climber in the camp, seven amateurs and nine Sherpas, perished in an avalanche which overwhelmed their tents as they slept.

One Englishman, two Gurkhas, eleven Germans and fifteen Sherpas had died in three attempts on Nanga Parbat. In 1938 Paul Bauer[1] led an expedition which was defeated by bad weather. In 1950 two Englishmen, J. W. Thornley and W. H. Crace disappeared on the Rakhiot Glacier, bringing the total death roll up to thirty-two.

Hermann Buhl has described not only his remarkable adventure on Nanga Parbat, but also his earlier life, in an excellent book, *8000 drüber und drunter*. Buhl was born in Innsbruck. His family lived on the margin of poverty and he was often in great trouble at home because his stockings wore out so quickly. He did not disclose the fact that having no money to buy *Kletterschuhe* he tackled the delicate rock climbs above Innsbruck in stockinged feet.

After matriculating on his native mountains he graduated on the terrible north faces of the Jorasses and Eiger. Money continued to be a problem, and it was with only five Swiss francs in his pocket he left Innsbruck and took the train to Landeck and in the late evening started on a bicycle ride to Promontogno, just under a hundred miles away. A friendly lorry gave him a short lift on the long climb to the Maloja Pass, 3000 ft. above Landeck. He reached Promontogno in

---

[1] *Das Ringen um den Nanga Parbat*, by Paul Bauer, is the standard work on this ruthless peak.

the late afternoon, spent four of his five precious francs on food, and climbed that same afternoon to the Sciora Hut. Next morning he ascended the north face of Piz Badile, one of the most tremendous of Alpine cliffs, in four and a half hours. The first party spent two nights on this grim face, and two of them died of exhaustion. Buhl rattled down to Promontogno, squandered the last of his five francs, pushed his bicycle up 3000 ft. to the Maloja Pass, and spent his third night bicycling down to Landeck. Falling asleep over his handlebars he awoke to find himself battling against the icy torrent of the Inn. He picked himself out of the river, and carried his damaged bicycle down the road to a small hotel where his clothes were dried.

Buhl is one of the most versatile of climbers, equally happy on ice, on rock and on ski. He has led many of the most extreme rock climbs, such as the "direttissima" of the Lalidererspitze north face, which is reckoned the hardest climb in the northern limestone Alps, and of which he made the second ascent. He had proved equal to the grimmest of Alpine north faces, Eiger and Jorasses. He is an expert winter climber. He made the first winter ascent of the terrible south face of the Marmolata, and he made a solitary winter ascent at *night* of the "Salzburg" route, reputed to be the most difficult of many extreme routes on the Watzmann. The precipice which he climbed is 6000 ft. in height. Winter—Alone —At night. One can condemn such desperate ventures as contrary to all sane mountaineering traditions, but one cannot withold one's admiration for Buhl's courage, endurance and fantastic skill. Buhl was to crown a career which has never been surpassed in mountaineering history by the most outstanding exploit in the story of Himalayan exploration.

The 1953 expedition to Nanga Parbat was the first major German expedition since the war and was led by Willy Merkl's step-brother, Dr. Karl Herrligkoffer, a Munich physician. The assault leader was Peter Aschenbrenner, one of the few survivors of the 1934 tragedy. Shortly after midnight, on July 3rd, 1953, Buhl left the highest camp (*ca.* 22,638 ft.) for the 4020-foot climb to the summit. His companion, Kempter, followed two hours later and was too exhausted by the time he reached the saddle to climb any further. Meanwhile Buhl was still climbing. In the late afternoon he was confronted with a narrow rock ridge and a 40-foot tower, an exacting test at 26,000 ft. It was 7 p.m. when Buhl's long struggle, sixteen and a half hours of solitary climbing, ended on the summit of Nanga Parbat.

He took a photograph which conclusively proved his claim to have climbed his peak. And then with what little strength was left he began to inch his way in the fading light down towards the rocks where the relentless night closed in on him. He was still over 26,000 ft. above the sea. Few indeed are those who have survived a night out high up on the Himalaya. None have survived alone and none have ever bivouacked in the open above 26,000 ft. and lived to tell the tale. Thirty-two brave men had already died on Nanga Parbat, but Buhl did not die there. He met his fate in June 1957 in the Baltoro mountains. I had met him two years ago in Zermatt where the centenary of the first ascent of Monte Rosa was being celebrated. Alone of the celebrants Buhl had marked the occasion by an ascent of Monte Rosa, or rather a traverse, for he came down to the valley after crossing Monte Rosa in bad weather from Macugnaga.

K2

Nanga Parbat to the Germans was "Unser Berg", the ruthless peak which had proved the tomb of so many Germans. And what Nanga Parbat was to the Germans, K2 was to the Americans.

The first American expedition led by C. S. Houston reached a height of 26,000 ft. The second American expedition was led by Fritz Wiessner, a German-born American, who had made the first ascent of Mount Waddington, a desperately difficult climb. His companions were Jack Durrance, one of the outstanding ski-ing cracks produced by Dartmouth College, Dudley Wolfe, whose wife, now Mrs. Kiare, organised the first team of American ladies who competed in World Championships, Eaton Cromwell and George Sheldon. Wiessner and Pasang Dawa Lama reached a height of 27,500 ft. at 6 p.m., and Wiessner decided to climb through the night but the Sherpa refused to follow and Wiessner was forced to retreat. The sequel was tragic, the camps to which they returned had been evacuated through a misunderstanding, as a result of which Wolfe and three Sherpas died on the mountain.

Fourteen years later Houston led another assault, with five young men, George Bell, Robert Craig, Arthur Gilkey, Dee Molenaar, Peter Schoening, and Captain Tony Streather, as British liaison officer. They had barely reached Camp VII about 25,500 ft. when a storm broke, a storm that raged with hardly a lull from July 26th to August 10th, when they finally left the camp, handicapped on their descent by the fact that Gilkey was suffering from an attack of thrombo-phlebitis, and was unable to walk. A stretcher was improvised to carry him down.

The problems involved in transporting Gilkey had forced them from the best line of descent, to regain which they had to cut steps across an ice slope fifty degrees in steepness. Bell slipped and dragged Streather with him. Their rope tangled with that of Houston and Bates, and theirs in turn with the rope joining Molenaar to Gilkey, all of whom were jerked off the ice-wall, but the entanglement of ropes which swept them off in succession created a single life-line and Schoening, by a magnificent effort managed to divide the shock between his shoulder, an axe jammed against a boulder and the boulder itself. The nylon rope held and Schoening held. Never before have a single climber and a belay held five falling men.

Many of those whose fall had been checked were injured and had to be helped down to the next camp, after which the uninjured climbers returned to bring down Gilkey, only to find that he had been swept away by an avalanche.[1]

In 1954, a strong Italian expedition, under the leadership of Ardito Desio, a professor of geology at Milan University, won through to success in spite of storms which raged for forty days. The summit team consisted of Achille Compagnoni and Lino Lacedelli. Nearly 800 ft. below the summit their oxygen supplies ran out. "Their bodies", writes Professor Desio, "began to be invaded by a kind of torpor, their heads felt as if seized in a grip of iron around their temples—and their breath failed." Lack of oxygen had so confused their minds that they still continued to carry the useless load of oxygen cylinders. This grim and heroic struggle against exhaustion and altitude ended at 6 p.m.

Most of the descent was made in darkness. They were caught in a small avalanche and all but carried away. They slipped and fell thirty feet down a wall of ice, but somehow they contrived to reach Camp VIII where their friends awaited them. Next day the brief lull in the unending storms ended, and the fact that the entire party fought their way down to the Base Camp without casualties is proof of outstanding courage, endurance and skill.

Though the Americans had earned the right to regard K 2 as *their* mountain it was not inappropriate that the first ascent should have been made by Italians, for K 2 is associated with two great Italians, the Duke of the Abruzzi, whose name is commemorated in the Abruzzi Ridge, and Vittorio Sella, whose famous photographs of K 2 are still by far the best ever taken. One is reproduced in this book.

Cho Oyu

A few weeks after K 2 had been climbed, the seventh highest peak in the world, Cho Oyu (26,750 ft.) was conquered by an Austrian party in the late autumn (October 19th, 1954). The first ascent was made without using oxygen by Dr. Herbert Tichy and Josef Joechler, with the veteran Sherpa Pasang Dawa Lama.

Kangchenjunga

Kangchenjunga (28,146 ft.) is the third highest mountain in the world, K 2 being the second highest.

---

[1] *K2—The Savage Mountain* by Charles S. Houston and Robert H. Bates, the story of the American expeditions, is a notable addition to the literature of Himalayan exploration.

Whereas K 2 is remote from the habitations of man, there is no peak which is so easily seen from the last outposts of civilisation as Kangchenjunga, or which is more majestic from the foothills. It is not height alone which determines the appeal which virgin peaks and virgin ridges exert over the mind of man. If the south face of the Eiger, which only mountaineers ever see had been as difficult as the north face it might still be unclimbed. The challenge of the Eigerwand was irresistible because this, the greatest precipice in the Alps, can be seen not only by every tourist who visits the Scheidegg or Grindelwald, but also from the shores of the lake of Thun, and from the terraces of Berne.

But it was not only because uncounted thousands had seen and admired Kangchenjunga from Darjeeling that Kangchenjunga was a prize which ranked second only to Everest in the mountaineering hierarchy, but also because it is the most difficult and dangerous of the 8000-metre peaks as yet climbed. "There is no doubt", writes Sir John Hunt, "that those who first climb Kangchenjunga will achieve the greatest feat of mountaineering, for it is a mountain which combines in its defences not only severe handicaps of wind, weather and very high altitude, but technical climbing problems and objective dangers of an order even higher than we found on Everest."

The British team which solved this problem was led by Dr. Charles Evans, a Liverpool surgeon of thirty-six who was the first to reach the south summit of Everest and whose *Eye on Everest*, a book of enchanting sketches, is an equal delight to children and to their elders.

The other members of the expedition were George Band, twenty-six, of the Everest expedition, Joe Brown (see page 183), Norman Hardie, John Clegg, John Jackson, Neil Mather, Tom McKinnon and Captain Streather, the transport officer (see page 220). Kangchenjunga was climbed on May 25th, 1955, by George Band and Joe Brown. Most of the climbing was on rock, some of which would be classified as "difficult" if it had been at sea level, some as "very difficult", but nothing could stop them, and at a quarter to three they had reached a point about five feet below the actual crest. They had pledged themselves to go no further for to the devout Sikkimese Kangchenjunga is a sacred mountain whose summit must not be desecrated by human feet.

On the following day the ascent was repeated by Hardie and Streather. A splendid follow-up to Everest.

Makalu

Makalu (27,790 ft.), a near neighbour of Everest, is the fifth highest peak in the world. A French expedition under the leadership of Jean Franco, after a preliminary exploration in the autumn of 1954, in the course of which Makalu's great neighbour Chomo Lonzö (25,640 ft.) was climbed, achieved their objective in May 1955. The planning, organisation and team-work were comparable with that of the Everest expedition of 1953. The success was in one respect without precedent. It was the first time in Himalayan history that every European member of an expedition, other than the doctor and geologists, attained the summit of an 8000-metre peak. On May 15th Jean Couzy, Lionel Terray, and on May 16th Jean Franco and Guido Magnone and Sirdar Gyalzen, and on May 17th Jean Bouvier, Serge Coupé, Pierre Leroux and André Vialatte climbed Makalu.

The Makalu expedition, precisely because it was a model of organisation, lacked drama, and Franco's book of the expedition, though admirably written is less poignant than Herzog's *Annapurna*. As Jean Franco ironically remarks, expeditions in which nothing goes wrong are as lacking in history as nations which are happy. A famous journalist asked him hopefully whether there had not been any incidents. "Alas!" replied Franco, "there was no crevasse into which we fell, no avalanche which swept away our camp. At 8000 m. we felt as though we were on the summit of Mont Blanc. Nine of us reached the top. Three ascents in three days. You can't call that a conquest. And we didn't even have frozen feet." "Well, then", said the journalist, "nothing happened." "But what he did not ask", comments Franco, "was why nothing happened."[1]

One reason why nothing happened was that they had profited in many ways from the experiences of those who climbed Annapurna. Franco's party, for instance, took far more trouble to acclimatise themselves.

Everest again and Lhotse

In 1956 the Swiss Foundation for Alpine Research organised, under the general direction of Ernst Feuz, an expedition of which the object was to repeat the ascent of Everest, to collect geological samples of the summit ridge, and to climb Lhotse (27,890 ft.), the highest unscaled mountain in the world. All three objects were achieved.

The expedition was led by Albert Eggler, and the Deputy Leader was Wolfgang Diehl.

The ultimate success of the expedition was the more creditable because of severe initial set backs. On March 24th Fritz Luchsinger was taken ill with an inflammation of the appendix. The expedition included a doctor, Eduard Leuthold, and a dentist, Hans Grimm. Leuthold had made preparations for an operation but his therapy proved so efficient that the patient suddenly recovered. The next temporary casualty was Wolfgang Diehl, who at forty-seven was the senior

[1] Hélas! Pas de crevasse où nous soyons tombés. Pas d'avalanche qui ait enseveli un camp. A 8000 comme au sommet du Mont Blanc. Au sommet nous étions neuf. Trois ascensions en trois jours, ce n'est pas une conquête! Et nous n'avions même pas eu froid aux pieds.

member of the expedition. He was stricken down with an inflammation of the lung, and he too recovered and was able to play an active and useful role in the expedition. The Sirdar Pasang Dawa Lama fell ill and finally collapsed at the Base Camp in May. Ten Sherpas and the doctor had to be detached from the expedition to carry him back to Namche Bazar.

On May 10th the weather broke, and there was good reason to fear that the dreaded monsoon had put in a premature appearance. Fortunately the pre-monsoon was followed by a brief spell of fine weather, but a foot of fresh snow aggravated the difficulties of the assault on Lhotse.

On May 18th the second objective of the expedition was achieved. Ernst Reiss and Fritz Luchsinger made the first ascent of Lhotse, and incidentally the first ascent of an 8000-metre peak by a Swiss expedition.

Reiss was the only member of the expedition who had had Himalayan experience. He had been a member of the Swiss Everest expedition of 1952, which attempted the mountain both in the spring and in the late autumn, and he had reached the South Col in winter conditions. At 5 a.m. on the morning of the 18th, Reiss and Luchsinger began their preparations, and it is a measure of the difficulties of high altitude climbing that cooking their breakfast, preparing their oxygen apparatus, etc. took them four hours. They left at 9 a.m., and lost an hour repairing Luchsinger's flow of oxygen. They climbed slowly to the foot of the Lhotse Couloir and were lucky to find good snow, for the couloir varies in steepness from forty-five to sixty degrees, and at one point it narrows to little more than a foot in breadth. Twice they drove in a piton for security on the trickier passages. They were again lucky in that the strong wind was at their backs, but even so their masks and glasses were soon crusted in ice.

A steep slope of green rock and a final snow funnel led them to the narrow ice-ridge of the summit, five and a half hours after leaving their tent. The wind had risen and on the descent they had to edge their way down, rope length by rope length, fully secured. At 6.15 p.m. they reached their tent, which had all but collapsed under the weight of driven snow. At midnight they had to force their feet into their frozen boots in order to free the tent from snow. The storm raged pitilessly throughout the night. It had been a great achievement to climb an 8000-metre peak on so cold and so stormy a day.

On May 19th they descended in safety to Camp III. They were both suffering from slight frostbite, but a few days later both of them had re-ascended to the South Col to support the parties attempting Everest.

On May 23rd Ernst Schmied and Jürg Marmet made the second ascent of Everest. Marmet has the guide's patent, and is also a chemist with a diploma from the Eidgenössische Technische Hochschule in Zurich, a world famous engineering University. Their highest camp was higher than the highest Swiss camp in 1952, and rather lower than the highest British camp in 1953. Its approximate height was 8400 m. (27,560 ft.).

They started their preparations for the climb at 3.30 a.m. and did not leave the tent until 8.30 a.m. The tent was broken in two places, and the wind had driven in so much snow that many of the cooking utensils were buried. Fortunately the wind dropped soon after they began to climb, and the sun shone from a cloudless sky. The South Summit was reached at midday. The chimney, which is the only technical difficulty on the final ridge, was mastered, and it is of interest to note that their estimate of its height, 15 m., is approximately the same as Hillary's (see page 207). They reached the summit in five and a half hours from their camp. After an hour's rest they descended to the South Col. Their oxygen was exhausted but they slept well without oxygen and, again without oxygen, descended next day to Camp III.

On the day that Everest was climbed, Adolf Reist and Dr. Hans Rudolf von Gunten, the brother-in-law of Ernst Schmied, climbed from the South Col to Camp VII, where they struggled for three hours to clear the tent from snow. One of the nylon sleeping-bags had been blown out of the tent by the wind and had disappeared with the result that the night was more than usually uncomfortable. At 6.45 a.m. they left the camp and ten hours later they were back on the South Col after making the third ascent of Everest. They spent two hours on the summit and during one of these hours they removed their masks and dispensed with oxygen.

Their times were good. Fifty minutes for the ascent from the South Peak to the summit, a vertical height of just over 300 ft., and they rattled down to the South Col, more than 3000 ft. below the summit, in two hours, an Alpine tempo.

On May 24th there were ten climbers in excellent condition on the South Col, and at least two more parties standing by in case of an emergency who could have attacked Everest, but the weather forecast was bad, and the leader, Albert Eggler, decided not to risk any further ascents which might have spoiled the record of an outstandingly successful expedition.

The triple success was due in the first instance to good leadership and splendid team spirit, and in the second place to improved oxygen apparatus. There has indeed been a steady improvement in oxygen equipment since the first Swiss expedition to Everest. The British in 1953 enjoyed the advantage of an equipment superior to the Swiss in 1952, and the 1956 expedition marked a still further advance.

Herr Karl Weber kindly invited me to the celebration at the Hotel Dolder, Zurich, to welcome the expedition on their return. I had some talk with Frau Reiss, whose husband climbed Lhotse. Frau Reiss had spent some time in England and speaks English well, but she was puzzled by the heading in one of our papers, "The Swiss do the Hat-trick". She was not quite sure whether the implications were not faintly leg-pulling. I explained that our rough islanders could not pay a more sincere compliment to the Swiss than to compare the triple success, Lhotse and Everest twice, to the achievement of taking three wickets in three successive balls.

Muztagh Tower (23,862 ft.)

Everyone who has read Filippi's book, describing the Duke of the Abruzzi's expedition to the Karakorum in 1909, will remember Sella's famous photograph of the Muztagh Tower, which did more perhaps than anything else to induce in the minds of mountaineers of the day, and later, the idea of an unclimbable mountain. And the written description by Filippi endorsed the legend, despite the fact that Martin Conway, in 1892, who discovered and named the peak, had correctly pointed out that the exceedingly precipitous appearance of the mountain, as seen from the upper reaches of the Baltoro Glacier, is deceptive.

Sella took other photographs, from different directions, but the extraordinary changes in appearance of the mountain when seen from different angles seem virtually to have been ignored and his most famous picture to have blotted out any alternatives. Yet the picture is a fraud, as can be seen from the Duke of Spoleto's photograph reproduced in *The Alpine Journal*, volume 43, page 7, where the apparently unbroken wall of Sella's picture is shown to carry a well-marked ridge (the south-eastern), with a high col from which, if it could be reached, the summit could obviously be attacked.

Nevertheless, the mountain has not proved easy to climb. It is, perhaps, the first of the greater peaks in the Himalayan-Karakorum massifs to be climbed which is technically difficult even by Alpine standards, and irrespective of the height.

By a coincidence, two parties from different countries embarked in 1956 to attempt the mountain, but only came across one another shortly before they achieved their climbs. The British party, under J.M.Hartog, had been establishing their camps during May and early June, and it was not till June 18th that they received word that a French party under Guido Magnone had arrived and were intent on the Muztagh Tower also, and from the Chagaran Glacier. However, a meeting on June 26th smoothed out rivalries, as the French had decided to make their attempt from the Younghusband Glacier, with the result that what might have been another Cho Oyu cause of irritation was to develop into a splendid instance of mountain friendship and co-operation, the French party coming to the aid of Hartog, who was badly frost-bitten on his descent from the mountain, in a most generous manner.

The Muztagh Tower was first climbed on July 6th by Ian McNaught-Davis and Joe Brown of the British party, and on July 7th by Hartog and T. Patey. The expedition was based on the Baltoro Glacier, and the route lay via the hitherto unexplored Chagaran Glacier and the north-west ridge. The first pair reached the west summit only at 6.30 p.m. and were too tired to proceed to the slightly higher (about 10 ft.) eastern summit. The second pair, profiting by the steps made the day before by the others, made better time and were able to traverse the summit ridge to the highest point. Both parties were benighted on the way down.

The French attacked the mountain by way of the south-east ridge on 12th–13th July and arrived at the eastern summit in a snowstorm, so did not proceed to the lower western point. The relative difficulty of the two routes must be matter of opinion, but both expeditions agreed that the Muztagh Tower, if not all it had been imagined in the past, was very far from easy.

CHAPTER XIX

MODERN TRENDS
IN MOUNTAINEERING LITERATURE

Of the many notable contributions to *The Mountain World*, published, as is the present book, by the *Swiss Foundation for Alpine Research*, the most notable was Geoffrey Young's essay *Courage and Mountain Writing* in the 1955 issue. Young's theme is the increasing "discontent with mountain publications", and his explanation is that "Mountain writing at the present time has more quantitative than qualitative merit and is usually only of ephemeral interest".

Now there is no necessary connection between artificial climbing and the impersonal description which one associated with technical notes in a Climbers' Guide. Gaston Rébuffat, for instance, who was born in Marseille and who adopted guiding as his profession as the only way of satisfying his passion for the mountains, has described supremely difficult climbs accomplished by modern methods in a book *Starlight and Storm* which, if it attains its deserts, will take its place among the accepted classics of mountain adventure. The demand that mountaineering expeditions should be recorded in prose which reminds one of an engineer's report—"using roped stirrups and the doubled rope technique Smith led into a narrow crack (Grade V and A 2)"—proceeds from those who are incapable of translating mountain adventure into anything which could be mistaken for literature.

Now there is, as Young observes, "a fair sized public for this sort of thing, a reading public greedy for technical details and for reports about peaks and precipices which they themselves have climbed or hope to climb.... To the young scientific mind in this 'machine age' the muscular movements in climbing are mechanical, explicable, and therefore sympathetic when described...." And because it is much easier to describe a climb in terms of graded difficulty and the number of pitons used than to interpret the emotions of the climber, those who cannot attempt Grade VI writing tend, as Young observes, "to condemn any writing which is not technical and impersonal as sentimentality, a superfluous display of emotion."

It is odd that those who believe that the opposition to modern developments of mountaineering is explicable by the fact that modern climbers have surpassed the standards which the critics of this method attained, should not realise that they invite a similar explanation of their own objection to standards of mountain description that are beyond their literary powers. These Alpine puritans who are suspicious of beauty and who dismiss as "Alpine Uplift" any narrative which deviates from what Clough calls "the merest 'it was'", found a brilliant advocate in the late Geoffrey Howard. I do not myself believe that he took his own thesis very seriously, but his paper, *Alpine Uplift*[1], provided the Alpine Club with one of the most entertaining evenings I can remember.

We can pity but we should not condemn those to whom art means nothing, and who are wholly unmoved, say, by the glorious stained glass windows of our old cathedrals, but we have every right to condemn the Puritans who destroyed so much of our medieval legacy. Similarly we have no right to condemn the mountaineer who dislikes any attempt to interpret in prose the response of man to mountain beauty, but we have every right to deplore an Alpine censorship which would restrict Alpine literature to the kind of writing which only appeals to one particular class of climber. The iconoclasm which swept away some of the finest sculpture and stained glass in our islands is closely akin to the iconoclasm which would reduce all Alpine literature to the Calvinistic plainness of a purely factual account of the physical details of a particular climb.

Rational criticism of Alpine literature is not rendered any the easier by prejudice-creating expressions such as "uplift". Many a mountaineer who has himself cut adrift from institutional religion has felt that his reaction to mountain beauty is in itself evidence that ultimate reality is not coterminous with the limitations of the physical universe. Metaphysics is by definition that which is "beyond physics", and *Alpine Uplift* is only a translation into prejudice-creating terminology of *Alpine Metaphysics*. Surely it would be more in accordance with the normal canons of literary criticisms to define the criteria which should enable us to distinguish between what is admirable and what is far from admirable in this particular genre of Alpine writing.

Geoffrey Howard failed to follow up one clue to an important criterion of good literature in general and good Alpine literature in particular. He remarks that Alpine Uplifters are mainly concerned with "a display of personality". Style is personal and therefore it is impossible to write without a "display of personality", but the discerning critic will distinguish between passages in which the display of personality is incidental and those in which the author is more concerned to exhibit his personality than to communicate a revelation. Wordsworth was a supreme egoist, but in his most inspired moments he was merely the medium for "some force working through him". Shelley's prayer, "make me thy lyre even as the forest is" sums up the ideal of all great art, for the great artist is an instrument through whom beauty is revealed.

[1] *Alpine Journal*, 57, 1. My reply *Alpine Puritanism* was published in *Alpine Journal*, 57, 231.

Wordsworth was at least as interested in his personality as Byron, but, at his best, an infinitely greater poet simply because, at his best, he was content to communicate a revelation. Who thinks of mountains when they read Byrons's?

> I live not in myself but I become
> Portion of that around me and to me
> High mountains are a feeling but the hum
> Of human cities torture

and who remembers egoistic Wordworth when he reads his lines on the Simplon?

> The immeasurable height
> Of woods decaying, never to be decayed
> The stationary blasts of waterfalls,
> And in the narrow rent, at every turn
> Winds thwarting winds bewildered and forlorn.

Byronic vanity is rare in Alpine literature. A far more frequent failing is timidity, that form of timidity which is provoked by a nervous conformity to intellectual fashion.

Alpine metaphysics is no exception to metaphysics in general. It is impossible to make up one's mind as to whether there is anything beyond physics without attempting to answer the ultimate question *Utrum Deus Sit*, as indeed many of the founding fathers of our sport fully realised. The sense of worship which mountains evoke presented no problem to men who believed, as Alfred Wills for one believed, that God revealed himself through the temporal loveliness of his creation. Here is Wills' description of the first moments on the summit of the Wetterhorn:

> "I am not ashamed to own that I experienced as this sublime and wonderful prospect burst upon my view, a profound and almost irrepressible emotion. . . . We felt as in the more immediate presence of Him who had reared this tremendous pinnacle, and beneath the 'majestical roof' of whose deep blue Heaven we stood."

It is no longer fashionable to refer to one's Creator in a book intended for an Alpine public.

I am, of course, far from suggesting that only theists can contribute anything of literary value to Alpine metaphysics. The one indispensable qualification is integrity, the integrity which accepts the logical conclusions which follow from one's basic premises, whatever those premises may be. Lucretius was an atheist but he was also a supreme poet and lines such as

Tantum religio potuit suadere malorum

or

O genus infelix humanum talis divis cum tribuit facta

will endure when most of our religious poetry is forgotten.

So long as mountaineers restrict themselves to a straightforward narrative of mountain adventure they are under no obligation to reveal what they believe, or indeed even to decide what they believe about the ultimate mystery, but those who cross the frontier which separates Alpine physics from Alpine metaphysics will find it difficult to carry conviction if they are unprepared to follow their own mountain musings through to their logical conclusion.

Let us begin by applying the criterion of integrity to the famous passages in Belloc's *The Path to Rome*, in which he describes the revelation of the Alps from the heights of Weissenstein.

> "Here were these magnificent creatures of God, I mean the Alps, which now for the first time I saw from the height of the Jura; and because they were 50 or 60 miles away, and because they were a mile or two high, they were become something different from us others, and could strike one motionless with the awe of supernatural things. Up there in the sky, to which only clouds belong and birds and the last trembling colours of pure light, they stood fast and hard; not moving as do the things of the sky. They were as distant as the little upper clouds of summer, as fine and tenuous; but in their reflection and in their quality as it were of weapons (like spears and shields of an unknown array) they occupied the sky with a sublime invasion: and the things proper to the sky were forgotten by me in their presence as I gazed."

No vagueness here, no religiosity. You know exactly what Belloc means, and if you accept his premise you will not find it difficult to accept his conclusion: "These, the great Alps seen thus, link one in some way to one's immortality."

Here is another passage, this time from a man who like Belloc was a poet and who like Belloc had the courage to draw logical conclusions from his premises but who, unlike Belloc, was an atheist. Llewelyn Powys died in Davos, and in this valley, which for Powys was the valley of the shadow of death, he sought, as so many others have done before him, for some clue to the ultimate mystery in the changing moods of peak and snowfield, but no touch of nature mysticism softens his austere repudiation of a Friend behind the phenomena of the visible world.

You will find in any seminary or common-room philosophers who can marshal the arguments for theism, but a generation may pass without giving birth to a poet who can express the Lucretian sense of an austere world from which "the parting genius is with sighing sent." Powys' meditation on the Aebi Wood can stand comparison with the noblest passages in Lucretius:

> "We were sage and we accepted the word of the uncouth wood. Whether wisely or no, let the forest judge. There is nothing better for us to do than to plot

for our own happiness, for the happiness of our companions, for the happiness of the whole human race. Our frights prompt us too easily to countenance illusions. Something can be done sometimes by far-seeing sagacious insights. We are too often taught to look up when we should be taught to look down. The spectacle of the unnervous, unideal confidence of nature should point us to a sounder doctrine.

"During the fair hours of the Alpine summer the Aebi Wood is as full of leaping laughing sap as is the comb of a bee with life-giving honey. Even to the stupid eye of man it is there visibly veiled in softest mystery. In December, January and February it is the austerity of the wood that becomes especially apparent. Then it is that the stately fir-trees, standing motionless in their white bondage, lift up patient heads of endurance in an astral universe without an end or a beginning, in a universe that to the fugitive race of men subject to death must for ever remain incomprehensible."

One knows exactly what Belloc meant and one knows exactly what Powys meant. The Christians and the atheists are equally precise, but too much of what may be called Alpine theology merely serves to illustrate the contrast that Croce draws between religion which is precise and irreligiosity which is vague. ("La religiosità è vaga, la religione è precisa.") Here are a few characteristic samples of Alpine religiosity culled from the pages of a widely read Alpine prophet: "Those who are impelled towards the hills seek something finer than the man-made dogmas now crushing and distorting the spiritual teachings of the universe." Does this mean anything? Or again: "The religion of the mountains is not one of cant or ritual" conveys no clear meaning to my mind.

It is all very well to tell us what the religion of the mountains is *not*—"not one of cant or ritual"—but surely the author should also have explained precisely what he means by the "religion of the mountains". It is a fact that men have been converted from a materialistic to a spiritual philosophy by their experiences among the mountains, but it is confusing to describe a religion which is reinforced by, or even derived from mountain experience as a religion *of* mountains.

In the very book in which we are assured that the religion of the mountains is "not one of cant or ritual" there is a spirited description of the descent of a great peak in a thunderstorm. "There with easy ground", writes the author, "separating us from the hut we shook hands not without feeling for it had been a close thing." What is a handshake but ritual? It is indeed ritual which differentiates man from the beasts. When dog meets dog there is no paw shaking, and bees do not curtsey to queen bees.

The vagueness of Alpine religiosity is partly due to the influence of fashion. Words which in my youth were classified as unprintable have obtained right of entry if not to *The Alpine Journal* at least to Alpine literature. Words which the pioneers often used would cause general embarrassment if introduced into a paper read before the Alpine Club. "Bloody" is an example of the first type of word, "God" of the second. In the last pencilled note which Mallory scribbled before leaving for his last climb he wrote: "It's a bloody load for climbing" but the facsimile which appeared in *The Alpine Journal* was cleverly faked and Mallory was credited with the remark: "It's a beastly load...."

The discreet censorship of Mallory's letter in *The Alpine Journal* recalled a sad experience of my youth. My publishers insisted that I should remove the word "bloody" from the dialogue in my book *The Harrovians*, and I spent a sad evening changing "bloody" into "ruddy" throughout the proof. I left one such "bloody" unchanged as a pretext for an erratum slip (On page 54 line 6 for "bloody" read "ruddy"), but even this consolation was denied me.

A modern editor of *The Alpine Journal* would be less squeamish about "bloody" but that useful little monosyllable "God" has vanished from the pages of Alpine literature. This would not matter so much if mountaineers confined themselves to describing their adventures, but those who attempt to interpret the spiritual message of the mountains are often handicapped by their timid subservience to a convention which is comparatively modern.

In my reply to Geoffrey Howard's *Alpine Uplift*, in which he tried to prove that the pioneers confined themselves to a factual account of their adventures, I quoted passage after passage from Wills, Hudson, Elliott, Birkbeck and others in which the forbidden monosyllable appears, as for instance in Alfred Wills' account of his first moments on reaching the crest of the Wetterhorn. And perhaps one reason why the Alpine pioneers were more intelligible than the moderns in interpreting their mountain philosophy is that they did not attempt the impossible task of trying to construct an Alpine theology without mentioning theos.

Here is another example of this curious shyness which afflicts our moderns when they cross the frontier from Alpine adventure to Alpine metaphysics.

> "... in a word, when we set our wholeness of conscious life in continuous moving contact with its differently timed existence, we are establishing a relationship between the mountain personality and our own; by which I mean between the rhythm of life and order which governs the mountain shape and duration and that by which we live. St. John, you will remember, postulated this λόγος, continuous principle of order, behind and within all living. To make contact with it, to arrive at consciousness of our community with it in other living forms of creation, is our reward for living contributively and vitally; it is the assurance to us of our participation in an eternal principle, call it beauty or truth or what we may."

But if St. John is to be subpoenaed as a witness against the exponents of artificial climbing (for such was the theme of the article) what he said should be quoted. St. John did not describe the logos as a "continuous principle of order". What he said was that "the logos was God".

In one of the most interesting papers ever read before the Alpine Club the late Michael Roberts, a distinguished poet, drew attention to a danger inherent in the vagueness of Alpine religiosity. "Mountains", he wrote, "may be symbols or images of some other reality, but the worship of symbols as if they were something more than images is a form of superstition." I am inclined to believe that those who write as if they were worshipping the symbol are inhibited by Alpine convention or shyness from explicit reference to the reality of which mountain beauty is only a symbol. Consider for instance the following passages from a recent book:

> "By the simple and delightful process of climbing mountains, getting to know them and loving to be with them, we are moving along a way which I think even the late Dean Inge might regard as a way of progress. For we are helping to give personality to these objects of our devotion, and so making our small contribution to the gradual permeating and final replacement of the material and perishable by the non-material and indestructible."

> "I reject altogether the idea that mountains can only give back to us the thoughts we have had about them."

> "Something of our personality has gone into every mountain on which we have spent our strength and on which thoughts have dwelt with admiration and love. And something of its personality has come into ours and had its small effect on everything that has come within our influence. These are fruits of mountaineering that nothing can entirely destroy."

The *Oxford Dictionary* defines *person* as an individual human being, and *personality* as "being a person; personal existence or identity". Dead matter cannot be said to possess personality and I find it difficult to believe that the author I have quoted means to suggest that mountains have reacted to our adoration by slowly coming to life. I do not deny that to the mountain lover mountains *appear* to possess personality, perhaps because the supreme Personality is reflected in the temporal loveliness of His creation. The author whom I have quoted seems to me to have evaded the problem by taking refuge in metaphor, and it is interesting to contrast the vagueness of his explanation with the clarity of Philo. "All Nature is the language in which God expresses his thoughts but the thoughts are more important than the language."

The same author compares, as did Ruskin, mountains to cathedrals but one does not worship cathedrals for, as St. Augustine remarked, *Quis comiscet artifici opera, nec artem intelligit, nec artificem.* (Whoever confuses the artist with the art understands neither the art nor the artist.)

I am reluctant to criticise by name authors whose works have given me so much pleasure, for I am concerned not with the criticism of individuals but with the establishment of the principle that no attempt to interpret our feeling for the mountains is of great interest unless it be distinguished by clarity and by integrity, clarity because you cannot convey to your reader what is not clear to yourself; integrity because you cannot convince your reader if you submit your mountain philosophy to the censorship of fashion. First, then, you clarify your own mind on the basic problem of philosophy. Is Nature her own explanation? Is ultimate reality identical with physical reality? Is metaphysics an illusion?

The mountain writings of an honest atheist such as Llewellyn Powys appeal to me far more than the woolly mysticism of those who are too timid to admit the theistic implications of their mountain creed.

If Nature be her own explanation, if metaphysics be an illusion, then Alpine mysticism is moonshine, and Geoffrey Howard's virile protest against "Alpine Uplift" was fully justified. If, in the other hand, reality exists beyond the physical realm, if metaphysics be securely founded on objective facts, the Alpine mystic is in touch with reality and has, at least, one link with the mystics who believe that the visible world is "the living garment of God". If this were more generally realised some of our Alpine mystics might have studied the subject of mysticism in general before expounding their own mystical approach to the mountains, and might not provoke, as did one of them, an unfriendly reviewer into quoting Samuel Johnson's "Beware of a man who writes more than he reads".

Mysticism is not peculiar to Christianity, and Alpine mystics would do well not to digress into discussion of the tenets of particular religions, if only to spare those who are well informed on these matters the tedium of separating the wheat of good writing from the chaff of ill-informed comments such as, for instance a statement by one of our Alpine mystics to the effect that the mediæval Church held views about "the opposition of the body and the spirit" which that Church consistently condemned, or the exhumation by another Alpine mystic of that venerable myth which credits mediæval philosophers with a vivid interest in the problem as to how many angels can dance on the point of a pin.

My own mind is so unsubtle that I have failed to detect the connection between mountaineering and mediævalism, but I commend to all those who ingeniously contrive to relate their mountain experiences, if only by way of complacent contrast, to mediæval thought, *Science and the Modern World* by the late Professor A.N. Whitehead F.R.S., a distinguished scientist and an agnostic with an odd bias in favour of studying mediævalism before dogmatising about it.

Here is a quotation from his book, obtainable in the *Penguin* series:

> The habit of definite exact thought was implanted in the European mind by the long domination of scholastic logic and scholastic divinity. The habit remained long after the philosophy had been repudiated, the priceless habit of looking for an exact point and of sticking to it when found . . . The greatest contribution of mediævalism to the formation of the scientific movement was the inexpugnable

belief that every detailed occurence can be correlated with its antecedents in a perfectly definite manner, exemplifying general principles.

Charles Meade, the famous Himalayan explorer, is one of the few mountaineers who has tried to relate Alpine mysticism to mysticism in general, and though he is sometimes betrayed into superficial comments, as for instance on page 61 of his book *High Mountains*, he has read widely, and what he writes is distinguished not only by knowledge but also by clarity and integrity. As a corrective to a certain complacency which the love of Nature sometimes engenders in Nature mystics I commend the following passage:

> The mere mountain-lover, limited as he is in his attitude to Nature, generally contents himself with the symbols without attempting a direct approach to anything beyond them. He may not even suspect that the object of his admiration is to be treated as a symbol and not as an idol or plaything. Whatever importance nature-mysticism may have in relation to religious mysticism is due to *its potentially preparatory character*, rather than to the resemblance there is between them. (Italics mine.)

In this chapter I am concerned less to praise books such as *High Mountains* or to criticise by implication what I once called "The Religiousity of the Mountains", than to protest against the attempt to impose a censorship on the free expression of what mountains mean to us. Alpine literature owes much of its interest to its diversity. There is something for all tastes. Those who only enjoy highly technical accounts are well catered for. Those who dislike what Howard called "Alpine Uplift" are under no obligation to read it, and have no right to complain if an occasional mountaineer refuses to be deterred either by Alpine puritanism or by Alpine theophobia from admitting that he has discovered among the mountains some clue to the ultimate mystery of life.

236

CHAPTER XX

THE ALPINE CLUB 1857—1957

Let me bring this book to a conclusion by an attempt to assess the contribution of the Alpine Club to mountaineering during the century which began with the foundation of the Club in 1857. Many of the great Alpine peaks, Mont Blanc, the Finsteraarhorn and Jungfrau, Ortler and Gross Venediger among others were climbed before the British invasion of the High Alps began, but mountaineering as an organised sport rather than as a succession of isolated achievements by individuals, none of whom founded a school or exercised any influence on the development of mountaineering as a sport, dates from the foundation of the Alpine Club. The pioneer role which members of the Alpine Club had played in the Alps was repeated in almost all the great mountain ranges of the world, in Norway, the Pyrennes and the Caucasus, in the Himalaya and in New Zealand and in the mountain ranges of the American continent.

The Club in its centenary year can recall with no less pride the contribution which her members have made to mountain literature. *The Alpine Journal* is the world's senior mountain journal. Ball's *Alpine Guide* and Conway's *The Zermatt Pocket Book* were pioneer publications, and no mountaineers have made a greater contribution than the British to books internationally recognised as mountain classics.

It is less easy to assess the influence of the Alpine Club on the traditions of our sport, and it will help the reader to arrive at a just conclusion on a debatable question if I begin by a long quotation from the valedictory address of Sir Edwin Herbert who was president from the beginning of 1953 to the end of 1955. Sir Edwin had the rare good fortune to be president during a three year period which was unsurpassed in the history of the Club for brilliance of achievement, the period which witnessed the first ascents by British parties of both Everest and Kangchenjunga. But if Edwin Herbert was fortunate to be president during this Elizabethan renaissance, mountaineering was no less fortunate, for the establishment of the Mount Everest Foundation, with its power to help finance future Himalayan genius, is due not only to the success of the Everest expedition but also to Edwin Herbert's administrative and financial talents.

"I have thought it worth while to pursue this train of thought because there is such a thing as a tradition in the Club. Traditions are good things, and one of the best things about them is that they can be followed with beneficent results without their being fully understood. It is important, however, sometimes to try and understand them, because a living tradition ought to be understood if it is to be an intelligible rule and a guide for the future. I will go so far as to say that, whether we know it or not, the things which really bind together the members of the Club are the recognition of the experience I have been talking about and an understanding of the conditions under which it is attainable. I t is for that reason that if you look at the things traditionally frowned on by the Club, you will find that they are just those things which make the full realisation of mountain joys impossible—national aggrandisement, self-display, publicity hunting, a neurotic search of danger for the sake of danger, attempts by artificial means to alter the conditions imposed by nature and all the rest. These things are silly and therefore unbecoming.

"It is a great piece of good fortune that so many of the early members of the Club who founded our tradition, were men of exceptional insight and understanding and far from inarticulate. By the accident of time and period they happened to be drawn largely from a certain social class. In these days that is no longer so, and therefore the distinction of class which was then relevant is no longer relevant. We intuitively judge the suitability of a man for membership of the Club by the extent to which he recognises and seeks to achieve the experience we have been discussing and observes the conditions that make it possible. If he has that quality he must be clubbable in the Alpine Club. He may be a brilliant climber and not have it. He may be a mediocre climber and have it to the full. But have it he must if he is to be at home with us or we with him."

It would be impossible to deny that the Alpine Club in the past has exhibited the virtues of conservatism in a slightly too extreme form. Guideless climbing, the use of crampons, ski-mountaineering and more recently artificial climbing were all initially condemned as undesirable innovations by the high priests of Alpine orthodoxy, but these delaying actions of the old guard did no harm. The development of ski-mountaineering is a case in point. Colonel Strutt's scepticism about the value of ski in the High Alps had a stimulating rather than a depressing effect on the present writer, and was indirectly responsible for the foundation of the Alpine Ski Club.

Next on the list of "things traditionally frowned on by the Club", is "a neurotic search for danger for the sake of danger". It is not, I am inclined to believe, the love of danger but the not ignoble ambition to be remembered in Alpine history which encourages too many young climbers to accept risks among the mountains, greater even than those which a man may justly accept in war. The case against this conception of mountaineering has never been better stated than in Geoffrey Young's famous paper which he read before the Alpine Club, *Should the Mountain be brought to Mahomet?* (*A. J.* LII, p. 180).

"No one, I hope, will claim for any game, or sport or exercise, that it should make the supreme claim upon any human life, that it should have an equal right to demand the sacrifice of time, labour and life itself, with the long duty which a man owes to his creative labour, his social responsibilities, or his own enduring part in vitality, in consciousness and in hope. If we begin to accept an interpretation that justifies young men in wagering duration of life and the duty owed to it upon a haphazard adventure so unchancy that it exacts sooner or later, the penalty of death from a large proportion of the players, we are outside any definition that seems applicable to the idea of a 'game'."

Admittedly the greatest sports are those which are exacting in their demands not only on endurance but on courage and which necessarily involve risk to life and to limb, and it is impossible to define the degree of risk which is justifiable. The pioneers of the Alpine Club may have exaggerated the virtue of prudence. They were a little too fond of quoting Melchior Anderegg's "Es geht, aber ich gehe nicht", and I agree with T. S. Blakeney's comment, in a private letter on A. W. Moore's criticisms of Jacob Anderegg's alleged lack of prudence, quoted on page 73 of this book.

"I've always thought old Melchior (writes Blakeney) got away with his reputation rather easily, not a little because he was such a nice, gentlemanly old man. But Moore's remark that in Jacob Anderegg, prudence was conspicuous by its absence seems to me rather unfair and absurd. Was Jacob imprudent? He may have had more dash and initiative than Melchior, but whereas I feel that dear old Almer would have held his own in a much later generation than his, Melchior would not have done so. No doubt he had all the technical skill one could want and was a first rate man in, say, an ice-fall; but I feel he lacked the nerve to be counted amongst the greatest guides."

Be that as it may, I am sure that T. S. Blakeney would be the first to agree that in the context of time and place Melchior's *Es geht, aber ich gehe nicht* (It goes but I don't) was defensible, whereas Hermann von Barth's *Wer mit mir geht, der sei zu sterben bereit* (Who goes with me must be ready to die), is an unbalanced aberration from the sane ideals which should govern our sport.

A note of proportion is as characteristic of sane mountaineering as of noble architecture, but it is easier to recognise this note than to define it. Even if the Alpine Club tended in the past to overstress caution this was a fault on the right side. There has perhaps never been a time when there were so many young and brilliant climbers in the Alpine Club as there are today, and it is all to the good that they are still influenced by a century-old tradition which the pioneers did so much to create, and which has been restated so convincingly in modern times by Geoffrey Young and Edwin Herbert.

The Alpine Club, as Sir Edwin rightly insists, has always resisted the attempt to exploit mountaineering in the interests of "national aggrandisement", but it

239

is as difficult to define the point at which pride in the achievement of one's countrymen degenerates into the exploitation of mountaineering for nationalistic propaganda, as to define the point at which mountain risks become justifiable. Once again it is a question of the note of proportion, the absence of which is obvious, but the nature of which is indefinable.

We have perhaps been more successful in convincing ourselves than our friends abroad that we are wholly uninfluenced by nationalism in our own mountain literature. I have already quoted Carl Egger's criticism—a criticism in which, however, he was anticipated by the present writer—of the myth which dates sporting mountaineering from Wills' ascent of the Wetterhorn. Walter Lehner, not without justice, complains of the fact that many of the great German and Austrian pioneers of guideless climbing were virtually ignored in *The Alpine Journal*. Other instances might be quoted of what appears to be a failure to give full credit to the foreigner, such as Leslie Stephen's claim quoted on page 57 that the Alpine Club "taught us for the first time really to see mountains".

It would, however, only be possible by diligent gleaning of our mountain literature to collect a few instances of the kind of thing which Edwin Herbert condemns as "national aggrandisement", and most of such cases are explicable by lack of knowledge. Leslie Stephen, for instance, knew nothing about art, and the occasional neglect of German achievements can normally be explained by the fact that comparatively few members of the Alpine Club could read German with ease, with the result that German mountain journals tended to be neglected. Moreover the note of complacency which is, or was, so often discernible in the references by Alpine Club members to the Alpine Club was inspired far less by national than by Club loyalty. It was analogous to the devotion which the great public schools inspire in those who wear "the old school tie".

Wilhelm Lehner, in his discerning and valuable history of mountaineering, from which I have quoted many times in earlier chapters, recurs again and again to what he describes as the competition for the blue ribbon of the Alps. He sees mountaineering in terms of an attempt to wrest an international challenge cup from the holders. Thus the blue ribbon which was in possession of the British in the Golden Age was wrested from them by the Germans and Austrians between the wars. It is fair to add that Lehner was always scrupulously fair and even generous to British achievements.

It would be an overstatement to claim that the Alpine Club has been wholly uninfluenced by the "blue ribbon" motive. The Club would have been disappointed had members of the newly founded Italian Club been the first to climb the Matterhorn, or had the Swiss in 1952 deprived us of the prize for which we had long contended, the ascent of Everest.

240

"*La vérité*", as Renan remarked, "*consiste dans les nuances*", and more than a *nuance* separates an openly proclaimed competition for "the blue ribbon of mountaineering" and a decent pride in the mountaineering achievements of one's countrymen. Such pride is consistent with the determination to de-emphasise international competition. The mountaineering world does not consist of national teams such as those that march in procession, bearing their national banners, through the Olympic stadium before the opening of the Olympic Games. On the contrary they are all members of one great brotherhood, like the Gothic chivalry before the Gates of Jerusalem, united as were the crusaders by a common purpose which should transcend inevitable national rivalries. Marcel Kurz writes: "This tradition of brotherhood or chivalry was easier to maintain when it was a case of exploration than when mountaineering became a competitive sport."

It was not only in mountaineering that the Nazis (and now the Russians) have tried to transform a great sport into a criterion of the merits not only of national but also of ideological competition. Before Hitler came to power the German skiers were primarily skiers, and then, as once again today, a friendly element in our ski-ing family, but we all felt during the Winter Olympic Games of 1936, which were held at Garmisch, that the Germans had been mobilised to demonstrate the invincibility of the Third Reich. Elsewhere I have described the tense atmosphere of those games and my reactions when invited after refereeing the slalom, to broadcast a few comments. All I could bring myself to say to the unseen audience was "Germans, let me tell you a little secret. There are still some people who ski for fun."

The Arlberg-Kandahar, which was founded by the British, ranks immediately after the Olympic Games and World Championship, but the Kandahar Ski Club has done what it could do to de-emphasise international rivalries and to insist that in the Arlberg-Kandahar racers compete as individuals and as members of the ski-ing brotherhood. No national flags are flown during the meeting and no national anthems are sung at the prize giving. Once again it is a question of the all important note of proportion. International rivalries are inevitable but they must not, whether in ski-ing or mountaineering, be permitted to obscure one of the main purposes of sport, the improvement of international relations rather than the intensification of international differences.

The Everest expedition provided a classic contrast between pride in a great national achievement and hysterical nationalism. It would be foolish to deny that Everest was the object of keen international competition, but the primary objective of the expedition led by John Hunt was not to defeat the Swiss but to solve a mountaineering problem. Of this expedition Edwin Herbert writes: "The party climbing a mountain is not carrying a national banner to wave in the face of less successful countries." The banner was not waved, but it was present if only in the hearts of every Englishman who rejoiced in the most felicitous coincidence in the history of sport, the coincidence summed up in the famous *Daily Express* headline on Coronation Day: "All this and Everest too." It would be hypocritical to deny that Everest was an omen of what we hoped would be a new Elizabethan age in our history. I was in Germany at the time in the temporary employment of the American State Department, and I listened to the Coronation broadcast in a hotel reserved for American personnel when I learned that Everest had been climbed and suddenly a line of Theocritus came back to me

"Thinkest thou that all our suns are set?"

I will not attempt to deny that it was my pride as an Englishman, and not only my emotion as a member of the mountain brotherhood, which was stirred by an Editorial which appeared next day in the *New York Times*:

> "In a span of less than twenty-four hours we lived through one of the most remarkable conjunctures of events in all history. Nothing less can characterize that wonderful combination of the conquest of the last unconquered spot on earth and the dawn of a new Elizabethan era.
> "Let us throw drab science to the winds! Anyone who tries to tell us that some mere fortuitous combination of weather and material circumstances brought about the triumph at Mount Everest on the eve of Queen Elizabeth's coronation might just as well save his breath. This was an omen. As long as men live, as long as there are pages to record the chronicles of the human race, it will be set down that man completed his conquest of the world while a young woman was preparing for consecration as Queen of England. Hillary, the New Zealander, along with Tensing, the Sherpa, 'Tiger of the Snows', will take his place with Sir Walter Raleigh and Sir Francis Drake. While such men serve the monarchs of England one need not worry about the decline and fall of the British Empire. It would be hard to say which event moved us the more. Indeed, we do not have to say, for they were of a piece and always will be."

None the less, nationalism was kept under control. John Hunt did everything he could to emphasise the great contribution of his predecessors, notably the Swiss, to the final victory, whereas fanatic nationalists made an hysterical attempt to exaggerate Tenzing's role. Had Hunt's motives been as base as theirs Hillary's partner on the final ascent would have been not Tenzing but an Englishman. It was the ideal of a mountain brotherhood which ensured that the gallant company of Sherpas should be represented in the final assault.

During the writing of this book I have tried not to forget that "national aggrandisement" is one of the things "frowned on by the Alpine Club", and I have done my best not to overstate our contribution to mountaineering and to do full justice to the contribution of other countries. Good intentions are, however, seldom realised, and I shall be happy if the contrast between what I intended and what I achieved is not too glaring. Be that as it may, I hope that I shall be forgiven by my foreign readers if from time to time my pride in the role which the Alpine Club has played is more apparent than my attempt to achieve the British ideal of understatement.

No mountaineer would deny that we have good reason to recall our past with pride, and even those who alleged that our reputation suffered a sharp decline after the First World War give us credit for a remarkable recovery. And it is not only on Everest and Kangchenjunga that this belief is based, for the reputation of our younger climbers in the Alps has never been higher. That great guide Camille Tournier who took me up the Aiguille du Goûter in my sixty-eighth year spoke to me with unfeigned enthusiasm of the recent achievements of our young men in the Mont Blanc range.

"Tradition", as Gilbert Norwood once said, "need not be a chain; it may be a life-line." And even those who have mastered the technique of artificial mountaineering are concerned not to reject but merely to modify the traditions which the founding fathers of the Club created.

All that is of value in those traditions will be preserved, for we may be very sure that the Alpine Club will continue to pass on the legacy which we have inherited from the past, a right knowledge and a discerning appreciation of

THE CHIEF THINGS OF THE ANCIENT MOUNTAINS
AND THE PRECIOUS THINGS OF THE LASTING HILLS.

GENERAL INDEX

INDEX A–Z

254